AWAKEN
TO YOUR
SPIRITUAL
SELF

M.J. Abadie

Adams Media Corporation
Holbrook, Massachusetts

Published by
Adams Media Corporation
260 Center Street, Holbrook, MA 02343

ISBN: 1-58062-000-0

Printed in the United States of America.

J I H G F E D C B

Library of Congress Cataloging-in-Publication Data
Abadie, M. J.
Awaken your spiritual self / M.J. Abadie. — 1st ed.
p.   cm.
ISBN 1-58062-000-0
1. Spiritual Life. I. Title.
BL624.A23   1998
291.4'4—dc21   98-16311
                              CIP

This publication is designed to provide accurate and authoritative information
with regard to the subject matter covered. It is sold with the understanding that
the publisher is not engaged in rendering legal, accounting, or other professional
advice. If legal advice or other expert assistance is required, the services of a com-
petent professional person should be sought.
—From a *Declaration of Principles* jointly adopted by a Committee of the
American Bar Association and a Committee of Publishers and Associations

Cover design by Barry Littmann.

This book is available at quantity discounts for bulk purchases.
For information, call 1-800-872-5627 (in Massachusetts, 781-767-8100).

Visit our home page at http://www.adamsmedia.com

contents

Acknowledgments

$\mathcal{M}$y enduring gratitude is extended to:

My nephew, J. Paul Abadie, whose generosity of spirit above and beyond the call of familial relationship provided me with extraordinary support on many levels, and whose own deep involvement with Spirit continually enhances my life and my work.

My dear friend, Chris Santini, who has enriched my life and work immeasurably through his devotion to the path of Spirit and who, when called to serve, responded with extraordinary generosity—of time, energy, and loving concern. For this gift, I offer him my most deeply felt affection and regard.

Pam Liflander, the editor of this book, who graciously handed me over the divide between strong opinions forcefully expressed in a sometimes complex way and the need to disseminate the ideas herein in a manner compatible with reaching as broad an audience as possible. And managing editor Linda Spencer for her blessed eye for detail and welcome attention to the small specifics.

Anne Sellaro, my agent and friend, who was at all times a bulwark of support, a beam of light in the darkness, always ready to rally to my side, and whose contribution of the original subtitle for this book, "Celebrating the Sacred Every Day" clarified my concept for it.

My assistant, Sarah Perry, whose cheerful and efficient dispatch of all things needful kept the ship of my life afloat during a time of dislocation and reorientation. She's now embarked on a new career in healing. I wish her the success she deserves.

Friend and fellow astrologer, Mary Orser, who kindly gave permission for the reprinting of her Moon Attunement and who also generously contributed some of her private research to my endeavor.

Last but not least, I acknowledge all the other forms of life that have taught me so much about Spirit, wholeness, and the connectedness of all life on this planet—my cat Mushkin especially, but also a varying assortment of animal and plant life that keeps me in humble perspective.

And, in a book of this type, it is also fitting to pay homage to the many sources of inspiration and support provided by Spirit itself, that most marvelous living intelligence that imbues and informs my life always.

preface
Awakening the Spiritual Self

Any discussion of Spirit, or that which is spiritual, is fraught with difficulty. Just *what* is spirit. And, *where* is it? Is it "out there," a great God in the sky—or is it "in here," located somewhere within us? Are we spiritual only when we are present in our formal place of worship, or when we are actively praying to whichever version of the divine we espouse as our God? Does spirituality require a formal discipline, a prescribed practice? Can anyone be spiritual, or is this quality difficult of attainment?

The simple truth is that we are *all* spiritual beings. The problem is that we are not fully awake to our own sacred dimension and that of the world around us. This point is illustrated by a story about the Buddha.

After receiving enlightenment, he radiated an aura of extraordinary power that gathered crowds around him. One man approached him and asked,

"Are you a god?"

"No," replied Buddha.

"Are you a holy prophet, then?"

"No," was the reply.

"Are you a powerful magician?"

"No," again.

The man, puzzled by these answers and dazzled by the glow emanating from Buddha, finally asked,

"What are you?"

And Buddha answered,

"I am *awake*."

Those three words are the essence of Buddhist teachings. *Buddha* means "awakened," and Buddha was a *human* who had become awake, or enlightened.

In 1945 at a village in upper Egypt called Nag Hammadi, an extraordinary find of papyrus books dating from the early Christian era was discovered. These came to be called the "gnostic gospels" based on their contents and age. Some scholars believe they may even predate the gospels of the New Testament, "possibly as early as the second half of the first century," according to Professor Helmut Koester of Harvard University. The gnostics of that era were considered a Christian heresy by the orthodoxy.

In one of these texts, many of which claim to offer traditions about Jesus that are secret, a disciple asks Jesus "When will the kingdom of God come?" and Jesus says, "The kingdom of the Father is spread over the earth and men do not see it."

And in truth, the divine is everywhere. We have only to look and listen. Most magnificently, the sacred is inside each of us, nestled in the most interior part of our beings. Alas, our perception of the sacred within ourselves and all around us is too often buried beneath an encrustation of the demands and expectations of others—family, teachers, society and its institutions, which serve to obscure our ability to realize and recognize the divine spirit glowing within ourselves. But, no matter how faint the ember, we have only to go deeply within to find its eternal spark and fan it into new and vibrant life. The Light is always there.

The day of God can come for anybody, anytime—right now. In Hindu terms, one need only hear the syllable OHM sounding through all things. This is the meaning of the word *gnosis* (direct knowing) and of *bodhi* (enlightenment).

To know one's self deeply and intimately is to know the divine Spirit. Orthodoxy insists that a chasm separates humanity from its creator, that God is wholly "other." The gnostic texts reveal a different belief.

The gnostics who wrote these gospels believed that "self-knowledge is knowledge of God; the self and the divine are identical," according to Elaine Pagels, author of *The Gnostic Gospels.* One gnostic teacher, Monoimus, says:

> Abandon the search for God and the creation and other matters of a similar sort. Look for him by taking yourself as the starting point. Learn who it is within you who makes everything his own and says, "My God, my mind, my thought, my soul, my body." Learn the sources of sorrow, joy, love, hate. . . . If you carefully investigate these matters you will find him in *yourself.*

Erich Neumann, the brilliant theoretical and philosophical analyst who studied with C.G. Jung in Zurich in the 1930s, states the problem thus in *Art and the Creative Unconscious:*

> We know that the core of the neuroses of our time is the religious problem or, stated in more universal terms, *the search for the self.* In this sense neuroses, like the mass phenomena resulting from this situation, are a kind of sacred disease.

And Edward C. Whitmont, M.D., another Jungian analyst, says in *The Return of the Goddess* that:

> *Search* is an expression of the urge to discover what "holds the world together at its inmost core" (Goethe, *Faust*) to establish an order and meaning for our place in the cosmos . . . man's thrust into outer space is the counterpart of the quest into inner space in search of integration and fulfillment.

Neumann further declares that, although our whole epoch is full of this "sacred disease," behind it stands the power of *a sacred center*, which can direct the individual through psychic crises and the process of transformation they engender—the disease, in other words, contains its own cure. Each of us is directed by this inner force—we have only to listen to its promptings. These transformations of consciousness enable us to experience the divine every day, each in his or her own way, according to our level of potential spiritual development.

The totality of the individual psyche takes form around this mysterious center in the Self, which, though it may seem to be chaotic and full of darkness, contains within itself the seeds of new life. This seeming void within is actually the center point of transformation and rebirth into the spirit; from it we can experience the sacred in our lives every day we live. As Neumann says:

> . . . when the phenomenon of transcendence occurs, the transpersonal seems, even though it has passed through the medium of the human . . . to have perceived itself and to shine forth with its own incandescence.

There is now a wide body of scientific evidence suggesting the existence of a living world organism based upon a universal flow of information acting as its substructure. In other words, the *subjective* has created the *objective*. As physicist David Bohm has remarked, "The universe begins to look more and more like a giant thought." These ideas suggest interplay of all levels of existence, within ourselves and in the entire cosmos.

In view of these similar ideas—emanating from religious, philosophical, psychological, and scientific sources—and in an attempt at clarity of terminology, I am proposing a new definition of the word *self*, redefining it as an acronym for **S**piritually **E**volving **L**ife **F**orce. This concept is meant to encompass the totality of the human being. It will be represented typographically as SELF throughout the book.

I am using SELF to include *all* of the complex and multifaceted being that each one of us is. There is more to "mind" than mere brain cells; more to body than mechanically functioning organs and glands; more to life than the interactions between the two. There is a spiritual dimension, which, no matter how you choose to define or identify it—as God, the Higher Power, the All One, etc.—cannot be ignored. This spiritual dimension is the creator of the objective world. But *where* is this located, and *how* do we contact it?

This often asked question reminds me of the story of an Eastern new student at Oxford University in England. His assigned preceptor was showing him around, helping him to familiarize himself in the environs of the great institution. After he had been exhaustively shown the buildings: housing dormitories, classrooms, lecture rooms, dons' quarters, examination rooms, libraries, chapels, he turned to his guide in utter bewilderment.

"But," he said, shaking his head in perplexity, "*where* is the university?"

The university was not in the stones of the venerable buildings; it was not contained within the many spaces he visited; it was not in the functions these spaces performed; it was not even in the rows and rows of books in the different libraries. Was it then in the learned masters, in the multitudinous students who came from all corners of the world to study at this university? No, it wasn't there either. Where, then, to look? It was everywhere and nowhere at the same time.

Lest this sound like a *koan*, the riddle form used by Zen masters to instruct their pupils, let me hasten to say that there is no puzzle at all. The university (from the root word *universe*), though it appears to be housed in a complex of physical structures, actually has its true location in the hearts and minds—and spirits—not only of all those students and teachers, past and present, who trod the grounds and corridors, but also of those whose lives have been touched in a significant way by their efforts. It is embodied in all those who came before, as it will be in all those yet to come. It is not only a physical place located in a precise geographical latitude but a place carried within, built anew inside each teacher and each student of every generation, from whom it goes forth into the world unconfined by its visible stone towers.

Temenos is the Greek word for temple, or sacred space. Outwardly, this can be a public place of worship—such as a church, cathedral, synagogue, mosque, tepee, a great pyramid, or a ring of giant stones. Inwardly, however, it is a place *within* where we experience the sacred dimension, no matter what form our outward worship takes. In this inner temple, we encounter the truth of our SELF, or Spiritually Evolving Life Force, which each of us *is*. From our inner temple we not only contact the divine light in ourselves, we have the capacity to contact it in our fellow beings. From a deeply understood connection with our *own* spiritual dimension, we are able to reach out and interact with the SELF—an identical spiritual energy—in others.

Just as the university consists of an invisible factor that transcends the physical buildings that house its daily functions, and is actually built by the hearts and minds of its residents over time, the true *temenos* is not constructed of bricks and stone, sand and mortar. It is not a product of priestly ministrations. It is a living force within us all.

Unfortunately, many of us are cut off from this vivifying flow of spirit. We are hampered and hamstrung by the notion that what we seek exists *somewhere* in time and space, or is to be found in a specific house of worship. However, today, disappointed and disengaged by institutionalized religion, many are seeking the wellspring of their own inner spirituality in their own individualized way. It is to these seekers that this book is addressed in the hope of providing the "something more" for which they quest.

In his exhaustive study *Recovering the Soul*, in support of the "nonlocal" view of man, which places mind and consciousness—and by extension spirit—outside the person, Larry Dossey, M.D., concludes:

> The "something more" that is needed is a vision that will transform our view of who we are and how we fit into the way of nature—a new world view that would redefine our very being. . . . The nonlocal view . . . leads to a theory of the One Mind, which is boundless in space and time. . . . [It] arises not only from the eternal intimations of seers and visionaries but also from modern scientific insights. . . . It lands us squarely in the lap of God—or the One, Logos, Tao, Brahma, Buddha, Krishna, Allah, Mana, the Universal Spirit or Principle. . . . Because nonlocal mind is *boundless* and *limitless*, and because these are precisely qualities of God also, this means that at some level we share something with the Godhead. To some degree, the borders of man and God overlap. This is a way of saying that there is an element of the divine within man. . . . nonlocality is the stage on which God and man meet.

Your personal *temenos*, or the temple within, is the stage on which that meeting takes place and reaches out, from you, to the whole world. As its designer and architect, you will there encounter the healthy, positive qualities of your SELF—body, mind, heart, spirit—and experience the "magic" of connectedness.

As we explore that borderland where body, mind, spirit, and soul merge into the One, where substance and spirit interface, it is my intent for you to gain new insights into what I call "the invisible world"—where Spirit resides and informs our daily life, if we will but let it. The Sufi tradition tells us that the central postulate of the Way is that there is a hidden meaning in all things, that every thing has an outer as well as an inner meaning, and every external form is complemented by an inner reality which is its hidden eternal essence.

Opening that previously shut door and making contact with your SELF—which contains within itself a perfect design for your life—can work wonders. Treat your SELF with compassion, gentleness, patience, and respect, and you will find the sacred all about you in your daily life with all of its mundane activities. You may be surprised at all the positive change that can come about as you open to the sacredness of everyday and discover that the living Spirit is everywhere, unbounded.

M.J. Abadie
Thanksgiving Day 1997

introduction
Preparation

our basic modes of preparation will enable us to reach the goal of living a life of sacredness every day. These are: *silence, solitude, breathing*, and *relaxation*. Each of these states is necessary for practicing the exercises that will be given throughout the book. By learning them in advance, and by giving yourself time to get acquainted with these fundamentals, you will be in a state of readiness to traverse the inner spiritual landscape and build your "temple within" on solid sacred ground from a universal spiritual blueprint.

⁂ Coming into Silence

Silence is golden, says the proverb. Yet today it seems as if we experience silence as terrifying. An increasing amount of human-made sound saturates our world, sometimes explosively. Once we were awakened by the cock's crow or birdsong. Today, we wake to the *buzz* of an alarm clock that turns on a radio so even the first few minutes of our day are filled with mechanically delivered sound. We get up and turn on the TV to accompany our ears while we dress and eat breakfast. Driving to work, we play the radio or a tape. Daily, our ears are insulted by blaring horns, screaming sirens, irate drivers shouting insults. Our children's music shakes the beams. No wonder 40 percent of Americans suffer serious hearing loss by the age of forty. Unsatisfied with all of this sound, we go a step further and, in our leisure hours, we wire our bodies for sound, strapping on the tape player as we walk or exercise. The CD collection becomes as much a part of our vacation luggage as our suitcases. We are constantly plugged in—and tuned out.

The average citizen in the United States views seven hours of television daily. Statistically, this means that many homes must have a TV on virtually twenty-four hours a day. Many people turn on the TV the minute they enter the house from work—not to sit and watch it but for the sound. Others play the radio or CDs no matter what else they may be doing—for "background" music. One cannot shop in a store without being subjected to some kind of recorded sound. Elevators play Muzak, and when you are put on hold while transacting business, your ear is filled with unnecessary and often unwanted music. The sound of music is everywhere it seems with no one able or willing to turn it off. Few question the need for meaningless sound in the background. (And we wonder why we feel a lack of meaning in our lives!) We have ratcheted up the noise so far that "noise pollution" has become a civil and political issue.

Silence causes anxiety. For example, in every conversation there is a lull. No one knows why, but it happens regularly, about every twenty minutes. People chattering away suddenly pause, making a still pool of silence in a previously animated atmosphere. This often makes them feel embarrassed, as if someone had committed a socially unacceptable *faux pas*. Looking anxiously about, laughing nervously, wondering who is to blame for the unexpected, unnerving silence, they struggle to get the conversation going again, not realizing that the intermittent silence comes of itself, for its own reasons—a natural pause that punctuates conversation.

Why is silence so hard to bear? Do we fear that in silence we will hear what we do not want to hear? Does the prospect of our own inner voice strike dread in us? Are we afraid of discovering that life can be lived at different levels? Pierre Lacout in *God Is Silence* says:

> Daily silence experienced in humility and fervour as an indispensable exercise in spiritual nourishment gradually creates within us a permanent state of silence. The soul discovers in such a silence unsuspected possibilities. It realizes that life can be lived at different levels.

A major component of the spiritual journey is reflection. Without silence one cannot reflect. As the popular culture does not value silence, it clearly denigrates reflection, which is seen as a threat to the established order of work and community involvement. Reflection leads to questioning—and questioning leads to independent thought, which in turn leads to weakening of social, political, and religious authority.

In order to experience the sacred in yourself, you must *dare to turn off the sound*. In order to come to your spiritual center, you will have to stake out a territory of silence, wage a war of personal independence over the tyranny of noise pollution. To experience the sacred is to be silent, at least some of the time. Try turning off all the electronic sound conveyors and listening instead to the simpler sounds around you—you might hear a baby bird peeping, a child babbling, a cat's footfall, rain dripping, or your own breathing. You might become aware of the natural silences that fall in the interstices of the flow of sound. Silence is the royal road to the center of the SELF.

The sacred is everywhere around us, but it speaks with a still, small voice that is drowned out by the level of noise we permit and even encourage in our lives. Contact with the sacred occurs in the quiet stillness, when mind and heart are at rest. This point of silence is comparable to the hub at the center of the turning wheel, "the still point." This center of stillness is the gateway to the SELF, which seeks wholeness and unity. To find our center, the striving ego must become quiet and still. Only then can we thread our way through the usual untidy jumble of our colliding thoughts to that place within where Spirit dwells.

It is in our silences that we experience unity and recognize ourselves as being part of the All. This is the essence of the spiritual quest. Almost everyone has had the experience of oneness at some time—perhaps sitting by a lake in silence and solitude, gazing at a sleeping child while preserving the quiet around its slumber, caught alone and awestruck by a magnificent sunset on a country road. These are mystical moments that connect us to the larger totality of which we are an integral part. We are transfixed—and we are transformed for the moment. It's difficult to describe the feeling, and we have no adequate words for that sense of having stepped outside our normal boundaries into something grand and inspiring. It always happens in silence.

Ordinarily, we slip accidentally into such experiences, and they are fleeting and ephemeral. But they can be found regularly if only we become silent and wait for them to appear before our inner eye. These hints of another reality—this momentary lifting of the veil between the worlds—come to us when we are aware and *listening* for their soft tread in our inner landscape.

Often, just slowing down enough to observe the mind at work is an illuminating experience. As we progress through our silence to the still point within, we peel away the layers of miscellaneous thought that have impeded our contact with the divine stratum which lies beneath our every thought and action. The practice of silence is how we open ourselves to direct experience of the SELF in the All.

Silence is not merely the absence of sound. It is a restful space which we inhabit when we are at our most free and uninhibited. Like a pointer on a spiritual roadmap, silence leads us to intuit the next step we are required to make for our continued growth and development. Silence is a great spiritual master who guides us and illuminates our way when it is dark. In the silence of the inner self, we reach *gnosis*, or truth, and in so doing we find the way—we know what to do or not to do.

Fortunately, you do not have to retire to a monastery or become a hermit to experience the contemplative silence that is at the heart of the spiritual path. You can achieve your own silence, contact your still center, and receive the guidance you long for by deciding to practice silence on a daily basis. Begin by asking yourself these questions.

- 🦎 What noise in my life would I like to eliminate?
- 🦎 What silence would I like to bring into my life?
- 🦎 How can I achieve a balance between necessary or unavoidable noise and the level of silence I desire?

Demanding silence for one's self in this society requires a major leap of faith. Not only must we overcome obstacles merely to obtain some silence in our busy lives, we must jealously guard against noisy invaders, including the ones inside who may try to sabotage our efforts to be silent. Given silence unexpectedly—whether a few moments or a few hours—most of us apprehensively reach out for the nearest sound with which to distract ourselves. Realize that silence is not the enemy: silence is the great mother lode of the sacred realm.

This focusing technique will allow you to make room in your life for the silence you need on your spiritual journey. It is especially helpful for people who are unclear about their own needs, usually because they have long denied having needs at all, or because they have spent their lives fulfilling the needs of others at the expense of their own. Really focusing in a sharp and clear manner, and writing it all down, seems to activate the SELF to provide solutions to everyday problems.

Confusion between what you really want and what you *think* you want or think you cannot change is a result of programming by outside influences.

 ### *Creating Silence*

To do this exercise, you will need pen and paper and at least twenty minutes of quiet, undisturbed time. After you have asked yourself the questions listed above, sit with them for a few minutes, turning them over and around to get a feeling for how you want to answer. Then, when you are feeling clear and relaxed, make three columns on a page and give each one of the following headings:

1. What silence I want to manifest in my life.
2. What noise I want to get rid of in my life.
3. What would be a good balance between sound and silence in my life?

Now, list everything you can think of in each column, including how you feel about each question. Let your imagination roam freely—don't worry about how you are going to achieve results yet. Just list what your true wishes are. Staying focused about what you want to achieve is the key to success. Knowing what you don't want allows you to focus more clearly on what you do want. Focusing on what you truly want will activate inner direction.

Once you have made your list, go over it carefully and ask yourself if you truly want to be rid of the things on your list. Look for modifications. For example, if you want to get rid of your son's blasting music, you know you aren't going to forbid him to play his CDs. However, you can insist that he use headphones. Next, ask yourself if you are willing to do what is necessary to obtain the silence you say you want, whether it is a mere half-hour a day or half a day twice a week. You have to be sure that you truly want to achieve the level of silence you have listed for yourself.

After reviewing what you have listed in the first two columns, write down whatever comes to mind about how you can balance the two. Then, put the list away for a day and don't think about it. Let your deep inner mind provide you with the answers you need. Review your list the following day and see if you want to make any changes, or if new ideas have occurred to you. Repeat this procedure for an entire week *without discussing it with anyone*. This process must be a reflection of *you* and your needs, not of anyone else's idea of how much silence you need or want.

After a week, take your list and work with in by arranging the items in columns one and two according to the following priorities. Give each an A, B, C, or Z code. A is for *Absolutely Must Have*. B is for *Better With than Without*. C is for *Can Do Without if Need Be*. And Z is for *Zilch*—you know this isn't important. If you have more than three entries in A, B, and C, reduce them to three and re-prioritize those three. Now, reconsider once more until you have two or three A items in both the "get rid of" and the "want to achieve" lists. This is your focus list. It tells you what your rock bottom demand for silence time is, where you feel you can be flexible, and where you will have to compromise.

In her book *Everyday Sacred,* Sue Bender tells the story of a trip she made to see the renovated warehouse that had become the downtown Guggenheim Museum. After describing the "uncluttered long white exhibition space," which "floated—a limitless expanse of calm and stillness," with white walls covered with white paintings, she says, "This was what a temple should feel like: a 'temple of the soul.'"

Who travels without an inner stillness is always at risk of being cut off from the wisdom of guidance, but once you allow yourself to claim your right to be silent, you will be in a position to access the "still, small voice" within your SELF.

🌿 Seeking Solitude

If silence is golden, solitude is a precious jewel. The historian Edward Gibbon called solitude "the school of genius." And the poet Rainer Maria Rilke, in *Letters to a Young Poet*, observes:

> The necessary thing is, after all, but this: solitude, great inner solitude. Going into oneself and for hours meeting no one—this one must be able to attain.

Solitude, however, is as difficult of attainment as is silence. If we fear silence, we see solitude as the ultimate negative state. Instead of being recognized as a treasure house of sublime gifts, being alone is viewed as a noxious condition to be remedied at once. And if we cannot fill our spaces with living people, the flickering color images on the TV set will do as well. Yet, like silence, solitude is "the necessary thing." Without it we are consumed in the backwash of others' lives. Lacking solitude, we are lonely despite the presence of others . . . lonely because we are not in touch with our deepest selves. When we fill up our hours, days, years, whole lives with the constant presence of others, we forfeit the opportunity to know ourselves. Neglecting or abandoning this innermost self reaps a bitter harvest. We feel we don't know who we truly are—because indeed we do not, never having bothered to find out by going within where the SELF dwells.

We somehow feel that the solitary individual is inferior, deficient in some way—unable or unwilling to make "significant" relationships with others. Yet, the world's most creative artists and writers have by and large preferred solitude to company. Abraham Maslow, the psychologist who identified "peak experiences" as those moments of unity, or a recognition of the self in the All, said that the ability to have peak experiences is dependent upon being free of other people, "which in turn means that we become much more . . . our authentic selves, our real identity." Maslow's approach differs considerably from those who propose that the entire meaning of life is derived from interpersonal relationships.

Complete happiness, that oceanic feeling of perfect harmony between the inner and outer worlds, is at best an infrequent experience, but the most profound psychological and spiritual experiences invariably take place internally, witnessed only by the "indwelling self." Rarely, and then only distantly, are these experiences related to interaction with other human beings. Adaptation to the world is largely a product of the imagination and the development of an inner world in which to shield the self from the vagaries of the outer world. Without this inner world, without a strong and well-built structure within, the outer world seems threatening and dangerous. The ability to remove one's self, to be totally immersed, fascinated and absorbed in the present, in the here-and-now, enables us to withstand the "slings and arrows of outrageous fortune."

It seems that the human psyche is so constructed that the discovery or creation of unity in the internal world produces a sense of wholeness or unity in the outer world, like a mirror reflection. This is what is meant by the New Age saying, "You create your own reality." Inner experience and outer happenings interact with one another. Mind and matter are not only inseparable, they affect one another. Thus, when the inner plane is in harmony with itself, the outer world seems to follow suit, almost magically.

How and *why* this works we do not know for certain, but the evidence suggests that communion with the inner self aligns us with the cosmos, with the right and natural order of all things. One might say that we are deliberately getting in tune with the harmonic chords of the universe. And when we are in tune, we produce effects.

For many people, solitude is a difficult commodity to come by—there are constant demands on one's time and physical presence. While you are working your way through to finding more actual solitude in your life, you can find a place of solitude within. Once you have done this and it has become real for you, a sense of calm and ease will suffuse you. Think of this as your inner sanctuary, a place where you can recharge your batteries and make contact with your deep inner self. Creating a place of inner solitude is not difficult. Here's how it is done.

 ## *Creating Your Sanctuary*

Find a time when you can be alone and undisturbed for half an hour. Spend a few minutes breathing slowly and rhythmically and allowing your body to relax completely.

Now, create in your mind a picture of a lovely place—it might be a secluded spot in a woods or a cove on a beach. It can be outdoors or indoors. Letting yourself feel relaxed and free, think leisurely about what a sanctuary would mean to you. As this picture emerges (you don't actually have to *see* it, you only have to *know* it), let yourself be absorbed into its quiet, beauty, silence, and sense of comforting solitude.

When you have an image in your mind or a feeling about what your sanctuary is like, continue to fill in all the details. Imagine what a "room of your own" would be and feel like. What would you put there? A comfortable chair, a bowl of fresh flowers, pictures on the wall? Make this picture as complete as you possibly can, with colors, smells, textures. Walk about the environment you are creating and claim it for your own personal place of inner solitude.

When you feel that you have taken complete possession of your special place, perform a symbolic gesture—such as writing your name or placing a favorite object there—that will enable you to return to your sanctuary at will. The purpose is to make it easy for you to recall this experience. After you have done this, breathe slowly and quietly for a few minutes before returning yourself to normal waking consciousness.

You have now created a place of inner solitude. It is yours to command. You can return anytime you want, whenever you choose or need a space to practice being alone and quiet.

✿ Breath as Spirit

Breath is life. When breath stops, life stops. The vital force of life comes into our bodies with our breath. Yet, we are mostly unaware of this and often neglect to breathe fully and deeply. Breath is something we take for granted—for we could hardly function if we had to consciously remember to breathe. Most of us are rarely aware of our breathing until it becomes impaired, by a cold or by shortness of breath. Breath is the gateway to the sacred dimension. When we breathe consciously, we connect to the link we have with our spiritual selves, for awareness and control of breath allow us to open ourselves to our innate sacred realm.

Most Eastern philosophies teach that we live in a sea of vital energy—and that we absorb and activate this with our breath. The Hindu yogi tradition calls this energy *prana*. Oriental mind-body balancing techniques such as acupuncture and shiatsu, refer to this vital force as *Qi* (chi). The Hawaiian Huna tradition calls it *mana* (*mana loa* in its highest form). In the Hawaiian language, the word for "to think" is *mana-o*.

Working with breath is a form of spiritual practice. Controlled breathing permits us to extract new energy from the air. Our physical bodies can store this energy in the same way food is stored as fat. When this subtle energy is in short supply, you feel down, listless, tired, and can get sick. When it is in abundant supply, you feel "up," energized, optimistic, and full of energy. Though the energy is subtle, it is very real.

You can prove this to yourself by paying attention to the ion content of the air you breathe. Air is charged with positive and negative ions and a surplus of the former results in an oppressively heavy atmosphere, like that before a thunderstorm. Positive ions sap our energy. Think of how you feel when a storm is brewing and the sky lowers darkly. Negative ions release uplifting energy into the air. When the storm breaks and the rain comes pelting down, the air is clear and refreshed. Your spirits lift and your mood brightens. You feel energized and ready to go. Proper deep breathing has the effect of saturating your system with negative ions, contributing to release of tension and mental calmness.

Yogis claim the energy generated by conscious breath not only gives vitality to the body, but also nourishes the spiritual self. A high content of *prana* in the system causes the unfolding of natural abilities—mental, physical, emotional, spiritual. *Prana* is there whether we are aware of it or not, like the oxygen in our lungs, but when we make a deliberate effort to increase it, blocked channels of information open. The breath is a powerful tool for bringing forth the sacred dimension in ourselves.

The following breathing techniques are simple, but if practiced daily they will release their power to you.

 ## *Rhythmic Breathing*

Most adults are shallow breathers. They sip the air the way a Victorian lady sipped her cup of tea, and for the same reason—not to appear coarse. Taking in generous amounts of air seems impolite to many people, especially those who feel socially restricted and insecure about how others will view them. A good belly breath, like a good belly laugh, seems not to belong in polite company.

Breath, like food, nourishes our every cell, and cleanses our blood. But, like anorexics, we insist on starving ourselves of this vital nutrient. The good news is that changing breathing patterns is easy. Anyone can do it. Changing your breathing starts with becoming aware of it.

This is a simple basic exercise, a form of relaxing meditation, a way to harmonize body, mind, and spirit. It can be used anytime and you can do this almost anywhere—sitting quietly at home, in your car, on a train. In the middle of a bustling city, I slip into a church, sit in a back pew, and breathe in spiritual energy.

Relax and close your eyes. Observe your breath pattern but do not make any attempt to alter it. Merely pay attention to the breath going in and coming out. Now, begin to breathe slowly and deeply. Breathe in through the nostrils and out through the mouth. Feel the coolness of the in-breath of fresh air coming in; feel the warmth of used air leaving your body. Imagine yourself being cleansed and energized by each breath.

Next, listen to any sounds you make while breathing. Do not judge, just listen. Also notice whether you breathe in shallow or deep breaths, where the air goes, into the diaphragm or into the belly. Does your chest rise and fall or does your abdomen rise and fall?

As you inhale each breath, be aware of the flow of air coming into and leaving your body. Follow the inhalation/exhalation cycle and see if you can find the point where they intersect. Actually, breath is one continuous movement, but we tend to separate the in-breath from the out-breath when we think about breathing. Continue doing this for several minutes. The object is to become aware of your own breath, to monitor its natural cycle of movement, nothing more. Imagine it filling up all the cells of your body like you would fill a balloon by blowing air into it. Let the sense of being filled with *prana* spread throughout your body. Do not force or strain.

What breathing consciously does is to develop a communications link between consciousness and the unconscious, between body and mind, between spirit and psyche. Adding the factor of imagination increases the benefit. The following is a yoga exercise known as "polarization."

Breathing with Color

To do this exercise, lie face up in a comfortable position, either on your bed or on a mat on the floor. Align your body with feet pointing south and head north, to the Earth's magnetic field. Let your palms rest face up with the arms stretched out alongside the body. Begin breathing as described above, slowly and rhythmically, and as you breathe, breathe in one *color* and exhale another. If you breathe in a warm color, breathe out a cool color, and vice versa. If you want to energize yourself, breathe in a warm color such as red, the strongest; orange, which enlivens; or yellow, promotes optimism. Breathe out a cool color, such a blue or green. For a calming or relaxing effect, do the opposite. Breathe in a cool color and breathe out a warm color. Think of the incoming breath as a positive current, the outgoing breath as a negative current. By breathing in these two polar opposites, you are balancing your energy state toward health. Imagine these polarized currents circulating through your body, one after the other, cleansing and purifying, healing and revivifying.

❧ The Royal Road to Relaxation

Relaxation seems to evade us most of the time. Why? The answer is not completely clear, but clues can be found in our outlook on life. When we look upon life as an adversary or threat, we are in a perpetual state of "fight or flight." Instead of releasing the tension when danger is past, we store it; the retention results in dangerous build-up that can bring on stress-related disease, such as high blood pressure, ulcers, and the like.

In the late 1960s, Harvard cardiologist Herbert Benson, M.D., was involved in some physiological tests on meditators. He discovered that relaxation methods, of which there are many, caused both psychological and *physiological* changes that served to counterbalance the body's "fight-or-flight" response. He called this the "relaxation response." Not a technique but a coordinated series of internal changes occurring when the mind and body become calm and tranquil, the relaxation response can be achieved by numerous means, such as deep breathing, muscle relaxation, meditation, visualizations, and prayer. The simplest of these is called "focused meditation." Benson's tests showed that persons who simply sat quietly with their minds focused on a single word, idea, or thought could markedly change their physiology, decreasing metabolism, slowing heart and respiratory rates, and exhibiting brain waves comparable to the dream state.

Physical relaxation can be an important adjunct to a spiritual practice, and we advise using a relaxation technique in conjunction with the exercises in this book.

There are two basic types of physical relaxation—*sequential* and *tension*. In sequential relaxation, you focus on each part of your body separately, from the toes up, allowing it to become limp and flaccid before moving on to the next part. In tension relaxation, you tense and release each muscle or muscle group in turn. Below are exercises for both types.

✸ Sequential Technique

To do this, lie comfortably on the floor or on a bed and breathe deeply several times, consciously inhaling fresh energy and consciously exhaling all negative tension. Then, starting with your toes, focus on each part of your body in turn: feet, ankles, calves, knees, thighs, hips, lower back, upper back, abdomen, chest, arms, hands, neck, spine, head. As you do this, mentally instruct each part to relax completely and linger until you feel your muscles loosen. Tell each set of muscles to go limp and feel yourself gradually sinking into an inert state of being. When you have finished with this sequence, do it in reverse, from head to toes.

Tense-and-Relax Technique

To do this exercise, choose a time and place where you can be alone and quiet for at least 30 minutes. Prepare your environment by lighting a candle, playing soft music, scenting the air, or anything else that appeals to you as an atmosphere in which to relax completely.

Sit comfortably in a chair or lie down on the floor or a bed. You are going to progressively tense-and-relax each of the major muscle groups of your whole body, beginning with the feet. Take a deep breath, let it out slowly, and gradually tense the muscles in your feet. Do this cautiously as feet and legs tend to cramp. Hold the tension for a count of three. Relax, tighten again, relax. Repeat this a third time. Leaving the foot relaxed, move up to the calf muscles and repeat the three-time procedure. Continue up to the thighs, the abdominal muscles, the buttocks, each time in sets of three. Proceed to your chest, arms, hands—tighten, relax, tighten, relax, tighten, relax. Next, go to your neck and shoulders. Move up to your face and make a "monster face" with open mouth and stretched muscles. This is known in yoga as the "lion face" and is used to prevent wrinkles and sagging face muscles. Lastly, squeeze your eyes tightly and then relax them completely three times. You should now be completely relaxed. Remain still for a few minutes enjoying this state of being.

Breathing Relaxation

This is a simple technique that takes only a little time. Sit or lie down in a safe and comfortable spot with no distractions. Loosen any tight clothing, unbutton or untie anything that is restrictive on your body. Begin to breathe *consciously*, following your breath in and out of your lungs. Breathe in through the nostrils, out through the mouth. Pay full attention to your breath, in and out, in and out. Listen to the sound and feel the rhythmic pulsing of it. Continue this until you begin to feel calm and relaxed, a state usually signaled by the breath becoming slow and even.

You can deepen your relaxation using breath by imagining that you are breathing in *prana*, or the vital force of life, and exhaling all tension and negative feeling or experience. One way to do this is to choose a color for both the *prana* and the negative energy and to see a stream of one color (positive) coming into your body as you inhale and to see a stream of the other color (negative) flowing out of you as you exhale. White and black are easy—white is the pure energy of light, while black represents any dark thoughts. But feel free to use any color that represents positive energy and release of negative energy to you. Don't worry if distracting thoughts arise. Let them float off (you can tell them you will attend to their needs later) like soap bubbles in the air and return to attending your breathing.

Instant Mini-Relaxation

Once you have fully experienced relaxation using one of the above techniques, and fixed this sensation firmly in mind as a mental picture, you can achieve instant relaxation simply by calling up the image you have created of your totally relaxed self. To do this, take a comfortable position and remember what it felt like to be completely relaxed. Your subconscious mind remembers everything. Tell it that you are now going to take ten deep breaths, and when you have finished you will be as completely relaxed as when you went through the entire relaxation process previously. Then, slowly and gently begin to breathe, counting to ten breaths.

❧ To summarize:

- ❧ Make room in your life for silence every day.
- ❧ Create a space in your life for the practice of solitude.
- ❧ Practice focused breathing daily.
- ❧ Practice relaxation meditations regularly in a calm, comfortable surrounding away from distractions.

We will be discussing advanced applications of these four basic fundamentals of the spiritual path—silence, solitude, breathing, and relaxation meditation—as we progress further along the way of creating the temple within for the purpose of bringing the sacred into our everyday lives.

part one
Transformations of the Inner Light

In order to effect a constructive and lasting change in our lives, we must strive toward a transformation [which] can occur only when we have gone beyond the personal dimension to the universal.

> Edward C. Whitmont, M.D.
> *The Symbolic Questest*

chapter one
Making the Daily Sacred

There is a sacred thread that runs through all life, from the largest, most lofty thought, word, or deed to the smallest, most humble daily chore. Everything with which we surround ourselves in our daily lives carries the potential for being made sacred. It is all in our attitude—toward ourselves, our lives, and the components of everyday. To experience *daily spirituality* is the goal of the sacred life. In the words of Taoist philosopher Chuang Tzu, "One has to be in the same place every day, watch the dawn from the same house, hear the same birds awake each morning, to realize how inexhaustibly rich and different is sameness."

Every area of life—home, sleeping and waking, our children and families; the chores of maintenance such as keeping ourselves and our homes clean, the purchase and preparation of food, upkeep of grounds; work, commuting, places we visit for business or recreation; the things we use in our daily lives; our relationships to others, to nature, to animals; our leisure and our creativity; the service we give to individuals and community; how we treat our bodies and how we use our minds—all have the potential for revealing their sacred dimension.

Everything we touch or encounter is made of sacred stuff. Wherever we set foot can be sacred ground.

The signals that confirm or point to the presence of Spirit are all around us. We need only become aware of what is hiding just beneath the surface of everyday life to realize that it is imbued with meaning, that it represents the sacred dimension.

There are three basic worldviews concerning the universe and all in it. The most prevalent of these today is that of *scientific materialism*, which holds that the universe was created by accident—by the "big bang," which brought it into being from mere *matter*, physical stuff considered dead and soulless. In this view the world is a vast mechanical clock in the process of running down. Scientific materialism attempts to eliminate the sacred from all but the designated precincts of formal churchgoing, which does not interfere much with the aims of the scientists to rob nature, not only of her treasures but also of her soul. It holds that the universe and everything in it—all of the marvellously complex forms of both organic and non-organic life, including ourselves and our wondrous brains and remarkable bodies—somehow evolved out of the primal soup by a series of mere happenstance interactions. Of this concept, psychologist Stanislav Grof says:

> The probability that human consciousness and our infinitely complex universe could have come into existence through the random interactions of inert matter has aptly been compared to that of a tornado blowing through a junkyard and accidentally assembling a 747 jumbo jet.

Today, most people accept the tenets of scientific materialism without dispute. Eager as we are for answers to life's perplexing questions, we have ceded to the scientists a near total authority to define "reality" for us, along with permission to denigrate, if not actually destroy, our perception of the sacred.

We continue to be dazzled by scientific "progress," despite obvious failings and great gaps in provable scientific knowledge. Take the brain—about which philosopher Authur Koestler said,"In creating the human brain, evolution has wildly overshot the mark."—as an example: the brain remains a mystery to scientists, who cannot figure out where memory is located—if it indeed is located in the brain at all. How we are able to recall information both deliberately and spontaneously; what the basis of feeling is; where thoughts originate; how we can discriminate musical harmony from chaotic notes flying through the air; where artistic talent comes from; how the brain mediates extrasensory perception—all remain unknown to the same scientists who purport to know the true nature of reality. They are apparently unaware that sages of all time, poets, and mythographers have made convincing arguments for the unity of body, mind, and spirit. All are one. The body is the physical manifestation of Spirit, mind its invisible form, and the quality of being human, with its multi-faceted capabilities, resides as much in the ether that surrounds and permeates us as it does in the physical organism.

The second worldview is that held by Western Judeo-Christian organized religions. This view holds that "creation" was an historical event that took place at some time in the past once and for all. It is fixed and unchanging. In this cosmological perception, the God who created the world is not a part of it but stands outside of his creation. This world, too, will end one day, at which time humanity will be reunited with its creator from whom it has been separated. A subset of this view is called *sacramentalism*, which is the concept that the entire creation is a sign pointing to God and that only through "sacraments" can one contact the divine. Another part of this view is *divinization*. Both Judaism and Christianity hold that humans are made in the *image* of God. Divinization, however, does *not* mean that we are God or in the process of becoming God. In it, we stand in a *relationship* to a God who is wholly other than we.

The third worldview, now becoming more prevalent, suggests that God and the universe are one and the same thing. We are cells in the body of God, psyche and substance of the divine energy out of which the entire universe is constantly being created, with us as participants in the divine work. Some like to use the term "co-creators," which indicates that we have more control and make a greater contribution to the totality of life than has previously been supposed.

In this view, which can be called *panentheism*, a term meaning "everything in God, and God in everything," what is emphasized is *immanence*, or God within the world, as opposed to the idea of *transcendence* espoused by the second worldview, which stresses the idea of a God *above and separate* from the world.

The worldview of an immanent God is not new but it is only now beginning to be more widely accepted in the West. A corollary of panentheism is the belief that all of creation—from the tiniest microbe to the furthest galaxy—is interconnected. And, most recently—in the wake of the new scientific paradigm which tells us that we live in an "intelligent universe" that is constantly in communication with all of its parts—there has evolved the sense not only of interconnectedness but of *communication*. In this view, the universe is like a cosmic Internet into which we are all hooked just by *being*. We don't need computers or a modem; we don't use software or a mouse. To live a sacred adventure every day, we need only learn to read the signs and pointers everywhere about us.

The word "read" has a common root with such words as art, skill, ordain, adorn, and ordinary. Think for a moment what your life would be like if you couldn't read. You would be lost on a vast sea of written words that would be utterly meaningless to you. You wouldn't know which bus to board because you couldn't read the route sign. If driving, you couldn't read the directional road signs. In a restaurant, you couldn't read the menu. You couldn't read your child a bedtime story. You couldn't read your mail or a book. You would know that there existed an entire world in print, one that had the capacity to open doors of information and inspiration, to provide personal independence and intellectual fulfillment—but you wouldn't have access to that world. Its doors would all be locked.

It is the same with reading the spiritual signs. If we do not teach ourselves to recognize them and read them, we become spiritual illiterates. We miss knowing about our interconnectedness. We cannot get on the worldwide web of Spirit. Just as the functional illiterate has to engage in all sorts of evasions and subterfuge to cover up the inability to read, we find ourselves constantly trying to cover up or compensate for the spiritual void we feel in our lives. We know instinctively that there is "something more," but look though we may, we can't find it.

Native Americans, who have always recognized that everything in the world is alive with Spirit, make their way through an untracked land by "reading signs." Ancient Polynesians navigated vast tracts of the open Pacific Ocean in canoes by their ability to "read the signs" of the seas without any navigational aids. The shaman, or priest, would put his ear to the waters and "read" the waves, listen to the whisperings of the mighty ocean, and take unerring bearings. By paying attention to the sacredness of their journey, and by respecting the life of nature all around, these intrepid voyagers crossed immense and unknown waters to settle the entire South Pacific.

When we learn to read as did these indigenous peoples, we discover that the whole world is charged with sacred meaning. We find that our inner spirituality is reflected throughout our ordinary, everyday experiences.

An example of this sign-reading comes from a recent experience of mine. While preparing a revision of this book to accommodate the editor's suggestions for improvement, I had become stuck and couldn't see how to proceed. At the same time, exacerbating the situation, an old knee injury had flared up painfully with the result that I was walking stiff-legged.

It was the time of the full Moon and, being in the country, I had the opportunity to observe and enjoy the glory of November's "frosty moon"—the shining, perfectly round orb hanging in a cold clear sky gave me a thrill. That night, the first cold snap arrived with temperatures dipping below freezing. The following morning I awakened inexplicably right before dawn and saw a bright white light coming through the west window of my bedroom. I thought: either I'm being visited by an angelic presence or the full Moon is still up. Stepping out on the back porch, my breath blowing frosty clouds into the air, I saw the setting Moon riding high in the western sky. The woods at the back of the house were silvered, as though by frost, but I knew a few hours of thirty-degree temperatures couldn't have deposited ice on the foliage. Then I realized that even though daylight was near the silvery effect was actually *moonlight*. It was magical, and I stood looking out over the western view. Suddenly, I saw *gold*, to the east. Turning, I saw the Sun coming up over the horizon, its light painting the sky pink and the trees a molten gold.

As if someone had drawn a line from north to south, the two sides of the landscape were separated by color. To the west, where night prevailed, the bright Moon turned what was beneath it to silver. In the east, the orange Sun was spreading out golden daylight. I looked from one side to the other and saw a phenomenon I had heard about but never before witnessed: the Sun and Moon stood exactly opposite each other in the sky, appearing to be the same size. This occurs once each month, at the time of the full Moon. I had observed it at night, when the Sun was the waning light and the Moon was about to become supreme, but I had never beheld the opposite configuration.

8

Despite the chill seeping through my pyjama-clad body, I stared awestruck at this division between the two worlds, of night and of day. As an astrologer, I'm always aware of the Moon's phases, from newborn crescent to full to shrinking into nothingness, but the significance of this dual-but-equal phenomenon had escaped me. I knew, of course, that the Moon represents what is hidden, i.e., night; that it is emblematic of the emotions, creativity, what is most deeply personal, while the masculine Sun represents objectivity, left-brained linear thinking, the "up and at 'em" point of view. Yet it had not previously been significant to me that the twain could, if not meet, at least stand as equals.

When I finally went back inside to warm up, I set to thinking of what the scene signified to me personally. If I waken at an odd hour, for no apparent reason, I always feel that I am being "called" to something. So it seemed now. I was *meant* to see that magnificent sight. There was a message for me in the experience. As I sorted through the symbolism with which I was familiar, looking for new clues, I was struck with the visual impression of equal size and the word *balance* leapt to my mind. I realized that what I had been lacking in my approach to editorial suggestion was balance. I was all on one side of the equation, and I was on the *Moon side*, which is to say I was involved with my internal feelings about the work rather than with its appearance in the world where its merit would be judged by others. As I thought about the idea of balance, and that I had seen a *setting* Moon and a *rising* Sun, it became clear that the message for me was that it was time for my emotional involvement to sink below the horizon and for the intellectual function to claim ascendancy.

As I switched my inner focus, I began to understand what had been murky, and the required new structure for the book began to take shape. What had been a tangle of emotions resolved into a state of clarity of mind under the sharp light of the solar approach of rational analysis. Though it could claim equality, the lunar aspect had already served its purpose by providing the creative impetus to write the book originally. Now it was time for it to drop below the horizon of conscious involvement in order for the book to "see the light of day."

This experience of reading the spiritual signs in the world around us taught me that what is common is not necessarily "ordinary." Also, that such peak experiences are readily available, if we are willing to tune into them. In *The Music of Silence*, Brother David Steindl-Rast says,

"Sometimes people get the mistaken notion that spirituality is a separate department of life, the penthouse of our existence, but rightly understood, it is a vital awareness that pervades all realms of our being."

Interestingly, once I had broken through the barrier that was giving me writer's block, the pain and stiffness in my knee disappeared. Since I believe that every illness, disability, or discomfort serves a spiritual purpose, I had previously attempted to understand why I was suffering physically, but I had not been able to get at the non-physical root of the problem until my Sun-Moon experience. As I pondered the idea of balance, I perceived that being stiff-legged and in pain was badly affecting my ability to walk, my *balance*. Symbolically, I connected this with my emotional one-sidedness and realized that I was being "unbending" in my approach to the editor's comments. It wasn't that I couldn't accept the criticism *intellectually*—what she said made sense—it was that my lunar self was holding on tight and wouldn't let go, wouldn't be flexible.

I will add that I have the Moon in the sign of Taurus, the same sign as that November full Moon was occupying! Taurus is the quintessential sign of inflexibility, hanging on to the past, refusal to change, stubbornness, and fixity. However, the Moon in Taurus is said to be "exalted," and that sign confers great strength and stamina. Therefore, my lunar self could survive

10

contact with the solar power and not be diminished by it, as was shown symbolically by the real moon riding high on her side of the sky, facing the blaze of the Sun as an equal across the horizon. Once I unbent internally, my knee returned to normal—overnight!

Signs are everywhere. To read them we have only to discern patterns. *Synchronicity* is the term for the principle that connects seemingly unrelated events, actions, and objects.

For example, someone finds a lone glove in the park, picks it up idly and wonders who lost it. The finder examines the glove to discover something about the personality of the wearer—is it a fine leather glove that would fit the hand of a woman? Or is it coarser leather, large and squarish, for a man's hand? Was it lost during a lovers' tryst, or dropped when reaching for loose coins or a handkerchief? Perhaps it is a workman's rough and dirty canvas glove, or a child's woolly mitten. Was the mitten one of a favorite pair and does the child now weep over the loss? This information is all contained in the glove, even though we term it an "inanimate object." Every object bears its owner's or maker's imprint.

The average person will leave the glove lying in the path to be trampled by the walking feet of the unaware, but the careful (meaning: *to take care*) person will lay it tenderly on a bench, knowing it is full of meaning for someone, in the hope the owner may seek and find it. So much of life is seeking and hoping to find, but how often it seems we find what we do not seek consciously.

Later that week, the glove finder has a fight with her lover at dinner and, while cleaning the kitchen in an upset and angry mood, she lacerates her hand badly and has to be rushed to an emergency room for twenty stitches. Emerging from the hospital into a fresh snowfall, the cold makes her aware that she cannot put her glove on the bandaged hand. So she wears one glove.

Coincidence? Most people would say it was and think no more about it. However, she is now wearing a visible reminder of the sorry state of her relationship, something she has been reluctant to admit. Every time she goes outside wearing only one glove she has to think about the circumstances that led up to her injuring herself. If she is tuned into thinking symbolically, she will see a connection. If not, she may only seethe and fume at the injustice of it all and blame her lover for the accident.

In this case, the woman was an aspiring poet. Reflective by nature, she mused on the curious incident of finding the single glove, and now wearing a single glove. She wrote a poem that began,

What so lonely as the single glove,
What so empty as a heart without love,

and came to realize that she had been holding onto a crumbling relationship because she feared the loss of love.

After breaking up the relationship, she offered the poem for publication and it was accepted. This boost to her morale set her life in a more creatively fulfilling direction, and she used her newfound insight about why she tended to stay in unsatisfactory relationships to change the old pattern.

All because an unknown someone lost a glove in the park one snowy afternoon. Was it just coincidence, or is there a pattern here, a system of signs pointing the way? Of course, the lost glove had no connection to her dissatisfaction with her relationship and certainly did not cause her to cut her hand. However, without encountering the lost glove, an experience that put her into a reflective state over the issue of separation, of the loss of a mate, she would have written no poem, found no new direction for her life.

Symbols in and of themselves have no meaning. They *point beyond themselves to meaning and significance*. The cross does not "mean" that Christ was crucified. Crucifixion was a common means of punishment in ancient Rome, and the Appian Way was lined with offenders hanging on crosses as a result of their crimes. The cross, as a symbol, meant something quite different to the Romans than to the Christians who followed Jesus. And something different still to the pre-Columbian Aztec people whose god Quetzacoatl, known as "Lord of Life and Death," carries a cross as his symbol. Interestingly, the legend of Quetzacoatl relates that he, like Jesus, was born of a virgin mother, Chimalman, who conceived him from the breath of the God-above-gods known as "The Morning." To the Christian believer today, the symbol of the cross tells an entire story of sacrifice and redemption. It points beyond itself to a sacred dimension, to meaning.

Symbols have always been essential for humans to relate to their gods and their environments. The earliest hunter cultures drew symbolic representations of the animals they killed for food, while plant-oriented cultures depicted the vegetation upon which they depended for sustenance and which they revered as symbolic of the ever-turning cycle of life.

A lovely representation of the Egyptian myth of Osiris in a bas relief from Philae, Egypt shows the dead god upon a crocodile, a symbol of the rising sun, with lotus and papyrus sprouts—symbols of resurgent life—springing up all around him. As a plant-dependent society whose rich agriculture relied upon the annual flooding of the great Nile river, these ancients showed that they knew and revered the connection between the plant world and themselves by using plants as symbols in their sacred art.

Throughout history, symbols have been a means by which humans could harness the mysterious powers of the unseen world. Symbols give meaning to the awesome mystery of the powers of the universe before which we stand helpless. They allow us to project our *intention* and through intention we discover meaning and significance. Says Lame Deer in *Lame Deer, Seeker of Visions*:

> We Sioux spend a lot of time thinking about everyday things, which in our minds are mixed with the spiritual. We see in the world around us many symbols that teach us the meaning of life. . . . Indians live in a world of symbols and images where the spiritual and the commonplace are one. . . . To us they are part of nature, part of ourselves—the earth, the sun, the wind and the rain, stones trees, animals . . . we need no more than a hint to give us the meaning.

The artist Andrew Wyeth has lived his entire life in a small town in Pennsylvania (spending summers in a Maine coastal village). When asked why he did not travel and see the world, he said that it would take an entire lifetime to really *see* the environments in which he lived and painted, and that seeing was his work. It is this "seeing," or the practicing of the ability to see, that makes Wyeth's paintings of simple, everyday objects—such as a basket of blueberries sitting on the kitchen table—or ordinary scenes—like a hay field or a chair leaning against a porch rail—so arresting. That he has truly *seen* illuminates the sacred dimension from which everyday life springs. This seeing imbues his paintings with a luminosity of spirit that calls forth deep emotion in the viewer.

Too often, we look but do not see—we are too busy, too preoccupied with our worries and our personal concerns to pay attention to the world around us with its multiplicity of wondrous forms, from the clouds passing overhead to the animal passing by. If you want to experience a creature that sees intensely, try watching a cat in the garden. The cat stalks through the grass, ears twitching to pick up the slightest sound, eyes brilliantly alert for anything that moves. It will crouch—and *watch*. Whether it is hunting or not, it looks at everything in its environment from the minute to the huge, not for opportunity but because it is in the nature of the feline to watch. A good role model for anyone truly interested in becoming aware.

Joseph Campbell, in speaking of the "dimension of wonder," suggested that one take a simple, insignificant object, such as a pencil, ashtray, or anything, and, holding it in both hands, contemplate it. He says, ". . . ask yourself seriously, 'What is it?' [and] its dimension of wonder opens; for the mystery of the being of that being is identical with the mystery of the being of the universe—and yourself."

George Washington Carver said, "If you love it enough, anything will talk with you." Below is a meditation I devised for experiencing this dimension of wonder.

 ### *Experiencing the Divine in the Ordinary*

First, choose an object upon which to focus. It can be anything out of your usual environment—something of which you are particularly fond or to which you have a sentimental connection. I find that beginners do well working with plants or flowers, because these are obviously alive. Items from nature, such as a seashell or a crystal, also work well, but any object will do.

Next, pick a place where you can be comfortable and remain undisturbed for about twenty minutes. It can be within doors or outside—in a garden or on the beach. Wear loose clothes and eliminate distractions.

Place the object in front of you on a table or the floor or ground and allow yourself a few minutes to relax and form a one-on-one relationship with the object you have chosen.

Now, take several deep breaths, exhaling slowly while clearing your mind of random thoughts. Begin to focus closely on the object and concentrate on it to the exclusion of all else, as if you were looking through a microscope which could reveal the smallest intimate details of the object. Through this concentration and attention, you are going to penetrate its essence and become one with it, coming to understand that you and it are of the same essential stuff.

As you view the object, try to sense what it would say to you if it could speak. Imagine the hidden knowledge it contains, which it has learned on its journey through life and time. If it is a plant, imagine the thousands of ancestor plants that grew and spread their seeds so that this plant could have life and be here with you now. If it's a rock, consider the eons spent building it and where it might have been originally in the geological strata.

Continuing to focus, really *look* at the object. If it is a plant or flower, examine each leaf or petal, noticing the delicate veins or shadings of color. Really look, as if you have never before seen anything like it. Make experiencing the object's reality something entirely new, as if it were transported to your hand from another planet. Imagine how you would consider a moon rock!

You might want to ask the object a question or try to communicate with it in some way. A name might occur to you. Remember that it was the task of Adam and Eve to name all the plants and animals. *Naming* is a powerful spiritual link with what is other-than-ourselves. In the story of Rumpelstiltskin, for example, the lovely queen keeps her child, who was promised as the price of turning the flax into gold, by discovering the name of the little gnome. Everything has a secret name. See if you can discover your object's secret name.

Take notice of its unique shape and other characteristics. Examine its construction for small details that set it apart from similar objects. Acknowledge its uniqueness. Like you, it is one of a kind (unless of course it was factory-made, but I suggest you choose a natural object).

Whatever it is, realize that it is made up of the same electrons whirling around the nuclei of atoms as are you, and envision these in both the object and in yourself as coming from the same universal source of pure energy that has been transformed into matter. Recognize that you and the object are one and interrelated. Credit your SELF with having the power to experience this unified life field. Reject the notion of being a separate being in a fragmented world and accept the reality that you are connected to everything in the universe, that your sense of apartness is merely the result of perceptual limitations which you can transcend.

Now, see yourself as able to perceive the true nature of the universe with everything in it as connected to everything else. Imagine what it would be like to live in a world where everyone realized this as the ultimate Truth. Envision peace and plenty for all as a result of the world being recognized as a unified whole, rather than merely a collection of separate and unrelated parts. Finish by sending love and harmony to the object and thanking it for existing and gracing your environment.

After you finish, do something very ordinary—like eating a piece of fruit, or taking a walk. Focus on the experience to the exclusion of everything else, noticing all the fine details.

If eating a piece of fruit, first examine the piece with care, noticing any tiny details. For example, if it is an orange look closely at the pores in the skin, or try to count the freckles on a banana. Feel the shape in your hands, imagine the tree upon which it grew,

17

the people who planted the tree, tended its growth, and harvested the crop.

Imagine the entire chain that brought the piece of fruit to you, from the person who picked it to the checker at the supermarket where you bought it, and everything in between. Maybe it came thousands of miles from a foreign country and travelled across an ocean to get to you. How might it have felt about its journey? How many hands did it pass through? Literally hundreds of people were involved in the process.

Imagine the fruit as a small seed and think about the entire life process that transformed that seed into a fruit-bearing tree. Eat the fruit slowly, in tiny bites, savoring each, noticing how you react to the experience of taking in life-sustaining nourishment from the life source. Imagine all the fruit trees in the world as emanating from the same energy and understand that you are incorporating that universal energy into your own body by eating the fruit.

Mentally celebrate the joys and benefits of the everyday reality in which you live and have your being. Consider that the flavor of the entire ocean is contained in but a single drop, that the entire mystery of life lies within a seed or the tiniest egg.

🌱 The World as Energy

Ancient shamanistic cultures like that of Native Americans understood that all forms of life—human and animal, plant and insect, the flowing waters of rivers and streams, clouds and trees—are but transient patterns of moving energy. This understanding can be traced to primordial times. It permeates native and indigenous cultures everywhere. That we live in a river of ever-changing energy is one of the most basic concepts underlying the practice of shamanism. This spiritual and intuitive knowledge is now being confirmed by quantum physics.

Underneath the visible forms of matter there are natural if unseen forces that possess both intelligence and purpose, as leading-edge scientists like physicist David Foster and biologist Rupert Sheldrake now assert. This is precisely what the magicians of earlier times believed and what shamans have always known. In an interesting twist, it is the ancient view that supports the emerging one, rather than the new disproving the old.

The current theoretical model of the universe is dependent upon the finding of a "sixth quark," which has been called the "God particle." This theory of particle physics, if proved, will explain what is so far a missing link in the universal model of existence. It may very well be that if this elusive particle is found it will substantiate the connection between ourselves and the universe.

The term "sixth sense" is often used to describe psychic gifts, but I believe that there is a range of subtle senses—that we may possess not only a sixth sense, but a seventh, eighth, ninth, and tenth as well. The physical senses—sight, touch, seeing, smell, and taste—might be regarded as the "gross" senses, while the *inner* ways of comprehending reality are governed by our subtle senses of perception.

There can be no doubt that primitive peoples, who were attuned to Spirit everywhere, were guided by such senses. They possessed powers that enabled them to locate favorable hunting grounds, and allowed telepathic communications. Hawaiian *kahunas* talked to the trees, the waters, the winds, and the *menehunes* (elemental spirits, or elves) in a most matter-of-fact way. If lost in the wilderness, a kahuna could ask the way of a tree, a stone, a vine, or a stream. The tribal shamans nurtured these powers and brought them to a high degree of development. Magic was not only used for religious purposes, it was an early form of science.

Magic teaches us that:

1. Everything is composed of a living energy that is constantly in flux.
2. There is no separation between creatures and the environment in which they live.
3. Everything, animate and inanimate alike, has consciousness at some level. The consciousness of animals may be somewhat similar to ours, but the consciousness of a tree or a rock is, though different, no less valid.

The chances are that we can never really grasp this intellectually. We must *feel* our way into experiencing this reality, through our emotions and our intuition. Nonetheless, I believe that we all somewhere *know* that we are connected to the whole and participate in it, else we would not be striving for an antidote to our sense of separation and loneliness.

We have "forgotten" the original Oneness. In our mad race for technological superiority, we have lost track of the universe as a unity, and of our beautiful planet as a living, pulsating Being. We must reconnect with the knowledge of the interrelatedness of all life and all things on our planet, affirming that nothing exists in isolation. The whole universe is living Spirit and everyone and everything pulses with this creative energy. Everything is relative to everything else.

chapter two
The Transformative Power of Prayer

Spiritual practice of whatever kind aims to balance—or, when difficulties arise, to rebalance—the person through communication with a higher power. *Intentionality* is a key—we seek to alter or uplift ourselves, or our conditions, through some form of spiritual communion.

The form itself is irrelevant—all roads at the bottom of a mountain lead to the summit. The key is to admit the possibility into our consciousness. Remember that, *where intention goes, Spirit flows.*

Does prayer work? Naturally, something so subjective, private, and personally intimate as prayer is extremely difficult to test in a scientific laboratory, although this has been tried. A group called Spindrift, located in Oregon, attempting to answer the question, Does prayer work?, has been pursuing testing the effectiveness of prayer, both directed (aimed at achieving a specific result) and non-directed ("Thy will be done.").

The researchers use very simple tests and low-tech equipment and conduct experiments with seed germination and plant growth. The basis of the Spindrift work is the central assumption that all humans have "divine attributes, a qualitative oneness with God." Human consciousness, in their view, is, like the Divine, infinite in space and time and both are a single unity.

They ask if there is a result that can be quantitatively measured, and, if so, can it be replicated? One of the simple ways they test this hypothesis is with sprouting seeds. If one tray of seeds receives prayer and another does not, does the rate of germination vary? Results have shown that it does.

Considering that fact that most of us pray for healing when someone is sick, the researchers set up tests that deliberately injured the seedlings and then measured the results of prayer for them to "get well." Results were dramatic. The "sick" seedlings responded even more to being prayed for than the healthy ones had. They then upped the ante and put even more stress on the seedlings, which indicated that prayer worked best when the stress level was increased.

The next question was: How much prayer? Some seeds received twice as much prayer as others and the results showed that the greater amount of prayer was more effective. This could be why we are given the admonition to "pray unceasingly." Apparently aware of this factor, Buddhist monks turn prayer wheels constantly, twenty-four hours a day.

Further experiments were directed to whether the seeds were effected by being identified to the person(s) doing the praying, and the researchers concluded that the more clearly the practitioner is conscious of the subject the greater the effect. "In order for our prayers to have any effect," they said, "we need to know who or what we are praying for."

The Spindrift researchers addressed the issue of directed and non-directed prayer and found that the "Thy will be done" approach worked better than praying for a specific outcome. In effect, what was happening was that the *law of the conceptual whole*, as they term it, was operating through the practitioner holding in his or her mind the overall concept of the system

22

involved. Both types of prayer were deemed effective, but the non-directed form produced quantitatively higher yields.

Interestingly, this approach is almost identical to that of the non-denominational Unitarian "Science of Mind." In this practice, according to Earnest Holmes in *How To Use the Science of Mind*,

> The basis of [the practitioner's] work lies in the assumption that we are now living in a spiritual universe, that the law of our being is the Law of Mind in action, that there is an exact parallel between thoughts and things.
>
> . . . One could not do this if he believed that things are independent of their silent, invisible causes. But if he really believes that the Law of Mind in action creates situations and conditions then he will know that . . . any state of consciousness consistently maintained, will produce a corresponding result. . . . the Divine Presence is the infinite Spirit from whose all-light, wisdom and love one may draw inspiration, guidance and a sense of certainty.

The concept that "thoughts are things" and that "you create your own reality" may seem to be very New Age, but Unity's co-founder Myrtle Fillmore discovered these principles and put them into practice over a hundred years ago, and the words quoted above were written in 1948.

Prayer is one of the most effective means of adding a spiritual dimension to our lives. It is a wonderful tool—easy to use, portable, requiring no special equipment, and it can be done any time and any place under any circumstances. You do not have to be in a special place such as a church, synagogue, or mosque to pray. Through prayer we contact our own Spiritually Evolving Life Force, and through contacting our SELF we contact the divine energy of which the SELF is composed. All matter is composed of energy, and all energy is divine energy.

23

Prayer comes in many forms. It can be formal or informal, directed or non-directed, simple or elaborate, silent or spoken, private or public. Here are some suggestions for how you can incorporate prayer into your daily life:

❧ Short blessing prayers are a part of many religious traditions. These can express gratitude for a thing or an event and also acknowledge that Spirit is present in it. You can create blessing prayers for the objects you use daily, for actions you perform regularly, for people and pets in your life. I make it a habit to end telephone calls with the words, "Bless you." You can bless those leaving your presence, bless your home when you depart. The term "goodbye" is actually a form of blessing. In Spanish, one says "Vaya con Dios," or "God go with you."

❧ You can include in your daily prayers awareness of the environment by blessing the streams and waters, plants and trees, wild life, and those whose efforts are directed toward healing our polluted environment.

❧ Make special blessing days. The feast day of St. Francis of Assisi, in the first week of October, is a day for the blessing of animals. You can take your pet to be blessed or create a private blessing ceremony in your home or neighborhood.

❧ You can create a blessing service for your home and each room in it. For example, you can do a blessing service for your kitchen. Bless the stove, refrigerator, freezer, appliances, your pots and pans, bowls and cutlery. You can acknowledge their role as co-creators in the meals you prepare for yourself and your family.

❧ Many people say a simple grace at meals. You can enlarge on your repertory by dipping into the grace sayings of other spiritual traditions, from past times to the present. *One Hundred Graces,* selected by Marcia and Jack Kelly, is a good reference.

🌿 You can become more aware of how you use the Sabbath. Even if you are not a regular churchgoer, you can "make holy the Sabbath," by making it a practice to spend some time in quiet meditation, turning off the television, forgoing shopping. These or similar actions may increase the meaning of the Sabbath for you.

🌿 One of the most sacred things we can do is to *celebrate*. Christians "celebrate the Lord." You can make any celebration sacred, or you can make anything sacred by celebrating it. Make it a point to celebrate one thing every day.

🌿 All service is sacred. Think about the work you do and how it serves others and say a prayer of blessing for your work and the benefits it brings you, your family, your community. Bless the "ripple effect" by thinking of how your efforts may be a blessing to people you will never meet.

🌿 Create a "living prayer" by rendering some service to someone in your neighborhood or community. Or, practice "random kindness" and bestow a blessing on someone you don't know. I once bought two dozen roses and walked along the street tucking one under the windshield wiper of each car I passed on my block. These little anonymous gestures of blessing confer benefits to the giver as well as the receiver. One man I heard about goes around putting quarters in expired parking meters to prevent the car owners from getting tickets.

🌿 Dedicate actions you perform throughout the day to Spirit. Bless and give thanks frequently for the ordinary good things in life. Praise the Higher Power frequently. Offer the first drink of the day in praise of the Goddess.

🌿 On the anniversary of a death, create a private memorial service for a person or a pet you loved who died. Invite others who knew the person or pet to join you. Do something that will reconnect you to the person or pet. For example, a very dear friend of mine, a confirmed chocoholic named Ari, was one of the first victims of AIDS. Though I'm not personally fond of chocolate, on the anniversary of his death I make or buy a scrumptious chocolate desert and invite some of his other friends to share it with me. Another deceased friend was an avid lover of classical music. On his day, I play the Brahms first piano concerto, which we once heard a magical performance of at the Dutch Concertgebouw in Amsterdam. It brings him back.

❧ If you live with a partner, consider sitting quietly together for a specific time daily or weekly in a prayerful silence. This may turn into a regular practice. You can also do this with your children.

❧ Practice wonder as a prayer. Let yourself be awed by a sunset, a moonrise, a flower blooming, a river rushing. Contemplate the divinity in all of nature. Become aware of Spirit flowing through everything.

❧ Say prayers of blessing over your house when you enter it or depart from it. After a long journey or vacation, do a "return blessing" and rededicate your house and the activities that take place in it to the Higher Power.

❧ Look for coincidences and delve into their hidden meaning. I recently did a Tarot card reading for a woman who had been brought to me by a lady who owns a healing gift shop. The reading was intense, provoking tears, and afterward, I felt strongly led to give my client a clear crystal, known as a Herkimer diamond. Saying, "For clarity of mind," I pressed one of these into her hand. She reacted as if I'd given her an electric shock. Tears came to her eyes. Her friend said, "Do you remember that candle you picked up in the gift shop? You wanted to buy it but it was too expensive. It was a

Herkimer diamond candle." She explained that the crystal within was revealed when the candle burned down. We were all touched and felt Spirit at work. Say a short prayer of praise and thanksgiving when Spirit touches you through a meaningful coincidence.

Prayer can also be used to open the gates of initiation. The term *initiation* refers to being inducted into the mysteries, of being given understanding of the higher order of things. The initiate is one who knows *internally* what cannot be communicated by mere words but what must take place at a deep inner level that connects the individual to the Universal Divine.

During a year-long sabbatical in Arizona, to where I had gone on a personal quest to encounter my own depths, I received several initiatory experiences. One of these, which came while I was in a profound, prayerful meditative state, showed me how the transmutation of "pure" or divine energy into physical matter worked. This concept was presented to me in the diagrammatic form shown below.

PURE ENERGY
[The Universal Source—God or Consciousness]
Becomes/is transformed into

THOUGHT
[Mind Stuff without Form]
Which inherently contains

STRUCTURE
[Corresponding to Matter]*
To activate physical manifestation

*Structure refers to the *archetypal patterns* already existent in Universal Mind prior to becoming manifest in material reality. For example, there is a crystalline structure in *unformed thought* that corresponds exactly to the physical structure of a crystal.

DESIRE
[To Manifest]
Uses thought structure to mold

SUBSTANCE
[Prana or Life Energy]
Which then becomes manifest in

MATTER
[Physical Reality]

Prayer and initiation are both magical practices. The word "magic" derives from the Persian *magi*, who were priests of the Mithraic religion. This sect was known for its ability to interpret natural phenomena. An example is the three Magi, or wise men, who followed a star to visit upon the birth of Jesus Christ.

Prayer has long been a component of the practice of magic, and magic was an important component of early religions. The practice of magic is itself a religious practice, although it has become associated with mere sleight-of-hand or with "wicked witch" notions. Magic is actually nothing more than the *conscious* use of mental powers employed for the purpose of aligning the magician with the natural forces of the universe. The German mystic poet Goethe called nature "God's living garment," and medieval monks referred to *liber mundi*, literally "the book of the world." They believed that nature was God's book, to be read through prayer, meditation, and the spiritual life.

This "book of the world" is hidden from immediate view, ates ordinary reality from our perception of the divine spirit that imbues it. As the poet-mystic William Blake put it,

> *To See a World in a Grain of Sand*
> *And Heaven in a Wild Flower,*
> *Hold Infinity in the palm of your hand,*
> *And Eternity in an hour.*

28

A more recent man of genius, Albert Einstein, expressed this concept by saying that, "Everyone who is seriously involved in the pursuit of science becomes convinced that a Spirit is manifest in the Laws of the Universe."

The actual practice (as opposed to belief in) magic calls upon higher states of consciousness than we generally use, and these can be activated through prayer, which tunes us in to guidance. This super-awareness is akin to religious mysticism. Both magician and mystic seek to transcend the "ordinariness" of everyday life and make it sacred. To do this, one must be able to "see" through the obscuring veil masking *true* reality, which is to say we must acknowledge the divine in all that we do and experience. Prayer is a means of lifting this veil and seeing through to the sacred dimension in all of life.

From time immemorial women have practiced the magical arts—healing wounds, curing disease, easing the pangs of childbirth—and millions of them were burned at the stake, paying with their lives for pursuing the ancient traditions and keeping magic alive. However, despite persistent efforts by church and state to obliterate magic, it refuses to die out—perhaps because it is truth—and the efforts of these countless unknown and unsung women have served to bring the tradition, today known as *Wicca*, or benign "white" witchcraft, to us in the present day.

An honorable craft and the fastest-growing religion in America today, Wicca carries on the great continuity of "earth magic," which stretches, like a long unbroken thread in the fabric of human history, from prehistoric times to our own. With its dedication to the interconnected sacredness of all things, this feminine-oriented belief system offers us much solace. With its resurgence, magic can have a successful and glorious future and take its rightful place once again among the useful pursuits of humans.

As we study the magical tradition and hear what our leading-edge scientists are saying, we come to the inescapable conclusion that we indeed do live in a "magical" universe, where, beneath the visible forms, an invisible support system of energy connects all to all. Magic and mysticism have in common the idea that there is an "inner force," an invisible underlying matrix out of which all the visible forms arise, of the universe and all in it deriving from the same source. In Hindu mythology, which is rooted in the concept of wholeness, the symbol of the goddess-as-lotus represents this concept of form rising out of the invisible life-giving source. In *The Art of Indian Asia*, Heinrich Zimmer gives this description:

> Rising from the depths of water and expanding its petals on the surface, the lotus . . . is the most beautiful evidence offered to the eye of the self-engendering fertility of the bottom. Through its appearance, it gives proof of the life-supporting of the all-nourishing abyss . . . the infinite ocean of that liquid life-substance out of which all the differentiated elements of the universe arise.

It is this underpinning that contains the sacred dimension that can inspire and inform our everyday life. The *mage* of earlier times believed that it was possible to transcend both time and space, which is what prayer does. Rather than ridiculing this notion, let us heed the words of physicist Russell Targ: "[Physics is] incomplete and inadequate to describe that kind of activity." Rather than fault those "magicians" of the past who have made the effort to observe and utilize this wholeness, the oneness of ourselves and nature with the divine spirit, we can choose to listen to them and learn from them.

How and *why* does prayer work—to heal or do anything else for that matter? Prayer aligns us with the cosmos, with the right and natural order of all things, or so I believe. When we pray for ourselves or others, we are putting ourselves into alignment with universal forces. One might say that we are deliberately getting in tune with the harmonic chords of the universe. And when we are in tune, we produce effects.

Cambridge University biologist Rupert Sheldrake, author of *A New Science of Life*, has proposed a fascinating hypothesis that provides a possible explanation for prayer's effectiveness. The type of prayer known as distant healing suggests the "morphogenetic fields" Sheldrake's theory advances.

According to Sheldrake, these immaterial fields are unbounded by space and time. They contain a feedback loop in which the field structures the matter within it and the qualities of the matter modify the field. All organisms are seen as dynamic structures continuously re-creating themselves under the influence of their own past states.

A key concept here is that *matter and energy cannot be separated.* The fields surrounding matter are basic to understanding the phenomena within these fields, including not only the fields for you and for me but those larger fields of the physical universe, all the way into the farthest reaches of space. New kinds of fields, both biological and consciousness-related, are being proposed, based upon the idea that the universe works like a hologram, in which every part interpenetrates every other part, thereby transmitting any change to the whole. Our brains, too, are holograms that construct "reality" by interpreting frequencies from a dimension transcending time and space. Thus, each of us can be considered to be a portion of the original Universal Hologram, which in some sense created us and everything else in the universe according to its holistic pattern. Prayer lines us up with this pattern, in ourselves and in the universe. As we resonate with the universal pattern, we influence our personal pattern.

Prayer is also a form of meditation. It puts us into an altered state of consciousness not unlike the ones used for self-hypnosis and visualization. When we pray, we are actually visualizing the result desired even if we are not doing so consciously. Claude Bristol in *The Magic of Believing* says, in relation to the law of suggestion,

> . . . forces operating within its limits are capable of producing phenomenal results. That is, the power of your own suggestion—starts the machinery into operation or causes the subconscious mind to begin its creative work [which] *leads to belief, and once this belief becomes a deep conviction, things begin to happen.* (Italics added.)

That we are all one is demonstrated by quantum physics—the science of the subatomic dimensions of the world. Recent experiments have shown that two electrons, having once been in contact but then separated—even by relatively immense distances—still have the effect of changing one another immediately and to the same degree, without any energy exchange or time elapsed. The implication is that in some way the two electrons remain *united* through the fact that there once was contact.

Brian Josephson, Nobel laureate physicist of Cambridge University's Cavendish Laboratory, suggests that this phenomenon, known as "quantum nonlocality," may one day serve to explain puzzling effects such as the effectiveness of prayer-at-a-distance. And Dr. Beverly Rubik of Temple University's Center for Frontier Sciences, believes that what makes *directed* prayer work is the transfer of "information."

Physicist David Bohm suggests that "Meaning, which is simultaneously mental and physical, can serve as the link or bridge between realms," connecting mind and body. Prayer brings us to meaning, for in prayer we address what is meaningful. According to Bohm, mind, body, and meaning together express a whole.

When we pray, we are addressing this "ground from which the whole of existence emerges." There are many names for this ground of being—God, Buddha, the One, the All, Source, Spirit—and each of us addresses it in our own individual way.

🌾 Healing Spirit

Prayer has been shown to heal. In a well-known experiment, by cardiologist Randolph Byrd of San Francisco General Hospital, people from across the country were asked to pray for approximately half of the nearly four hundred patients in coronary care. This was what is called a "double-blind" or controlled experiment in which no one involved, except the researchers, knew who was being prayed for and who was not. The prayed-for group did better on several counts. The death level was lower, they did not require life-support systems, and they needed much less medicine.

Research has also shown that it doesn't matter what the person's religious belief is, or even if they believe, in order for the healing to work. Though some, such as born-again Christians and Buddhists scored higher, even agnostics can pray successfully. Prayer need not be in the format or context of any formalized ritual or organized church.

Many "nondenominational" groups, such as Unity, use prayer as part of regular healing services, as do "spiritual" churches that practice prayer healing.

Prayer seems to work from some deep well of humanity's ability to feel compassion and empathy for those in need. It is the same impulse that acts when in an emergency situation a person risks life and limb to rescue another person from peril.

Here is a list of affirmations to be used in conjunction with your prayer, or to get you started praying if you don't already do so, and some meditative mind-prayers adapted from *Spiritual Mind Healing* by Ernest Holmes.

I am healthy, strong, peaceful, happy, and at rest.
Spirit, which is active in me, flows throughout.
I am well, buoyant, happy, free, and full of joy.
My days are filled with energy, radiance, and health.
My prayer now removes all obstacles to my healing.
The purifying energy of Spirit moves through me.
I give praise and thanksgiving for all blessings.
I bless myself and all others.
I invite the healing power of Spirit into my life.

§§§§

Everything that I believe to be true about the Spirit, I understand is also true about myself. Its Goodness is my goodness. Its Power is my power. Its Presence in me is my true self. There is only one True Self.

Every day I believe I am receiving Divine Guidance and inspiration. I realize there is nothing in the universe opposed to me other than my own doubt or any negative force in my own mind. There is nothing that can hinder, impede, or impair my progress.

I shall remember at all times that it is Life that gives. I am its beneficiary. Quietness, confidence, and peace are mine. My every tomorrow is better than today. I now accept that I have an Infinite Power at my disposal.

In Spirit, all is perfect. In Spirit I am perfect. Spirit is at the root of my being. I have an intimate Source from which I may draw strength and inspiration. This universal "I Am" finds expression through me as the individual "I." It is the very essence of my being and in it I realize my true nature.

Another way to include prayer in your life on a regular basis is to choose as a focus word for your relaxation response exercises one that is spiritually meaningful to you. Here are some commonly used terms that will help you to choose one for yourself.

Non-Denominational Focus Words
ONE . ALL . SOURCE . SPIRIT . INFINITE

Christian Focus Words
FATHER . CHRIST . LORD . MARY . JESUS

Jewish Focus Words
SH'MA YISROEL . SHALOM . ECHOD

Islamic Focus Words
INSHA'ALLAH . MOHAMMED . PROPHET

Buddhist Focus Words
OM MANI PADMI HUM . OM

🌿 Prayers of Thanksgiving

Thankfulness is a potent form of prayer. We recognize this annually as Thanksgiving Day, originally a prayerful occasion rather than just a feast, and many people repeat a simple prayer of thanksgiving daily at meals.

Sometimes, however, if life is fraught with difficulty, being thankful for *anything* may seem but another difficulty. But if you practice "an attitude of gratitude," no matter how rocky the path seems at the moment, you will soon find things are improving.

There is always *something*, no matter how small, for which one can give thanks and feel grateful. Once when I was quite ill and bedridden and things seemed dark indeed, I searched for something to give thanks for. I was nestled comfortably in a mound of soft pillows and down quilts, and it occurred to me that the very bed which contained my sick body was something for which I could express gratitude. I did so, adding prayers of thanks for every little thing around me that served to ameliorate my discomfort. The more thanks I gave, the better I felt.

When you give thanks, you are praising, and praising is a form of prayer. Many people go to their place of worship and offer prayers in a formal way and then come home and set about complaining and grumping about all sorts of things. If you are guilty of this transgression against good sense, begin now to praise and give thanks to all about you. Your words of thanks-giving will sink into your subconscious and do their trans-forming work. Dr. Masaharu Taniguchi, a Japanese metaphysician who has had remarkable success in the healing of cancer, says in his book, *You Can Heal Yourself*, "These ideas of . . . 'Thank you' cure all diseases." Here are some affirma-tions you can use.

> *I give praise and thanksgiving for every good thing.*
> *I give thanks for (list everything you can think of).*
> *Today I find many positive things to be thankful for.*

 ### How to Pray Thankfully

This exercise is easy to do, and you should do it often. You need only to be comfortable and relaxed. You can even do it while walking around or performing simple chores or errands.

Mentally go through all the rooms in your house, your work space, your property. Give thanks for each and every item or function you are glad you have available to you. Go into your kitchen and give thanks for your stove, refrigerator, the food in it, your dishes, cutlery, appliances and conveniences. Tour your living room and the other rooms of your house or apartment and give thanks for the furniture, lamps and the electricity to run them, your appliances such as the TV, VCR, or air conditioner. Do this for every room—give thanks for the clothes in your closets (even if you perpetually have "nothing to wear"), the linens on your bed, the rugs on your floors, every comfort and convenience you enjoy. Think of what you would miss especially if you did not have it and give thanks specifically. So many of us take so much for granted until we find ourselves without the common amenities. Just having a roof over your head is deserving of your profound gratitude.

Then work through your garage, and any outside property, giving thanks for your car (if you have one), lawnmower, and so on. Give thanks for your work space and whatever you have there, such as a computer, fax machine, telephone, comfortable chair, good lighting, even tape and paper clips.

Next, turn to the people and animals that populate and benefit your life and give thanks for them one by one.

Don't forget to praise your own personal attributes, from whatever you like about your looks to your skills and abilities. Be thankful you have a brain that can learn and solve problems for you, a heart that can give and receive love, a body that houses your SELF. Give praise to your bodily functions, for without those you would be miserable indeed! You will be amazed how long a list you can compile.

By the time you have finished this inventory, you will be much happier and have gained some necessary perspective. and you will have given your immune system a boost. Do this exercise every day, more often if you are under the weather. Once you have done it a few times, you will be intimately familiar with all you are grateful for and you can take a shortcut. Simply say, "I give praise and thanksgiving for every good thing in my life."

🍃 Love as Prayer

The Greeks recognized different forms of love: the intensely personal feeling we have for someone with whom we are closely related, especially in a romantic or sexual way, they called *eros*; the generalized feeling of love we have for fellow humans, *philia*; and spiritual love, *agape*. To this I add another category—*self-love*, for which the elegant Greeks had no name, but which is essential for effective prayer. Logically, if we are praying for ourselves, we must love ourselves. This is easier said than done. In fact, psychiatrist M. Scott Peck flatly states in his bestseller, *The Road Less Traveled*, that

> The feeling of being valuable [i.e., worthy of love] . . . is a direct product of parental love. Such a conviction must be gained in childhood; it is extremely difficult to acquire it during adulthood. . . . As a result of the experience of consistent parental love and caring throughout childhood, such fortunate children will enter adulthood not only with a deep internal sense of their own value but also with a deep internal sense of security. . . . When these gifts have not been proffered by one's parents, it is possible to acquire them from other sources, but in that case the process of their acquisition is invariably an uphill struggle, often of lifelong duration and often unsuccessful.

That doesn't seem to offer much hope to those among us—a majority—whose parents fell short of Dr. Peck's standard. However, I disagree with his pessimism on the grounds of personal experience. To my mind, where Peck goes wrong is in saying that a sense of worth and security must be acquired from "other sources," presumably outside one's self, for to be dependent upon the love of others is to fear loss of that love, to court disaster, and be in danger of serious disappointment. The proper aim of the loving parent is to teach the child to love *itself.*

I would dispute Peck's theory that loved children always develop "a deep internal sense of their own value," because dependency on the love of another creates fear of the loss of that love, which engenders a sense of *insecurity.*

Love between humans is a variable thing. All such love is by its nature colored by the personality, character, and integrity of the person doing the loving. Although we cherish the notion of "unconditional" love, there really is no such thing. It is common, and self-serving, to deny that our feelings of love for others in our lives fluctuate, but they do—constantly. It is all a matter of degree. There is no one alive who has not at some moment felt a negative feeling toward the most dearly loved person in their life, whether child, parent, lover, or friend.

In point of fact, self-love is the only kind you can ever count on. The love of others can grow cold, be withdrawn, have strings attached, or be snatched away by an unkind fate. Other-love can also cripple. If we are forever seeking love from outside sources, we are on a lifelong search through a minefield that, with a single misstep, can blow up in our faces. Perfect love from another person simply does not exist. But perfect love is possible—from you to your SELF. The love you generate and give to yourself is pure and inexhaustible, like the life force itself, from which it emanates.

Peck suggests that the void can be filled by psychiatric counseling such as he practices. Unfortunately, a great deal of such therapy fails. Peck himself says,

> No matter how well credentialed and trained psychothera-
> pists may be, if they cannot extend themselves through love
> to their patients, the results will be generally unsuccessful.
> Conversely, a totally uncredentialed and minimally trained
> lay therapist who exercises a great capacity to love will

achieve psychotherapeutic results that equal those of the very best psychiatrists.

Certainly many of us, and especially women, have been taught and trained to regard ourselves as dispensable, even disposable. We are supposed to take care of the needs of others, giving out love and nourishment, while taking in little or nothing, receiving only lip service in return for depriving ourselves. Though the word *sacrifice* originally meant "to make sacred," it has come to mean forfeiting one's own legitimate needs in the service of attending the needs of others. This road-to-martyrdom style of life is about as far from sacred as one can get. It is ultimately destructive, not only of the person making the sacrifices but also of those for whom the sacrifices are made. There is a hidden price to be paid—always.

Experience has shown me that the sense of self-worth that is the basis for self-love can be had by recognizing ourselves as a SELF—as a **S**piritually **E**volving **L**ife **F**orce, a work-in-progress, so to speak. As such, you are already a worthy person, one who has a purpose for being on the planet, one who deserves love, no matter how your parents treated you or what wrong notions you absorbed in the past. The act of loving is a *spiritual* act, one of self-evolution. And as we contact our loving SELF, we come to recognize that self-love and love of others are woven from the same thread—that ultimately they are indistinguishable.

The secret that is here revealed is: you already have all the love you need within you right now. Love is your birthright, and you don't have to wait for it to arrive via another person. You can give it to yourself. You can actually generate a flow of love by releasing it from within. Love can be produced deliberately just as thought can be produced on demand. We have only to turn on our "love spigot" and let it flow into us and then out into the world, from where it will return multiplied. A friend once quipped, "Cast your bread upon the waters and it will come back buttered."

The first step in generating the flow of love from within is to realize now that that love is there within you and is waiting to be released into circulation through your prayers, feelings, words, and actions. Once you have learned to generate love, you will never be short of it again. You will become free of the crippling demands of others and you will never need to enter a relationship with anyone in order to receive love. Not only that, but once you have acquired the knack of generating love to yourself, you will see that the outer world responds in kind. Since you will have plenty of love—"to share and to spare"— others will feel loved by you and act accordingly. As you radiate love first to yourself and then outward to the world, every part of your life will begin to right itself—you will attract the right people, right situations, right conditions for your full health and happiness.

This love you can generate is *agape*, or divine love. You have only to call upon it and it is there for you to use. Do not wonder how love works, or where it comes from, but have the boldness to know you can release it from within yourself now and forever. It is a well that can never be empty. It does not depend on persons, places, or things. It is as free as the air you breathe, and just as necessary. It is, for example, a known fact that women who get breast cancer suffer from a lack of love. I'd like everyone to know a wonderful truth—that when there is need for love we can supply it from within ourselves, to ourselves (as well as to others). Begin now to speak words of love to yourself, especially to any afflicted part of yourself.

Wherever you are in your life, whatever problems you have now or have faced in the past, love is a powerhouse of spiritual energy. It connects you to all good in the universe, from which you can draw at will. When we love we feel transported, as if into another dimension, and we truly are in a

higher place. You can climb to the stars on a beam of love.
Love can be your secret weapon with which you vanquish the
sorrows and ills of life. Practicing generating love on a daily
basis is a powerful and effective means of prayer. Like pouring
a healing balm over yourself, you will become quiet, peaceful,
and filled with harmony. You will be in sync with your SELF.
By becoming a constantly radiating center of love, by filling
yourself with the love you carry within you, you heal what ails
you and better your life in all ways. Here are some prayer affirmations you can use.

> *I generate love from the inexhaustible supply that fills the*
> *universe.*
> *Love flows through me at all times in proportion to my*
> *needs and desires.*
> *The love within me is mine to have and to use for all*
> *good purpose.*

How to Generate Love

You have the ability to generate love at will. To
experience this, sit, recline, or lie down in a comfortable position and close your eyes. Begin with a
breathing or relaxation exercise. Then picture your
dominant hand in your mind. Find your hand mentally and begin sending it love. Radiate love out of
your heart center to your hand. Soon it will begin to
feel warm and alive. It is responding to the love you
are generating. Now, send love to other parts of
your body at will. Just concentrate on sending the
love out and feel it being received. Continue sending
yourself love until you feel filled with a glowing
warmth, emanating from your heart center. Picture
this love as a beautiful, pure, white light cascading
through your entire body, loosening tension,
soothing emotional hurt, healing pain or discomfort.
Say, *"I give this total pure love to myself. I honor*

myself with love now." Feel this love energy pulsating through your entire being while you imagine it as a beam of light streaming out of your heart center and filling every cell in your body, every crevice in your emotions, every thought in your mind. See this beam of powerful light leave your body and flow out to the universe, filling it with radiance. Now, see the radiance returning to you, entering your heart center, and filling you with even more love, connecting you to the meaning in yourself and the meaning in the universe.

🌿 Prayer in the *Huna* Tradition

The Hawaiian tradition of *Huna* teaches that we are composed of three "beings" that interpenetrate each other. One is the *unihipili*, or elemental/animal self, called the "low self" (not because it is inferior but because it is basal); unihipili correlates with the subconscious; the second is the mental self, called *uhane*, the "middle self," or the ego/personal self that deals with the outer world; the third is *aumakua*, or the spiritual self, which could be likened to the superconscious. It can be considered as your divine potential—*akua* means "possessing the attributes of a god." Each aumakua belongs to "The Great Poe Aumakua," the family of High Selves. These are always in contact with each other.

In addition, you may have with you an *akuanoho*, or guardian angel. This being is under the direction of your aumakua and acts as an intermediary. It assists you, protects you, and guides you.

In the hierarchy of the low self (unihipili), the middle self (uhane), and the High Self (aumakua), each has a task to perform so that the whole runs smoothly. The low self takes care of bodily needs, is instinctual and runs the autonomic systems. Our physical life—the need for action and rest, tension and relaxation, food and water, elimination, protection from the elements, and sex are all under the control of unihipili.

The middle self, uhane, deals with our personal and social needs—ego needs and relationships with others. The psychologist Abraham Maslow identified "mega needs," which are the demands of the High Self—truth, beauty, justice, wisdom, and humor. He also pointed out that the basic needs for sustenance and shelter and the societal needs for ego fulfillment and financial security must be met before the needs of the High Self can be attended. To meet the meta needs of aumakua, we first must have a healthy body and a developed ego (ego here used in its proper connotation of that part of us which makes conscious choices). Then, we can have close communion with our high self, or in my terms the SELF.

Prayer is a wonderful way for connecting all three of our "selves." In this ancient tradition, to pray is to engage all three selves simultaneously through the life energy called *mana*. In the Hawaiian language, the word for "to pray," *wai-pa*, also means "to divide the waters." This is a reference to the practice of sending mana from the low self to the High Self for its work.

There are many terms for this life energy in different traditions—yogis speak of *prana*; the Chinese call it *chi*. Others have identified vital force, orgone, odyle, or psychic energy. It is the energy that creates and maintains your SELF.

The image of water is used as a metaphor for mana, or prana, or chi. Water flows, has waves, reaches its own level, permeates substances, goes where it will, seeks out hidden crevices, is the mother of life. So to "divide the waters" is to activate the flow of this life energy.

The practitioners of Huna believe that the low self controls the supply and use of mana. A related Hawaiian word is *mana-o*, "to think." In order for you to have the energy to think, your unhipili must send mana to your uhane, which converts the mana to *mana-mana*, a higher voltage form.

If you want aumakua to answer a prayer, you must send a supply of mana, which aumakua converts to the higher frequency of *mana-loa*. According to huna, this frequency is so powerful it can be used to dematerialize and rematerialize matter, including living flesh. There are stories about great Huna priests, known as the *kahuna*, who could apply mana-loa to a broken or gangrenous limb and dematerialize the wounded or affected portion and rematerialize it whole and perfect.

To pray effectively using this method, it is necessary to sacrifice some mana from the low and middle selves to supply the High Self for its work. To do this, we start by creating energy.

 ### Creating Energy

This is a simple exercise. Precede it with a breathing and/or relaxation technique and when you are completely comfortable and relaxed, tell your SELF to generate energy every time you draw a breath. This will be a *superabundance*, or surplus, over and above the daily energy you normally require. You are generating it specifically to send *mana* to aumakaua for the purpose of making a prayer.

Begin to breathe *slowly* and *deeply*. Do not force anything. As you breathe in, imagine the vital force coming into your body and spirit, filling you up like air fills a balloon. Hold each breath to a count of two as you let this image fill your mind. See this energy as the pure divine stuff which created you and the universe. It is all-powerful, the life force itself. Let the air out of your lungs easily while being aware that you are retaining the vital force within yourself.

Stand up and, with feet wide apart and arms extended at shoulder level, palms up, continue breathing and say to yourself, "The divine life force is flowing into me now. I can feel it." Repeat this statement several times while you continue to breathe slowly and easily. Pause briefly between each repetition. As the energy builds inside you, you may feel some bodily sensation, such as a prickling in your hands or a tingling in your scalp or elsewhere.

The kahuna technique for generating energy, or mana, is described by a Hawaiian word that means "to rise up like water in a fountain until the water overflows." To amplify your energy surcharge, use this image.

Either stand or sit while you continue to breathe as before. Now imagine the energy you are creating as a flow of water, starting at your feet and rising up like a fountain, up through your body and up through and over your head. Feel this energy/water overflowing and showering you with abundant mana.

You can now send this mana to the High Self and make a prayer.

"The Fountain Rite" Prayer Technique

The following technique for sending a prayer was recommended by Max Freedom Long, who first recounted the Huna tradition for outsiders. To perform the Fountain Rite, you speak your intention for the prayer aloud. As you speak (either from memory or reading), feel the import of each word (remember the importance of words!) and put that feeling tone into the words you say, letting the meaning of each word resonate with your SELF. Your statement of intent might be something like this—but write your own words in your own way.

> We are now asking for contact with the Universal Life Force through our High Self. We are now sending an abundance of extra mana for this work to be done. We offer this mana as a sacrifice and ask that it be used to manifest the prayer for the benefit of all.

After stating your intention, mentally give the prayer to your unihipili to send. After a quiet pause, say "The flow stops, the action is finished, let blessings rain. *Au-ma-ma* (amen). After sending the prayer, sit quietly and relax.

Prayer is like planting a garden. You don't rush out and pull up the seedlings to see if they are growing roots. You wait patiently for the crop to ripen so you can harvest it. So, after you have made your prayer and sent it, leave things alone. Don't worry it, like a dog with a bone. Give it peace and time. Rest in the certainty that the work is being done. Your confidence in the wisdom of your High Self will enhance its ability to manifest your desires. Patience and optimism are needed. Affirm that you are confident of your aumkua's ability to complete the prayer rite correctly and effectively. As you work with this technique, and find yourself delighted by the results, you will become even more skilled at using prayer to bring forth the sacred.

chapter three
Soul and Self

ow do we define spirituality in the context of experiencing the sacred every day?

Experiencing the sacred, living spiritually, is most of all a matter of *seeing*, of a worldview, of perspective. The contemporary Catholic theologian John Shea tells us that, "The spiritual life . . . is all of life seen from a certain perspective," which includes waking, sleeping, dreaming, eating, drinking, working, loving, relaxing, recreating, walking, sitting, standing, and breathing. He says, ". . . spirit suffuses everything; and so the spiritual life is simply life . . . seen from the vantage point of spirit."

Echoing this, Jungian therapist Jeremiah Abrams defines spirituality as a "holy longing, a yearning to know the meaning of our lives, to have a connection with the transpersonal."

Others have called it "the art of making connections," "awareness of the 'more than meets the eye' in daily life," and psychiatrist and director of spiritual guidance Gerald May links it to "our deepest values and desires, the very core of our being."

Thus, spirituality can be seen as how we are in the world and who we are in ourselves. For me, the essence of spirituality is the journey into wholeness and wellness. It is the essential *quest*, or Path or Way. It's been said that as you follow the Path you find that the goal recedes. But as you continue, you discover that the Path *is* the goal.

Everyday spirituality, then, is the Path as well as the goal. Many religions emphasize this. To Christian monks common everyday acts such as gardening and cooking are to be hallowed as an important component of the devotional life. Judaism calls itself "a way of life," and teaches that ordinary experiences are holy; Islam teaches believers that signs of God's presence are visible in everything around them. In Hinduism, an enlightened person recognizes manifestations of the divine in cows, plants, and small objects in everyday use; Buddhist masters regard the chores and activities of daily life as themselves spiritual practices: "Before enlightenment, chop wood, carry water; after enlightenment, chop wood, carry water."

People come to a spiritual quest from many different points of view, and from many roads of life. Many come via therapy and transformational psychology. They are looking to become all that they can be—who they really *are* beneath the underlays of past trauma and social conditioning. Their quest is to take responsibility for their lives and how they experience both events and emotions. In their search for a way to become whole, they call upon many resources—dreams, mythology, creative endeavor. From whatever background they emerged, whatever different traditions, convictions, interests, values, beliefs shaped their worldview, they are looking for that "something more." They seek to live purposefully and thereby to access their own sacred dimension.

Others approach spirituality by way of a twelve-step program, while still others are drawn by their concern for ecology and their love of the Earth. By seeking to live in harmony with nature, they develop a spiritual perspective, which they believe is the route to reclaiming the global environment.

Early feminists pioneered women's spirituality which has been an active force for decades. By gathering in groups, comparing experiences, creating rituals, dialoging about the interpretations of myths and other sacred stories, these women are reconceptualizing God by following their own inner lights. Some follow Wicca, or the Goddess religion of the ancient past, seeking to revive the feminine-oriented traditions.

Men, too, have realized the importance of spirituality to their lives and have been making their own spiritual journeys to experience new ways of being intimate with their inner selves and with other men, as well as with their wives and lovers. Through meetings and weekend retreats. they are discovering ways to bring out the sacred dimension in their lives.

What is called New Age spirituality is a multifaceted phenomenon, what has been called "freelance spirituality." It includes healing and transformation, dreamwork, contact with angels and guides, astrology, and the seeking of information from beyond the physical realm, such as through psychics or Tarot card readings. Whatever form it takes, New Age spirituality emphasizes both personal and planetary transformation through a wide variety of avenues now open to seekers who are eager for a holistic worldview that includes the holy in its vision.

Many people have become trans-traditional, going from the religion with which they grew up out into the world to experience another tradition. Christians have become Buddhists. Others have gone to India to meet with a guru and develop a wider viewpoint. Some incorporate these "foreign" teachings into their own spiritual practice, another form of freelance spirituality. One Protestant theologian, Harvey Cox, says that spiritual seekers are free to move in and out of different religions without losing their spiritual balance in the process. This is eloquently stated by Ewart Cousins:

It may well be that the meeting of spiritual paths—the assimilation not only of one's own personal spiritual heritage but that of the human community as a whole—is the distinctive spiritual journey of our time.

From all of this, it would seem we are in the middle of a veritable spiritual renaissance. The evidence is all around us—from a spate of books on the subject to churches offering their congregations programs in spiritual formation. Prayer groups abound, as do adult education classes for the study of sacred texts, sacred art, and sacred ritual. People use their vacation time to go on retreat, where silence and solitude are their primary companions, or they attend workshops, conferences, and seminars with spiritual themes. Spiritual counsellors offer guidance to seekers, many of whom have become disaffected by soulless therapies. Spirituality has even gone on-line—individuals can communicate with others across the world and keep up-to-date on the burgeoning field of spiritual resources. Even popular culture reflects this new desire for spirituality in everyday life. Movies now offer storylines about how life's traumas can set the character on a spiritual journey, and several recent films have had specific spiritual themes; even television series characters get into the spiritual act.

Why then, with all of this spiritual activity going on all around us, do so many of us have difficulty both in understanding "spirituality" and in achieving it? What blocks us from perceiving—and thus experiencing—our spiritual selves?

If we accept the term *wholeness* as a definition of spirituality, remembering that *whole = holy*, we see that Spirit and psychology are linked. It is not that we fail to be spiritual. It is that we view the spiritual as something *separate and apart from ourselves*. We are fragmented—not whole. In truth, our spirituality is an integral part of who we are. We are made of spiritual stuff—how could we *not* be spiritual? For those still struggling to attain their spirituality, the task is to remove the inner blocks to the experience of the sacred self.

One of the most prevalent blocks is the sense of *sin*, of perpetually being unworthy. So many of us are guilt–ridden, crippled by a sense of being not worthy. Whether we consciously believe it or not, the sense of humans as being sinful by nature is deeply embedded in our Western culture, as is the idea of nature itself being anti-divine or without spirit, which is a legacy of the predominant scientific mode of scientific materialism.

The concept of "original sin" has been handed down the generations of Judeo-Christian peoples for two thousand years. A poisonous notion that came into being through the biblical story of Adam and Eve, it holds that these original parents of humankind offended their God by eating the forbidden fruit of the Tree of Knowledge (of good and evil), and God, fearing their effrontery would embolden them to partake of the fruit of the Garden's second Tree (of Immortal Life), and become like Him, banished them from the Garden of Eden. Ever since, according to Judeo-Christian tradition, every human child has been afflicted with the original sin of the first parents. Further, Western religious tradition teaches that we are all sinners in need of redemption.

When I was a child, I was taught that because of Adam and Eve, I was permanently stained with black *sin*. There was no way to cleanse this ineradicable mark from my soul—not by prayer or penance. Only God could forgive me for what I had not done myself but inherited by mere fact of being born. Unlike sins I committed myself, such as telling fibs or filching candy from someone else's Christmas box, which could easily be absolved by going to confession and making an act of contrition, this monster sin could only be erased by God's *grace*— and there was absolutely no guarantee He would grant me this pardon, for grace can never be earned. What is a child, who earnestly desires to be "good," to do?

The most common reaction is *guilt* accompanied by a sense of being unworthy which engenders low self-esteem. Psychology and Spirit cannot be separated. We experience the sacred through our personal history. These early influences are strong and difficult to overcome because they are so deeply embedded in our psyches, often at an unconscious level. If our upbringing has caused us to experience the world as evil, sin-ridden, dangerous, and a playground for the Devil, we will find it difficult to embrace the world as glorious and full of wonder. We cannot access an inner positive view if we think we are innately "bad."

Another factor in the sin equation is our *physicality*: our sensuous nature and our sexuality. Prior to their expulsion from Paradise, Adam and Eve had gone naked, but afterwards, shamed, they covered the parts of themselves designed to procreate their own kind. Thus did sex get irrevocably tainted with the notion of sin. The very nature with which the Creator endowed us became a thing to be ashamed of, or overcome, or thrust aside, hidden, or negated entirely.

Unfortunately, in our society there are many sins—societal sins which get transmogrified into personal guilt. We have lost the ability to differentiate *real* guilt, which is a natural feeling when one has transgressed one's true self or done harm to another's true self, from *social* guilt, which derives from breaking rules made by others and imposed on us from the time we are children.

Social sins come in many guises. When we make mistakes, we feel guilty. When we indulge ourselves in "forbidden" pleasures, we feel guilty. To compensate for these feelings of guilt, we impose new, often impossible, standards of perfection upon ourselves, which serve to guarantee guilt production in a never-ending vicious cycle. When we then don't—because we can't—live up to our own demands for perfect behavior, guilt comes crashing in and we feel worse than ever, more a failure, less a person. The need to be right all the time becomes a stressful

54

taskmaster, pushing us into just the behavior we most deplore in ourselves and others. We become the policemen for our own social programming.

From earliest childhood, we are programmed to accept a set of values already established by others. We are told what is right and what is wrong, what is acceptable and what is unacceptable, not only in terms of behavior but even to how we appear to others, what we weigh, how we dress. And, tragically, we are also judged on what we think and feel.

As children, we internalize these social standards because our survival depends on doing so. Too many of us, however, do not take the next necessary step of integrating these social rules into a personal system of values, discarding what we consider irrelevant or harmful. Thus, having accepted the social norms in youth, we continue to be dependent upon them, thinking they belong to us and unaware of their true origins.

Undiscriminating, we believe without examination with the effect that the garment becomes the person rather than an artifact that can be donned or removed at will. Acceptance of someone else's set of values is a dangerous thing for it stifles self-development. Negative connotations notwithstanding, he or she who does not develop a SELF never becomes a fulfilled person and is stunted on both the personal and societal level. Without a firm sense of SELF we cannot become either fully human nor be contributing members of our communities.

Our personal worldview, therefore, dictates how we encounter ourselves as spiritual beings, how we experience the world around us, and whether we are able to believe that the spiritual is integral to and not separate from daily life. If we hold a negative image of the world, we cannot experience it as meaningful, nor interpret the signs we encounter as being pointers to the spiritual realm. And if we cannot open ourselves fully to the wonder and mystery of the world, we cannot express our spiritual selves through it.

Physicist Albert Einstein once said that the most important question we can ask is, "Is the universe a friendly place or not?" and poet Mary Oliver expands on this by saying, "There is only one question: How to love this world." We can look upon the world as a friend; we can see it as the body of God; we can envision it as a living being as proposed by James Lovelace's *Gaia Hypothesis* that views the earth itself as *alive* a being in its own right.

The ancient Chinese image of *the world as self*, is expressed in the *Tao Te Ching* by Lao-tzu, who says: "See the world as your self./Have faith in the way things are./Love the world as your self; /Then you can care for all things." For me this is the most meaningful and comprehensive interpretation.

Unfortunately, the word *self* has long been used pejoratively. We are accused of being "self-centered," or "selfish," or of thinking only of ourselves. These negative connotations of the self have done much spiritual damage, which is why I have redefined self as SELF, or **S**piritually **E**volving **L**ife **F**orce, to emphasize that the SELF is imbued with Spirit. If we first recognize the divinity in ourselves, we cannot fail to acknowledge it in all others. In fact, it is but a short step from accepting that each of us is a SELF to the understanding that all of life is imbued with Spirit, as Native Americans believe.

It is time to change our concept of *sin*, with its attendant guilt, which serves mainly to hold us back from the life we long to live. Too many of us are dragging around a load of guilt, like a vagrant with a wagonful of miscellaneous junk collected at random from others' refuse on the streets. We've got it—but we may not even know where it came from. Our efforts to rid ourselves of it may take us to therapy or church, but this rarely helps for the simple reason that it doesn't get to the root of the matter. Once we realize that guilt is *junk*—usually other people's junk—we are in a position to discard it forever.

In the Hawaiian tradition of Huna, there is only one sin: the harming of one's self or the self of another. Though I had rejected the Catholic concept of original sin as being both toxic and ridiculous, it was not until I discovered Huna that I found my sin-eraser was something I possessed myself. When I learned of the great kahunas, or shamans, who had immense power to heal I found the philosophy I had been seeking—a kind and gentle, wise and commonsensical, totally coherent approach to life that centered on the SELF.

Are you sick and tired of carrying around a load of guilt and the hurt that accompanies it? If you are, get ready to change your attitude toward both yourself and your world by accepting that you are a SELF. Welcome to the wonderful world of the sacred! Be aware, however, that the hurt and guilt are so familiar one can feel quite bereft without them. Sometimes they are our closest companions and giving them up, let alone shoving them firmly out the door, can be a difficult under-taking. Give yourself time. Rome wasn't built in one day—it didn't fall in one day either. In fact, the famous "fall of Rome" took five hundred years! *You* didn't gather all that negativity overnight and you won't jettison it overnight. But, with stead-fastness and practice, I guarantee you can live guilt-free and hurt-free and experience the benevolent sacred every day of that kind of life. As mature adults with an ability to reason, feel, and respond, we have only to open ourselves to the SELF within and it will guide us to our truth, enabling us to live guilt-free and productive lives.

Let's examine more thoroughly the effects of being hurt and not openly expressing that hurt. Hurt and anger are counter-parts. Rarely do you get one without the other. Hurt which is tucked away inside and not given expression turns into anger that is often turned against one's self. Often, we are afraid to express anger because we have been taught that it is "wrong" or "bad" to be angry. If a parent slaps a child and the child slaps back, another parental slap is sure to follow. Thus the child learns that anger is unacceptable, even when it results from being hurt. All too soon, this lesson is internalized. When we are hurt, we don't fight back because doing so is "not nice." Usually, the hitting parent claims to love us, with the outcome that we connect abuse with love and feel more guilt because we are supposed to love the abuser—or we blame ourselves for the abuse, thinking we deserve it because we are innately bad.

The logical extension of this psychological assault is hostility, which in turn leads to destructive behavior as unexpressed hurt and anger build and build to explosive proportions. We've all had the experience of someone blowing up at us over a trifle, or of ourselves blowing up over a trifle. Usually, we recognize that there is a build-up, but often it's too late to prevent or repair the damage.

Astonished by an outburst, we might say, "Why didn't you tell me something was wrong?" *Because I thought you wouldn't love me if I did* is often the unspoken answer. The trick is to start expressing hurt and anger when they first occur and are at the smallest stage, at which time it is still possible to be pleasant, rather like issuing a reminder. "I don't like it when you do that. I feel hurt and it makes me angry," can be said gently but firmly, putting the other person on notice without causing a conflagration. By calling attention to hurtful behavior at the time of its occurrence, you do the other person a favor. So often we are unaware that our behavior or our words hurt another person.

As an adult, it is your responsibility not to allow others to hurt you, just as it is your duty to refrain from harming others. When we refuse to allow ourselves to be hurt, we encourage others to refuse as well. Learning not to mask feelings is an essential part of healing the soul. When you let others know they have hurt you, expect them to take notice and not repeat the behavior. Repeated hurtful behavior, after a notice has been given, is a warning signal that should be taken with utmost seriousness. Many people get in trouble because they do not heed their own warning signals. Making excuses for another who hurts you not only assures you will continue to be hurt, it sanctions bad behavior that should not be tolerated. Doing this makes us the author of our own woes.

You can eliminate conditions that permit you to become a target for another's anger, resentment, or hurt feelings. When these result in put-downs, halt them in their tracks immediately. At the same time, be sure you take responsibility for your own feelings of hurt, anger, guilt, and self-recrimination. No one can change your feelings but yourself. When you honor your SELF, you commit to changing your worldview so that you become aware of all hurtful deeds or words issuing from others or from yourself. And, it is of primary importance never to hurt yourself. Don't ever "bad mouth" yourself. Be honest with yourself about your faults or things you want to change, but don't ever criticize yourself unfairly.

When we disobey our authority figures, whether real or imagined, guilt and shame result. Original sin is another way of saying that disobedience to authority carries heavy penalties. The antidote to this is to become your own authority, to act and feel only from the deep authenticity of the SELF. By so doing, you have the opportunity to eliminate any fear of authority and its power to punish and hurt, which is the state of the helpless child dependent on others for survival. This condition experienced so early remains embedded in our forgotten memories and forms a substructure of the unconscious that produces fear.

Fear is a slow-moving poison that inhibits the expression of true feelings. When we hold back our natural impulses, we suffer on many different levels—emotional, mental, physical, and spiritual. If we accept the notion that doing what we want

59

for ourselves is sinful because it contradicts the desires of others, we shut off an essential part of ourselves, stunting our personal growth and becoming prey to a multiplicity of ills.

What happens then is that we suffer *soul damage.* In the shamanic tradition, this is referred to as "soul loss." Psychologist Jeanne Achterberg, in *Shaman's Path: Healing, Personal Growth and Empowerment,* identifies soul loss as "injury to the inviolate core of a person's being [which] does manifest as despair, immunological damage, cancer, and a host of other very serious disorders." Soul loss also manifests as a sense of something being missing, as though we have lost an intangible but important and very real part of ourselves. In seeking to find it, we often come to our spiritual journey.

Our soul work, then, is to repair ourselves, to heal into wholeness. It is, simply put, to identify and remove whatever gets in the way of being truly who we are. It is the task of uncovering our *authentic self* from the encrustations that overlay it, concealing it from us. Our culture does not provide us with tools for reclaiming lost souls, but we can learn from other traditions and also invent our own devices for soul retrieval.

One of the best of these is simply to *accept* who we are, warts and all. It may seem strange, but acceptance is a most powerful aid to soul retrieval. Many exhaust their energies by trying to "keep up a front," because they feel unacceptable as they are. By acceptance, I most emphatically do not mean resignation, which means giving up and becoming powerless—acceptance carries with it the possibility of saying "no" to what damages the soul. We *can* change our value systems and create more whole—and therefore holy—ways of experiencing our lives. Acceptance means to *first* accept what is and then empower yourself to make the changes you seek. Here is a simple meditation that will help you achieve this goal.

Acceptance Meditation

To do this exercise, find a comfortable position and begin by taking several deep breaths to relax yourself completely. Close your eyes and imagine yourself standing before a magic mirror that has the power to show you your true self—not just your physical reflection, but a reflection of your innermost reality—how you are when you are most yourself. Look carefully at this reflection and examine what you see without making any judgments or criticizing. Just look.

Now, while looking at this reflection of your true self, say softly and gently in your mind, "I accept you. I truly accept you for who you are and who you can be. I accept all of you. I know that by accepting you I empower myself to make any changes that I choose."

Repeat this several times until you feel that you are speaking the truth to yourself, and that you are genuinely able to accept yourself with all your pain and shortcomings, but also with all your wonderful spiritual potential to develop and grow.

Now, slowly breathe yourself back to normal consciousness and revel in the acceptance of your true being.

Another powerful tool to use in soul work is that of *forgiveness.* Odd as it may seem, the act of *forgiving* has immense power. When we carry within us—encoded into our flesh and bones—hate, anger, grudges, and other negative feelings about ourselves and others, we are doing serious damage to the SELF. Remember that in Huna the only sin is to harm the self or to hurt another self.

But how is one to forgive heinous crimes against one, or even lesser incursions that have caused us to suffer? The secret is that "forgive" does *not* mean to *approve.* Nor does it mean that we are to welcome the perpetrator back into our affections and regard. It only means that we must *let go within ourselves* of the negative emotions that are poisoning our systems. If we hate and resent—no matter how rightly and justified these feelings are—we do the most harm to ourselves. Unless we act out in a violent way, the hated person suffers far less than we ourselves do. Hate acts like a corrosive on both spirit and body, a contaminant that flows through our cells like acid, burning everything it touches. To paraphrase, the road to the SELF is paved with forgiving intentions.

When I first learned of the power of forgiveness, I was most skeptical. My anger and hate had previously served me as a source of strength and even survival during some pretty tough times. It got me going when there was no discernible reason for continuing on. Like many protective devices erected in childhood to defend against the onslaught of conditions over which the child has no control, mine had worked for a time, when crisis was a way of life.

But, like all defensive constructions, those emotions of hate and anger began to strangle me once they had served their survival purpose. I had used them when I had no other defenses, but they had outlived their usefulness. I recognized it was time to let them go. And letting go is what forgiveness is all about—flushing that corrosive acid out of *your* system, for *your* own purposes, to help *yourself*. It's not about the other person.

As I began to practice forgiveness, consciously calling to mind those who had caused me soul damage, some very interesting things began to happen. Inside, old tensions loosened and relaxed; self-destructive behaviors or ones I didn't like were easier to control or forgo; and, I began to see the entire world in a new and more positive way. You don't have to believe it to try it. Practicing forgiveness is risk-free. You have nothing to lose and everything to gain.

It is not only others who need to be forgiven. We must also forgive ourselves. Apologize to your SELF for any past harm you have done it, and ask it to forgive you. As you practice the following exercise, you will begin to actually feel that forgiveness flowing upward from your solar plexus, where angry feelings are stored.

Repeat this exercise daily until you feel the flow upward, feel the loosening of old tensions. Explain to your SELF that you hurt it out of ignorance, and resolve to make amends. Affirm that your intention is to avoid any speech or action that hurts your SELF or the SELF of any other person. As you do this, you will become sensitized to the inner experiences of yourself and of others. When you become aware of hurt feelings, move immediately to alleviate any harm done. Apologize and forgive in the here and now—don't store anything away for later. Get rid of the feelings from the past and they will not color your actions and reactions in the present.

Forgiveness Affirmations (Use daily.)

I invoke the healing power of forgiveness.
I forgive everybody and everything that has hurt me.
Forgiveness cleanses my SELF and brings me peace.
I resolve to live in a state of forgivingness.
I ask my SELF to forgive me for all harm done to it.
I now live a guilt-free, hurt-free life at all times.

How to Practice Forgiveness

Your "forgiveness ritual" can be very simple. The great Hawaiian kahunas knew principles we are now rediscovering. They practiced "burning the rubbish in the mind" techniques to cleanse the mind of guilt and hate, whatever was "eating up inside" the person being treated.

Burning the Rubbish in the Mind

After breathing quietly for a few minutes, imagine yourself gathering up all the unwanted material in your mind, just as you would gather up dead leaves and fallen tree limbs to make a bonfire. Now, take all of these old, unnecessary thoughts and pile them up in a place where you can safely start a fire—a fireplace is good. As you collect them, say to yourself, "I now let go outworn thoughts, outworn emotions, outworn attitudes." After you have piled up your mental rubbish, strike an imaginary match to the pile and as it goes up in flames say to yourself, "I now return this to the universe for cleansing. I need it no more."

Set aside half an hour each day and sit quietly and mentally forgive everyone you can think of who has ever hurt or harmed you in any way whatsoever. Start with the lesser and more recent experiences—the small hurts and stings which nonetheless can be painful. (There is an old saying, "We can sit on a mountain but not a tack.") Perhaps you were snubbed by someone, unfairly criticized by a friend, fired from a job. Begin along these lines and work your way back to the most painful and deepset traumas of your life. One by one, like counting beads on a string, forgive each person and tick off the name.

Forgiving need not involve the other person in any way. This is a private matter, your own personal housecleaning. It involves only the letting go of bad feelings resulting from past experience. And if you happen to encounter someone who was on your list, you will be pleasantly surprised to discover that your reaction to that person will be different than before. Not only that, but as you change your attitudes toward others they will automatically respond by altering their attitude toward you.

Resentment can lead to the desire for vengeance. So long as you are involved with resentment, you are controlled by it, which wastes vital energy. Mired in the past, you cannot move freely into your future. Releasing resentment has nothing to do with the other person—*do it for yourself.*

Affirmations for Releasing Resentment

I now reclaim my own power in this situation.
I release all that is not positive for my life.
What happened in the past is now over and
    done with.
My love for myself overcomes all resentment.
I now release and let go of all resentful feelings.
The divine in me now releases me from all resentment.

Resentment Neutralizing Exercise

To do this meditation, first breathe deeply until you feel relaxed. When you feel ready, allow yourself to sink into a deep state of relaxed consciousness. Tell your SELF that you are now ready to let go of all resentments.

Imagine a bubble of beautiful royal purple, like a magical carriage, drawing up in front of you. Step inside. There find an altar on which is a flame of purple fire. Speak your resentment to the flame, which will consume it.

Next, see a pool of purple-tinted water and allow all resentments to come to its surface. Transfer them one by one to the purple flame and watch them go up in lavender smoke.

Finally, when the water in the pool is clear of all your resentments, wash your hands in it and proclaim, "I am now free of all resentment. I am cleansed and purified of all past resentment. I now release all resentment forever."

Let the purple flame flare up, burning higher and higher until its peak has reached your Higher Self. Give thanks and slowly allow yourself to return to consciousness.

Self-blessing is another way of restoring the soul to wholeness. When we bless the totality of ourselves, we acknowledge the soul and its needs. When we bless, we invoke the sacred, and connect to it. In so doing, we reconnect to our innate whole selves—and this acts as a healing balm that is especially useful when we are in psychic or emotional pain, a condition Jungian psychologist James Hillman describes as, ". . . the soul in neurosis trying to make itself heard." Soul wounds cannot be treated with superficial means: we must go deeply and clean them so they can heal completely. Blessing the self helps do that. It is a form of self-absolution.

Self-Blessing Technique

To do this, you need only assemble some common household items: salt (symbolizing wisdom, the "salt of the earth"); water, preferably pure (which symbolizes life itself, for without water there would be no life on Earth); wine (representing transformation, the transmutation of one substance into another); and a white candle (representing the element of fire and symbolizing the ongoing, everchanging creativity of the divine nature); a flower or small bunch of grasses or fresh herbs (symbolizing Nature); a clean white cloth (to cover the table or space upon which you will set the items); and an attractive cup or glass (to serve as your chalice—a crystal wineglass is nice).

After you have assembled your items and chosen a place to serve as your altar (if you don't have a home altar, this can be a small table or even a dresser top cleared for the purpose), take a bath or shower (representing purification) and, if weather and privacy permit, remain naked. Otherwise wear something loose and comfortable, preferably white. Arrange the items on the cloth on the table to suit your taste, with the flower or herbs in the center, the cup, containing the wine and water mixed together, in front, and the salt on the floor in front of you. Stand barefooted on the salt in front of the altar for a moment and center yourself to give the blessing. Then step forward and light the candle. Holding your index finger and middle finger touching your thumb (a boon-bestowing position known as a *mudra*), dip your fingers into the wine-water mixture and touch your forehead, saying, "Blessed be my mind and its ability to form thought, which forms my reality."

Continue to bless yourself with the blessings given below, each time dipping your fingers into the wine-water mixture and touching the part of your body mentioned.

- Blessed be my nose, which breathes Spirit.
- Blessed be my ears, which hear the sound of Spirit.
- Blessed be my eyes, which see Spirit everywhere.
- Blessed be my lips, which speak Spirit's truth.
- Blessed be my heart, which gives and receives divine love.
- Blessed be my body (touching your abdomen), which is the temple where Spirit dwells.
- Blessed be my genitals, which have the power to bring forth life as I was brought forth into life.
- Blessed be my legs, which give me the ability to stand up to all challenges I face.
- Blessed be my feet, which walk the path of Spirit.

Remain standing quietly for a few moments to let the blessing penetrate deeply, and then say, "I give my self absolution. I am one with Life. I am one with Spirit."

After finishing this blessing, remain standing on the salt and feel the earth-power flowing through you. Bless the Earth on which you stand, and of which you are a part. Accept the reality of yourself as a Spiritually Evolving Life Force, with reason and purpose. Reflect that whatever your mind thinks, your feet will follow. The aim is to empower yourself to create a life orientation toward yourself and your world that will allow you to bring forth the sacred in your life every day. You *are* divine—you have the power.

You can use my words or words you choose yourself, but remember that words have enormous power, so choose your blessing words carefully. "Thoughts are things," and the conscious manifestation of thought is words—we are told that "In the beginning there was the Word. . . ," so when you speak words do so with the knowledge that you have a responsibility for choosing them wisely and well. The Hawaiian *kahunas*, and other cultures as well, believe that, words—or any sounds, whether speech or music—once uttered continue forever: the vibration released never stops.

chapter four
The Authentic Self

The spiritual quest is a journey, and every journey contains the seeds of transformation. The hope of tomorrow is planted in the seeds of today. Whether we allow them to sprout and then water and tend them to the fulfillment of bloom is up to us. Just as a seed contains within it the invisible pattern of the whole plant—root, shoot, stem, leaf, bud, flower, fruit—we contain within ourselves the blueprint for what we are capable of becoming.

When we travel, either physically or mentally, we open ourselves to new and transformative experiences, which is what the hero journey is about. Once we embark on this spiritual journey, or quest, there is no turning back. The decision to live by the light of Spirit is irrevocable.

Joseph Campbell once astonished me by saying that I was one of only five or six true heroes he had ever known. Mystified by this unexpected accolade, I asked *why* he considered me a hero. He answered, "Because you never turned back, no matter what happened."

I make no claim of heroism for myself, but I do know that illness, trauma, failure, and defeat can draw out the best in us.

Trauma of any kind, be it severe disappointment, serious frustration, physical debilitation, or having all one's hopes dashed is—or can be—a call to the hero journey, which is no longer one of outward feats of braving danger and overcoming odds, but an inward quest, to the center of one's being.

If we refuse this challenge, what Campbell terms "the call to adventure," to participate fully in our own process of becoming who we are meant to be—we cannot experience our own sacred realm. Only acceptance of the necessary process of transformation and *cooperation with it* can achieve that.

The first stage is mythologically represented as the descent into the underworld, which is analogous to a trip to the underworld of our being.

An example is the myth of the Sumerian goddess Inanna, beautiful queen of the light-filled upperworld, who goes to visit her ugly sister, Ereshkigal, queen of the damned, in her hellish subterranean region for the purpose of rescuing her young lover.

When one is in Ereshkigal's realm, life comes to a standstill. We experience paralysis of the will, inertia, immobility, depression. Everything seems stuck and we cannot move forward until we have satisfied her demands. All interests fall away and become superficial as we are pulled into our depths to deal with what has been buried, denied, or neglected. And, like Inanna who must remove all of her emblems of power in the upper, or outer, world, we experience a letting-go—of aims, ambitions, desires, expectations, demands—in order to touch ourselves at our own base where the power of renewal resides.

Just as the hero must encounter the Goddess in her unloveliest of forms—for the processes of Nature from which new life arises—death and decay, decomposition, malodorous waste—are disgusting to us, in her descent to the realm of her dark sibling, beautiful Inanna must pass through seven gates, at each of which she is stripped of some of her queenly raiment, until she arrives naked in the underworld and, having left all of her outward identity behind, is hung upon a peg to die and rot in hell.

The spiritual journey, which is an attempt to cope with the experience of soul loss, whether in childhood or as later trauma—we become ill, or depressed, lose a job or get a divorce—can be a means of stripping away the outer shell of unnecessary accumulations that have impeded our lives and our spiritual growth. Sometimes the necessary solitude is forced upon us. We are separated from the mainstream of life as we knew it before. We may have lost our means of livelihood, our beauty, or our usual occupations. Sometimes we lose our friends and find that family members avoid us. Without energy to cope with these losses, we turn inward—descend into the netherworld of our being and there confront our own dark sibling in the long and despairing dark night of the distressed but still unconquerable soul.

This withdrawal, or detachment from the world of ordinary life, is, like the trip to the alpine sanatorium described by Thomas Mann in *The Magic Mountain,* analogous to the descent into the underworld. To abide there is to make a radical transfer of emphasis from the external to the internal world, to retreat from our accustomed other-oriented duties and activities to a place where the whole attention is concentrated upon the self.

Before embarking on her journey to hell, Queen Inanna had the forethought to call upon the water god Enki and make an arrangement with him for help should she fail to return. When the Queen did not reappear, Enki fashioned, from the scrapings of his fingernails, two small mourners to grieve for the lovely Queen, now stripped of her outer powers and privileges. He sent them down to the underworld to sit beside her as she hung mournfully on the stake, waiting to die. Upon seeing these compassionate companions attending her bright sister, weeping tears of sincere sorrow for her unfortunate condition, the angry Ereshkigal relented and released Inanna, explaining that she had only wanted to be acknowledged by her sister, recognized as being part of the family. Lacking this recognition, she let loose on Inanna her dark powers, which are formidable.

Ereshkigal is emblematic of all that we have repressed, denied, left unshriven, hated, failed to mourn, and what has shamed us, wounded us deeply, and been left unfelt or unexpressed. Hers is a realm to which each of us must descend, not only once but periodically, for renewal, for these emotions sink deep into the unconscious where they build a charge of negative power, which, finally, erupts into the upperworld, sometimes using the body as its vehicle of expression, sometimes the mind, sometimes both. When illness strikes it is often because our dark sibling is trying to get our attention—"I am here," she says, and we can no longer ignore her but must meet her long-denied demands for recognition. She symbolizes the abyss, which is not only the dark realm but also the ultimate Source, the ground of all being.

"When there is an impasse . . . we must look to the dark, hitherto unacceptable side which has not been at our conscious disposal, and see that the shadow, when realized, is the source of renewal," says Jungian analyst Edward C. Whitmont. In Jungian terms, the "shadow" is the repressed or unrealized part of the personality, which goes underground and causes no end of trouble. It is that element in us which we are least willing to admit is a part of us. It consists of personal qualities that constitute the part of ourselves we consider "dark," or unacceptable, and therefore reject or refuse to acknowledge: "I am *not* . . ." Fill in the blank.

This dark part is often represented as one of a pair of brothers or sisters, as in the Inanna-Ereshkigal myth. The way out of the impasse is to "own" the shadow. Recognizing our shadow-self and acknowledging its legitimate role empowers us to become whole. As Whitmont states in *Alchemy of Healing,*

> The unfolding of our life's development ever and again leads us into critical impasses that cry out for resolution and healing. Some form of assimilation by personal or vicarious surrender to the entelechy of the Self-field is then required, or even forced upon us by illness or relationship problems. These are bent upon connecting and reconnecting us to the implicate essence and its reordering stream of information, psychologically and/or physically.

Inanna represents energies that are in constant flux, the very flow of life which is never static nor reliable no matter how much we attempt to hedge ourselves in with "law and order." She symbolizes transition and borderlessness. With these go creativity, change, and all the multiple joys and sorrows of human consciousness. The transformative process represented by Inanna and Ereshkigal is an expression of the deepest mystery of the life force, in which the making and unmaking of forms— change brought about by destruction and re-creation—are seen to be variations within unity.

But before we can return to the light of the upperworld, we must, like Inanna, make peace with our own dark twin in the underworld. We must meet the ugly Goddess and realize that she has a legitimate part to play in the totality of our lives. In order to do this, we must fashion our own mourners out of the scrapings of our souls, to bear witness to our losses and travail and to give us the compassion we require to accept the unpredictable and recognize that life is an ever-changing process which goes by its own rules.

🦁 Through the Seven Gates

At each of the seven gates through which Queen Inanna must pass to reach her dread dark sister, she sacrifices something symbolic of her high estate in the daylight world—her crown, her necklaces, her breastplate, her gold ring, her rod of lapis lazuli, and her queenly robe—to finally stand totally naked before her sister.

We, too, pass through seven gates of our inner being before reaching the transpersonal level represented by the underworld. At each of these inward portals, we are called upon to recognize certain qualities and surrender them for transmutation into their higher forms.

The Gold Gate

At the Gold Gate, we are asked to give up our attachment to authority and power. We are also required to surrender our attachment to money and material goods. Just as Inanna gave up her scepter, or emblem of power and authority in the upper world of queens, magistrates, and religious leadership, we must consciously eliminate our drive for power and sublimate it to the Higher Power within ourselves. It is here that we are to submit our individuality to the unity in order to realize our life's true purpose.

The Silver Gate

The Silver Gate is where we give up our attachments to the merely physical aspect of life. It is also where we surrender our attachments (or over-attachment) to the fulfillment of our needs by others. It is the "link breaker," which allows us to give up living vicariously or expecting others to take care of us. It is where we determine to take full responsibility for ourselves. Here, we accept that we must learn to fulfill our own needs, to not demand that life be predictable and comfortable all the time, to allow others to live their lives freely so that we can move into our own rebirth.

The Silver Gate represents shedding the old to bring in the new. It's about whatever is growing in us, what has been conceived and is in the gestation process. It initiates us into both the labor and triumph of new birth.

The Mercury Gate

At the Mercury Gate, we are to give up our attachment to the intellect and recognize that we are multifaceted beings who also have hearts and souls. For many of us, the intellect is not only king but tyrant. We constantly analyze—and consequently paralyze—our feelings. Reason and the rational mental processes must give way to a more holistic concept that includes all of our facilities, including those which "science" tells us do not exist. Here we must abandon any notions that people who relate to the unseen, or who are open to other realms we don't understand or accept, are not to be labeled "weird," or not normal. We must learn to respect those other realms by letting go of the habit of intellectualizing. We must cease our dependence upon only spoken and written communication and be open to the fact that other forms exist. We are required to accept that mind, logic, and reason do not constitute a total picture of human faculties.

The Copper Gate

At the Copper Gate, we are to give up mere adornment for its own sake, as Inanna removed her jeweled bracelets, and confront ourselves without cosmetic enhancement or the camouflage of clothing. We are in short to drop our masks, those disguises we don to present ourselves to others, not as we are but as we wish them to think we are. Here, at the Copper Gate, we are asked to identify what deeper or more amplified identity we possess, one that is a true expression of the SELF. Here, relinquishing our concealing masks, we are given the opportunity to relate to others through genuine love and to recognize the beauty in our unadorned selves. At the Copper Gate, we learn

75

about real *love* that comes directly from the heart. It is this love that fills us with a sense of beauty and pleasure and tells us what we truly want from our lives.

The Iron Gate

At the Iron Gate, we give up aggression, negativity, and all forms of conquest. We surrender that part of the ego which constantly demands more and more gratification, even at the cost of injuring others. Here we submit our anger to be transmuted into intelligent action. We are required to abandon old patterns of doing, making, building, fighting, defending in order to re-create ourselves as people who know how to take action peacefully. The Iron Gate is the place where we confront our sexuality and transmute rigid definitions of male and female into understanding, harmony, and balance. The Iron Gate demands us to shed old patterns, which may include abuse or being abused, or denial and non-acceptance of the legitimate needs and desires of others. Here we must strip away our painful past and risk telling the truth about ourselves in order to restore our ego to proper functioning.

The Tin Gate

At the Tin Gate, we give up our reliance on the laws of men and realize that the law of the sacred is greater. We must abandon our ideas of "justice" as being a system of crime and punishment and understand that justice for one must mean justice for all. The Tin Gate demands that we substitute universal law for ordinary law in order to expand ourselves on the spiritual, mental, and psychological levels. Here, we must accept that "truth" is not something solid and fixed, carved in marble or written in a book, but must be sought and found by each individual person on his or her own spiritual quest. At the Tin Gate, we give up any attachment to our own

76

particular truth, whether it is theological or philosophical, in order to learn to understand the greater truth of the whole.

The Lead Gate

As the last gate, the Lead Gate is the most difficult. Here, we encounter death and dying, which are only forms of letting go and surrendering. At this gate, we give up our attachment to life itself, we acknowledge that one day we must shed the "garment" of the body, as Inanna put aside her queenly robe. Naked we are born and naked we die, even though we may be very well dressed in our coffins. At the Lead Gate, we give up the need to control. We understand that Time through its passage brings us wisdom as well as taking us closer to our final transformation. Here we meet the Lord of Karma who teaches us the self-discipline which leads to the liberation of the soul.

Psychologist Lawrence LeShan, who has done much work with cancer patients, comments that, although pathology must be taken into consideration, it is to be viewed in context, "as the process that blocks the perception and the expression of the individual's special song to sing in life; as the cause of his or her loss of contact with enthusiasm and joy." He says that some patients have negative reactions to the idea of singing their own song, feeling that it would be ugly and unacceptable, or impossible in this society, or so full of contradictions as to be useless. However, he says that he has *never* seen anyone who, upon finding their own special song and style, remained negative. *Never.* In addition, he says that "in every case the song was socially positive and acceptable."

Though it is natural to crave simple solutions to complex problems, ignoring our soul wounds will not make them go away or be less complex. Jung has said that "neurosis is a sub-stitute for legitimate suffering." We must learn to legitimize our soul's neurosis by accepting our "dark" selves and discovering that our journey to retrieve our soul can free us from what inhibits our spiritual growth.

According to Campbell, the hero's first work is to "retreat from the world scene of secondary effects to those causal zones of the psyche where the difficulties really reside," there to clarify them and "break through to the undistorted, direct experience and assimilation of . . . the archetypal images."

The descent to the underworld presents an opportunity to recognize that dark sibling self, so long repressed and ignored. To acknowledge its power is to enlist it in our aid. To consciously reach this mythic ground is to be purified by the ordeals you have experienced, to see clearly—often for the first time—what is of true value.

Recognition of the needs and claims of the self who dwells in the underworld of our being can lead to renewed life, for it is there transformation takes place, through a process of pruning that gradually reveals the powers that generate and sustain life; it is thus a form of initiation.

In the Eleusinian mysteries of ancient Greece the last trial of the initiation required the candidate to spend one night alone in "the valley of the shadow of death." When he emerged into the light from this frightful experience, he was shown a sheaf of corn—the emblem of the Great Mother Goddess, who gives life to all on earth but also eats back the dead. It is said that the shock of recognition of this basic life-death power changed the consciousness of the initiate forever; having glimpsed the powers of creation, he was transformed.

Our task, at the same time both simple and extremely complex, is to ferret out an approach to ourselves that takes all of our "parts" into consideration—with gentleness and love. Jung says,

> The serious problems of life . . . are never fully solved. If
> ever they should appear to be so this is a sure sign that

something has been lost. The meaning and purpose of a problem seem to lie not in its solution but in our working it out incessantly.

When we have passed through the seven Gates and confronted the dark Ereshkigal in ourselves, seen our shadow, and divested ourselves of outward coverings, we are ready to find our *authentic self*.

Arriving at an authentic self means honoring one's emotional needs and desires. However, to honor them we must first know what they are. Often, we are operating using a false set, either one grafted onto us when we were children or one we have assumed ourselves for some purpose, most often to please or mollify others in the mistaken notion that this is the only way to get love.

Our needs are biological, intellectual, emotional, and spiritual. All of these areas demand satisfaction and they can be in conflict with each other. But the way to resolve conflict is not by means of denying that our needs exist, nor of sublimating them to another's more pressing demands. Healthy human function is based on self-authenticity. To be one's authentic self should be recognized as a basic human right. Unfortunately, this is not the case. We are taught from an early age to deny our needs, to stifle our authentic self in service of some ideal— usually created by another person or an institution such as society, state, church, or tradition.

The person in quest of the authentic self must, like the hero, confront demons and overcome them, must encounter the dark Goddess within the psyche and recognize the beauty inherent in the ugliness. Our innermost hidden self, that place where we hide the things we find gruesome or unacceptable, must be honored with our compassion. Then, our inner demons turn into helpers and we see revealed the bright face of the Goddess of Life.

Jung says in relation to the therapeutic work, "The labours
. . . are directed towards that hidden and as yet unmanifest
'whole' man, who is at once the greater and the future man."
Through facing our own darkness, we enable the light of the
spirit to shine through us, and we are transformed into the gold
of spiritual realization. So it is with all of us. It does not matter
what work we do as we practice the art of living our lives. In the
transformational process, we achieve the desired end by sub-
mitting to the requirements of our authentic selves. Our
authentic soul-directedness—what I call the "internal imperative"—is like an inborn compass that serves to keep us on the
course that will fulfill who we truly are.

The search for the authentic self draws forth the spiritual
energy that engenders wholeness. This implies a definite will-
ingness to yield to our own inner process. This conscious surrender never comes without a concomitant struggle. However,
unless we are willing to submit to the larger order of ourselves,
little will be attained. It is this very stance that reveals the sacred
realm we seek. This larger order—our inner dynamic—leads us
to who we really *are*, to the authentic self latent within.

The medieval alchemists were keen observers of the inner
process of transmutation that accompanies spiritual growth.
They believed that, if the work were to be effective, it required
complete integration and total emotional and psychological
honesty. It was essential that there be no separation of spirit,
body, soul, and substance. To fail in this endeavor was to fall
into illness of both substance and spirit. Taking half-measures or
shirking the full responsibility would not do. Therefore, if the
sacred is to become meaningful in our lives, the transformative
experience must be sought after and fully accepted.

To find the authentic self, we must listen to our own individual
voices, not be swayed by the monolithic tone of the crowd, nor
determined by those ever-running "parent tapes" in our heads.

So long as you look for an *outside* authority to tell you who you are (or who you are supposed to be) rather than looking to your own *inside* authority, your authentic self will elude your discovery.

Here is a meditation I devised to help find the authentic self. It is a good idea to tape this meditation or have someone do it with you. It can be a wonderful experience to share with a friend or a lover with the understanding that you have the right to keep what you discover private if you wish.

 ### Finding the Authentic Self

You will need half an hour of quiet time to do this meditation. It can take you very deeply into yourself, so be prepared for some surprises. Above all, do not be frightened or repulsed should you encounter anything you don't expect. We all have dark corners, and the only way to light them is to inhabit them. On the other hand, you may be quite pleasantly surprised to discover your authentic self is quite to your liking, only waiting for you to uncover it and be your friend.

Find a time when you can be alone and undisturbed. If possible, take a leisurely warm bath or shower using scented soap or salts. Dry yourself gently and dress in something soft, loose, and clean. Cotton or silk is best. Next, prepare for the meditation using a breathing technique and a relaxation exercise. (Always precede any of the exercises in this book by breathing and relaxation.)

Now, breathe deeply several times and allow yourself to drift into a state of deep meditation. You are going to find a lovely spot somewhere outdoors—it could be in a woods, a park, a garden, on the beach, by a lake, or anywhere else you fancy.

After you have envisioned this place, take a walk and look around. You are going to find a small, secret door someplace. It might be in the ground, under the water, in a tree, hidden under fallen leaves, under a hedge, or be the entrance to a secret garden.

When you find the secret door, open it carefully. It isn't locked, but it might have rusty hinges from lack of use. When you open the secret door, you will find a passageway leading downward, a spiral staircase. Follow it down, counting from ten to one. As you descend this staircase clockwise in a spiral traverse, at ten you allow your body to relax further; at nine, your awareness sharpens and anticipates; at eight, you are enveloped in silence; at seven, you feel safe and comfortable; at six, five, four, as you descend the spiral way you are in a state of complete relaxation and begin to sense there is magic here. At three, two, your senses tingle with expectation as you prepare to meet your true self. At one, as you step from the last rung of the spiral staircase, you have left the upper world behind and find yourself in a beautiful room that houses your authentic self.

Look around at this room. You have seen it before. It was there the day you were born. Before you came to this Earth plane, you knew who you were and you still know, but you have forgotten. This experience is like meeting someone you knew as a child and loved very much but have lost touch with over the years. Now you will meet yourself again and for the first time.

Take a comfortable seat in this lovely room and ask your true self to come forth. Imagine this self standing in front of you and observe its form, figure, posture, and pose. Tell yourself you will recall this experience completely and that all the observations will remain as vivid memories, which you can call to mind at any time in the future. When you see an image of your authentic self, observe details—clothing, facial expression, age, style. Allow this image to move and change and stay with it for a few moments.

Acknowledge this self and take some time to get to know him or her. Ask your authentic self if it has anything to say to you at this time. Express your love for your authentic self and affirm your determination to live by and for it. If at first you feel uncomfortable, be patient until you become accustomed to this person, who is you at your best, the *you* you truly are, the person you came to this Earth to be.

Before beginning your ascent back to the ordinary world, make a symbolic gesture to your authentic self. You can hug him or her and promise to return often. You might want to place a vase of fresh flowers on a table there as an indication you have visited. Do whatever comes to your mind at the time that expresses how you feel about the meeting.

After making your symbolic gesture, slowly ascend the spiral staircase, counting from one to ten going upwards, breathing evenly as you do, and return to the secret door, which is a sacred portal. Follow your footsteps back to where you started and gradually bring yourself back to normal waking con- sciousness. Write down what you experienced and read it over frequently.

You can do this meditation as often as you like. As you become better acquainted with your authentic self, you will learn more and more and develop a rela- tionship. You can always go through the secret door and down the spiral staircase when you want to commune with your deepest, truest level of being, which will provide you with comfort and guidance.

Jung believed that psychoneurosis must be understood "as the suffering of a soul which has not discovered its meaning." He asserts that, ". . . all creativeness in the realm of the spirit as well as every psychic advance of man arises from the suffering of the soul and the cause of the suffering is spiritual stagnation or spiritual sterility."

"Spiritual sterility," it would seem, is the neurosis of our time. Ours has been called the age of anxiety, and millions depend on drugs such as Prozac to alleviate their suffering, which may be due to "spiritual stagnation." But no drug has ever been invented that will substitute for our necessary journey into Spirit.

To recover the soul, we must delve deeply to find the authentic self, the foundation for our temple within.

Opening ourselves to the vast possibilities inherent in our own natures releases great spiritual power. The "lotus" meditation below is one I evolved from working with those suffering from what I call "concretized" thoughts, emotions, and attitudes, usually a product of having internalized the standards set forth by parents, church, or society. A major factor in both discovering and activating the authentic self is being open to new possibilities.

 ### *Lotus Meditation*

Prepare for this meditation by choosing a quiet place where you can be alone and comfortable for half an hour. If possible, first relax in a warm bath scented and softened with salts or oil. This meditation is best done without clothes or only lightly clad or covered, preferably in white. Light a white candle and arrange yourself in a comfortable position lying down or reclining. If the air is cool, cover yourself; if warm, remain nude.

Now, breathe slowly and deeply several times and allow your body to relax completely. Imagine yourself a seed at the bottom of a deep pool where all is dark and tranquil. Feel yourself begin to put out roots into the nourishing bottom and anchor yourself there. Next, feel a stem begin to grow up and out of you, reaching upwards for the light above. Feel it move through the abyssal water until it breaks the surface. Then, feel yourself putting out little new leaves on the surface of the water, stretching in all directions.

Say to yourself, *I open to the possibilities within myself.*

Spirit flows through me as I open to my authentic self. All obstacles to the experience of my inner truth are now permanently removed.

As these leaves grow larger and stronger, feel yourself growing into the bud of a beautiful lotus. Let this bud rest on the surface, in the light, for a few minutes and then—slowly—begin to open up your petals, one by one, until you have unfurled a glorious blossom, fully opened and gently floating on its undulant stem, but firmly rooted in the earth at the bottom of the pond. Feel the light on your petals, soak up the warmth of the sun, breathe in the cool of the air.

Say, *I am open. I am open. I now open fully to all my possibilities. I open to my inner healing powers. I release and let go all constraints, restrictions, limits. Whatever comes, I welcome. My openness brings happiness, pleasure, reward, and healing. I remain open to the light at all times. My roots are strong so I have no fear of being open. My state of openness brings me all good things.*

Remain with this feeling of being totally, safely and completely open for as long as the feeling lasts. When it begins to fade, *slowly* return to waking consciousness by breathing gently and easily, continuing to feel yourself as open to your inner possibilities. Write down what you felt and thought during the meditation so that you can recall it.

Rest quietly until you feel yourself retracting into the bud state. Now that your lotus self has blossomed fully, you know you can always open when you wish. You do not need to be fully open all of the time—you can rest in the bud state, or even return to the seed state to gather new force.

chapter five

A Journey into the Self

A unique characteristic of our minds is their *power to make images*. Sinking thought-images deep into the mind causes them to work their way upward into manifestation. In the classical drama *Medea*, the great Greek dramatist Euripides has the nurse warn the raving, betrayed Medea that, "Images the mind makes work into life."

Symbols are images that arise from the deepest levels of our beings. They carry with them great power to affect our emotions and bodies. Our ability to program—or reprogram—our deep inner minds with images connects our conscious minds with the unconscious substructure—the gateway to the spiritual realm.

Alas, few of us feel free to use our imaginative powers. Especially, we don't associate our powers of image-making with the sacred as did those who came before us. Their art was not used for mere decoration or aesthetic pleasure; it was the vehicle by which the sacred tradition was transmitted to the populace. Before general literacy, the only way to instruct the illiterate masses in the religious forms of their culture was through images. Thus, much of our knowledge of the culture of ancient Egypt has come from the sacred texts and images inscribed on

87

the walls of the pyramids and other monuments. The great Gothic cathedrals of Europe are called "books in stone." The images they contain, first conjured in the minds of the artisans who produced them, were intended not for visual enjoyment, like pictures in a gallery, but to instruct the illiterate multitudes about their religion and its stories.

By using the powers of your mind to spontaneously generate specific and meaningful symbols, you give yourself the power to change negative images into positive ones that will promote your spiritual growth. This process is not to be confused with ordinary positive thinking, which tries to replace a negative idea with a positive one. The difference is that you are here using the power of your own mind to produce images. By use of your conscious imagination, you can change the images you carry within *permanently*. When you have replaced a negative image with a positive one, the new image sinks deep into your very being and becomes your sacred truth.

The following self-guided inner journey will help you to identify those areas of your life that can benefit from the use of image consciousness.

Each of the experiences you will encounter in this journey into your inner symbolic dimension has a specific correspondence to how you truly feel about the different areas of your life, which will be revealed after you have finished. It is easier to do this with another person, asking them to guide you through the steps. However, if you prefer to do it alone, you can memorize the steps or tape them. If at any time during the meditation you feel uncomfortable, *stop*. You are in total control. If bad feelings emerge, notice them and wait for another time to complete the exercise.

Read the following outline carefully. It tells you exactly how you will proceed through the meditation.

FIRST—Get into a comfortable position where you can remain for about thirty minutes. It can be sitting, reclining, or lying down. Make sure you are totally comfortable physically and that you will not be interrupted. Eliminate all outside distractions, such as noise, before you start. Do not do this if you are tired or hungry.

SECOND—Relax your body and mind using a breathing exercise and a relaxation technique. Gradually, let your breathing become slow and deep. If you are doing this with a partner, arrange a hand signal to show when you feel ready to begin. If you make a tape of the sequence, leave sufficient blank time at the beginning for the relaxation. With another person, arrange a hand signal if you want to stop.

THIRD—Know that in this exercise whatever imagery you produce and your response to it is perfectly all right. Nothing is right or wrong. This is about *you*. Approach the entire episode in a playful mode. You are going to have a fantastic adventure.

FOURTH—When you have reached a state of deep relaxation, signal your partner or wait for the tape to begin.

FIFTH—When the exercise is over, return slowly to full waking consciousness and describe your experiences to your partner; make notes for your own later use. Or, remember the experiences and write them down in detail.

SIXTH—Compare your experiences with the symbolic meanings of the imagery given at the end of this section. Reflect upon the images you produce to reach their meaning for you and your life.

Important: Do not peek at the interpretations in advance. It is vital that you complete the fantasy without knowing the symbolic interpretations to assure that you get a spontaneous reading of your own inner landscape.

❧ The Adventure Trip

One—Your Special Place (Allow three minutes.)

You are going to find a wonderful, special, secret place. It can be anywhere you choose—a beach, a woods, a park, a forest. It is a place you like to be, where you feel comfortable and safe. It at any time during the exercise you feel uncomfortable, you can instantly return to this place. When you have found a locale, spend a few moments experiencing it. Notice how it looks, feels, smells. Are there trees, birds, flowers, water? Smell the air, pick a flower, listen to a bird singing, hear the roar of the ocean waves or the lapping of a lake's waters. Maybe there isn't any water. Maybe you have chosen the desert, or a hidden-away garden.

Two—Your Personal Path (Allow two minutes.)

Now that you have found your secret place and feel comfortable and familiar there, look about you for a path. There will be a path somewhere. It might be right in front of you or it might take a little poking about to find. Take your time. The path is there and it is the right path.

Once you have found the path, notice everything about it. Is it broad or narrow, smooth or rough, paved or dirt, straight or crooked, open or obstructed? Are there any people or animals on the path? If so, feel free to interact with them and remember the experiences later. If not, go on alone. Notice how you feel about the path—is it nice, or is it difficult? Do you like walking there or would you prefer to be elsewhere? Do not analyze your response, merely notice it.

Three— Finding Water (Allow two minutes.)

As you proceed along your path, noticing the entire environment, you will encounter a body of water. Describe the water to yourself. It might be a placid lake, a burbling stream, a rushing river, the crashing ocean, or a fresh spring. You may or may not be able to see the water. It might be hidden or in the distance. It doesn't matter. If you like, spend some time with the water. Get in it, go wading, splash around, gaze into its depths, or listen to the sounds it makes. Again, if you meet any people or animals—perhaps see fish swimming—take note.

Four—Finding the Key (Allow two minutes.)

Leaving the water when you are ready, continue once more along your path. Find a key. Describe the key. Is it large or small, plain or ornate? What is it made of? How do you feel about it? Where was it, in the open or hidden? Put the key in your pocket and continue along the path.

Five— Finding the Chest (Allow two minutes.)

As you walk along your path, continue to notice the details— sights, sounds, smells, other creatures. Now you find a chest. Describe the chest. Is it wood or metal, large or small, open or locked? Does the key fit the chest? Is it full or empty? Examine the contents, if any, and see how you feel about the chest and what it contains. If you like, you can take something from the chest along with you on your journey.

Six—Finding the Cup (Allow two minutes.)

Continue to proceed along your path, noticing if there are any changes. If the path started broad, does it now narrow, or vice versa? If it was smooth, is it now rocky? Continue to be aware of your surroundings as you stroll. Now, you find a cup. Examine the cup. What is it made of? Is there anything in it? What? How do you *feel* about the cup? Is it pretty or plain, clean or dirty, used or new, whole or damaged? Is it something you'd like to keep or want to leave behind? Describe it.

Seven—Encountering a Bear (Allow two minutes.)

Continue along your path, keeping aware of what is around you and how you feel about it. Now, you encounter a bear. Describe the bear. Is it on the path coming toward you, or off in the woods going away from you? Is it a large bear or a small one? What color? Does it notice you or is it intent on its own business? Do you feel threatened by the bear? How do you react to finding a bear on your path? Are you scared? Thrilled? Indifferent? Does the bear smell? Does it make any noises? Do you make eye contact with the bear? Remember the details.

Eight—Reaching a House (Allow three minutes.)

Soon you will see in the distance a house. Describe the house, what it looks like, what it is made of, how you feel about it. Is it large or small, wood or brick, old or new, empty or inhabited? What about the grounds? Landscaped or overgrown, spacious or cramped, inviting or dismal?

When you reach the house, check to see if the front door is open or shut. If locked, see if your key fits the lock. Describe your reaction to the house. Enter the house and look around. How many rooms? How furnished? Any people? Is there an upstairs level? Go exploring.

Nine— Finding the Vase (Allow one minute.)

As you explore the house, you will find a vase. Describe the vase. What is it made of? Large or small? Beautiful or plain? Ornate or serviceable? Is there anything in it? How do you feel about it?

Ten—Seeing the Fence (Allow one minute.)

Go to the back of the house and look out the window. You will see a fence. Describe the fence. High or low? Wood or rock? New or old? Well kept or run down? Nearby or at a distance? Pleasant to look at or ugly? What is your reaction to this fence? How does it make you feel?

🌿 Interpreting the Symbols

Now that you have taken this inner journey, read through the symbol correspondences below. Remember, there are no right or wrong interpretations. This exercise is to give you information about yourself and your perceptions of various areas of your life where negativity may reside. If there is anything you do not like, remember that you can always change it. Life is not static, it is always in flux. You are in a continual process of growth and change, even when you are not aware of this. Once you have done this meditation, you can re-enter the experiences you encountered and make any changes you desire. It is our ability to change the images we produce that gives us the power to bring forth the sacred in our lives.

This exercise is a powerful guidance tool to show you where you are in your attitudes at any time. You can repeat it as often as you like. Once you have learned the steps, you can activate your symbol-making faculty to tune into your current inner state, changing anything you want. That's the beauty of the sacred mind—it's there to help. Its power to create images allows us to reprogram ourselves by changing images we carry that are not right for us. While you cannot change your past experiences, you can rearrange how your *think about them*, thereby releasing feelings that may inhibit you from becoming your authentic self.

One—The Starting Place

The Starting Place represents the environment to which you naturally resonate. This is important information. If your Starting Place gave you any discomfort, you may fear beginning new things. If the experience was unpleasant in any way, or unexpected, you may feel timid about embarking on a new course of action in your life, such as taking up a spiritual practice.

If your Starting Place was comfortable and felt good and safe to you, you are already on your way to accepting the great adventure of living through your SELF and building a temple within.

Two—The Path

The Path represents your life's path as you currently view it. If your Path was open, broad, smooth, and free of obstacles, you view your life as proceeding along quite well. However, a Path free of obstacles may indicate that you are unwilling to take risks or forge ahead in new directions. It can indicate a satisfaction with the status quo.

If your Path was narrow, difficult, hilly, rocky, or otherwise difficult to traverse, you are generally unhappy about your life as it is now unfolding. You see your way as difficult and obstructed. However, a difficult Path can indicate that you are a person who overcomes obstacles and does not fear a rocky or uncertain way.

One client's image was of a deep rut in which she was walking two feet below the surface of the surrounding ground. The message was unmistakable: she felt she was in a rut—and she was. This information, revealed by her sacred mind, enabled her to face a reality that she had been refusing to acknowledge and make corrections.

At a time of transition in my own life, I entered this meditation and found my Path to be a level bricked walkway, very pleasant and lovely for walking. On one side it was landscaped like an English garden, with neatly clipped hedges and well-tended flower beds—tame and civilized and totally in order. But the other side (the left side) was bordered by a virgin forest—dense, dark, unknown, wild. The garden side held no charm nor challenge, but the wild side pulled me to want to know what was beyond the safe, neat path I had chosen. I could hear rushing water in the distance, deep within the forest, and I imagined a swift-running, deep, clear river of great power.

The imagery told me that I had a choice between continuing on a safe and orderly but unchallenging way or risking the adventure of going off into the unknown, uncharted region of myself, which promised exhilaration as well as hinted of possible dangers. I chose the forest of living by my authentic self, no matter what others thought or how it affected what gave me order and safety. I found the wild side to be full of exotic flora and fauna that I would never have experienced in the English garden, and peopled with magical beings I would never have met except in the mysterious dark forest.

The image of the Path is an important one. It can reveal a great deal about how you approach the spiritual journey that is your life. Examine your feelings about your Path. Did you enjoy being on it? Would you like to continue on this path or create a different one?

Three—The Water

The Water represents sex, how you feel about it, how you experience it in your life. Attitudes and feelings about sexuality are deep and far-reaching. They can cause conflicts and inhibitions. There can be compulsions, obsessions, fear, or lack of interest. Again, nothing is right or wrong. This is all information to enable you to release blocks so that you can become your authentic self and bring forth the sacred in your life.

Water that is calm and placid, such as a quiet lake, represents a passive (or inhibited) sexual nature, one that is not easily aroused but that gives little trouble. Or, it might represent a temporary period of quiescence or abstinence when sex is not an issue for you. A rushing river, deep and dark, can mean a turbulent sexual nature, exciting but at the same time frightening. The ceaseless ocean indicates a restless sexual nature that makes it difficult for the person to settle into a monogamous relationship. A country pond bordered with flowers, with ducks swimming on it, suggests a person who is either sexually content or not sexually adventurous, preferring to remain with what is traditional. A fog-shrouded bay indicates someone for whom sex seems mysterious or unobtainable. A stagnant pool, where nothing grows, implies being cut off from spontaneous sexual feelings. A cascading waterfall represents abundant sexual energies that need to be appropriately channeled.

Your image must be interpreted by you. What you *feel* about the image you produce is key. Sexuality is a vital and intimately personal element in our makeup. No two people are alike in their inner sexual beings. Like every other human energy, sexuality ebbs and flows—with the days, with the months, with the seasons, with the years. How we use our sacred sexual energy is up to us, but it is important to realize that this is a power source within, never to be misused or taken lightly. It is worth pondering the image your sacred mind gives you for the Water. Ask yourself how you felt about the image, whether you liked it, if you wanted to immerse yourself in it, if you wanted to leave or linger. Were you comfortable with it, or did it make you feel uncomfortable, shy, or embarrassed? Did you enjoy the experience? Was there anything about the water you'd like to change?

Four—The Key

The Key represents the value we place on ourselves. The image you received tells you how you feel about yourself and its worthiness, way deep down. It is not the description of the Key that matters, but how you react to what you find inside yourself.

For example, one woman found a Key that was ornate and beautiful, but she didn't like it because it seemed useless. She was a "trophy wife"—young and beautiful and decorative to her rich older husband—but she felt herself to be of no use or value in any significant way.

On the other hand, a man found an ordinary-looking house Key. It seemed uninteresting—merely utilitarian. But upon careful examination and reflection it proved to be a master Key capable of opening all locks. Because he considered himself to be just a plain and simple guy, his self-esteem was low. But his sacred mind knew better, and it showed him that he was a master in his own right, possessing many abilities, which he did not value because they seemed ordinary. After doing this meditation, he began to appreciate himself more.

An artist who felt that her talent was limited in comparison to what she wished to achieve found a very small Key. It was, however, made of solid gold and beautifully worked. This image allowed her to acknowledge that her talent was, if not commercial, nonetheless genuine and valuable.

Consider your Key carefully. What feelings does it call up in you? Are you happy to be the possessor of such a key or dismayed to own it? Would you be upset if you lost it, or does the Key generate negative feelings in you? Do you dislike it? What would you change about it? Would you prefer a substitute? If so, what?

Five—The Chest

The Chest represents the value we put on our mind/brain and the knowledge it has gathered to date. An open Chest signifies that we feel we can access and use our mind/brain freely. If the Chest is locked, it tells us we feel locked away from our own inner resources, an indication we do not feel that our mental faculties are readily available. When the Key fits the lock of the Chest, it is an indication that we are in possession of the key to our own minds. If the Key does not fit the Chest, we feel we may mistrust our mental abilities or feel they are unavailable to us.

The contents of the Chest give clues about what we think we possess in the way of mental attributes and about how we value those, such as knowledge and experience, our intelligence and intuition.

The size and shape of the Chest are indicators of our attitude toward our mind and its abilities. The Chest can be old or new, large or small, plain or fancy, open or closed, full or empty. You must interpret the symbol your sacred mind gives you in the light of your own self-knowledge. An empty Chest need not be a negative—it might just be waiting to be filled up. A student just beginning school, for example, experienced a shiny new Chest, like a footlocker, that stood open and empty. He interpreted it as waiting to be filled with knowledge and experience to see him through his life. An overflowing Chest may indicate a cluttered mind, or one filled with inappropriate knowledge, or it may indicate an abundance of mental riches. No one but you can say what your Chest means to you.

One client's Chest was locked tight and bound with iron. Her sweet little key, the kind a young girl has for her diary, was totally ineffective for the huge rusty lock. As she had never been good at left-brain, rational-type schooling, this woman felt her brain was a cumbersome thing of no use to her at all. Although she had artistic leanings, she had never bothered to try to discover or develop any talents she might possess for fear of failing. Her parents had made her feel small and childish (the child's key), even in adulthood. At age forty-two, she did not feel like a grown-up. Once she saw what was blocking her, she was able to access her sacred mind and discover the truth about herself. Her artistic talent flowered as she progressed on her spiritual journey into the SELF.

Another client, an accomplished intellectual, not surprisingly encountered a Chest both open and well stocked with books. What was surprising was that this man found the book-filled Chest a burden and kicked it off his path. I instructed him to dump out all the books to see if there was anything else at the bottom. There was—a music score. He was a frustrated composer who had been forced into an academic career by his father—and he had lost his authentic self along the way. But though it was buried under the books, his sacred mind showed him it was still there. He now plays in an amateur string quartet and writes music on weekends.

Six—The Cup

The Cup represents our attitude toward the positive/negative polarity of life. Was your cup half-full or half-empty? Was it a sturdy mug, a fragile china teacup, or a throw-away styrofoam container? Did it contain something lovely to drink, like fragrant tea? The cup is how we feel about the hand life dealt us, and the experiences we have sustained. Remember, whether your cup was full or empty, beautiful or ugly, you have the power to change the feeling it represents by changing the image and recovering your authentic self.

As with all of these symbolic representations, you are the best interpreter. You are already the world's expert on yourself. Meditation upon the images you receive will clarify their meaning. What is "good" for one person may be negative for another, and vice versa.

For example, one woman's Cup was a lovely piece of Limoges porcelain, of great monetary value. It was a delicate teacup. A nice image, isn't it? But she hated it because it represented her constricted lady-like life which required her to give "proper" tea parties and always be the soul of decorum. Wife of a rich man with traditional values, she was restricted to doing charity work and caring for a large, expensively furnished house. She was slowly dying, she said, of *things*. In a return to the meditation, she smashed the Limoges cup—to break out of her restraints. Now she has a job and a sturdy earthenware coffee mug.

In another example, a young man, who thought life had given him a raw deal, found a discarded styrofoam Cup that had once held coffee. A cigarette had been crushed out in the bottom, leaving a disgusting-looking mess. He was revolted by what he saw and threw the cup away, which was what he wanted to do with his life. In a return meditation, he decided upon a brand-new Cup— white, clean, shiny—which he could fill with his authentic self. By contacting the feeling that his life was fit only to be discarded and using his sacred mind, he found the strength to make changes.

Seven—The Bear

The Bear represents the outside world and our feelings toward it. It also stands for authority of all kinds imposed upon us from without. The Bear gives important clues about the factors that have prevented us from realizing our authentic selves and how they operate in us. It also shows the way to reconciliation of the inner world with the outer world. Bears come in all guises—cuddly teddy bears, fierce and scary wild beasts, threatening, neutral, or friendly. If *your* Bear was a mean one—well, just remember he is your Bear and you can change him at will. Sometimes we don't actually see the Bear—he is off in the woods somewhere and we only hear him crashing around or sense his presence. Again, the important thing is not the bear itself, but how we feel about it.

A talented singer who had run aground in the commercial music industry had retreated to the safety of giving music lessons. In her fantasy, she dressed as a little girl and when she saw the big bad Bear coming, she scampered up a tree. Safe upon her high and remote perch, she watched as he went his way. Later, we returned to the meditation so that she could confront her fear. This time, she offered him a large jewel she had taken from her Chest. He ate it with relish and gave her a bear hug!

Her talent—represented by the jewel from her Chest—served to neutralize the Bear. By eating it, he was saying he wanted to assimilate it into himself. She realized that withholding her talent from the world was harming her authentic self, a performer who wanted to be onstage.

An actor, in a constant and unsuccessful struggle to get good parts, saw his Bear as an adversary whose intention was to block his path. This Bear made him very angry. He wanted to kill it, but he realized he was not strong enough, which engendered a high level of frustration. On a return trip, he took the Bear a large pot of honey and made friends with him. The experience allowed him to accept that the world was not against him, that struggle is part of life. It is our attitude toward adversity that either gives or removes its sting.

Eight—The House

The House represents your goals in life. You may be surprised at the difference between the image your inner mind presents to you and the conscious image you have of your aims in life. Remember, your sacred mind gives you the true picture.

One man, a powerful lawyer, saw his life goals as becoming politically powerful and being able to help other people. He considered himself an altruist, interested only in the "welfare of the people." However, the image presented to him told a different story. His house was an old stone hut, almost primitive, in a remote place where there were no people at all. The territory was rugged and demanding, the ideal place for a loner who wanted to seclude himself away from all humanity. He became a lawyer to please his liberal parents and devoted himself to *their* code of altruism, under which cloak his authentic self was hidden from him.

Your House may have one or many rooms, be a cottage or a mansion, full of laughing people having a party or uninhabited. It may be cozily furnished with everything to make you comfortable, sparsely furnished, or totally bare. What is important about this image is what you make of it, how you react to it.

One client found a houseful of partying guests—and was dismayed. She wanted to be left alone to do her painting, or so she thought. The fact was that she had retreated into her artwork to avoid the pain of shyness and difficulty making friends, yet her authentic self loved being around people and longed to have a house full of friends all having a good time. The image distressed her so much she burst into tears. They were healing tears, however, for the image allowed her to glimpse her authentic self and its needs.

Whatever your image of your House is, it is a vital component of who you are and where you are going on your spiritual journey. If your conscious goals conflict with the aims of your authentic self, you are going to have difficulties reaching them, or if you do reach them you will feel dissatisfied because they are not what your true self desires. Finding out what blocks you on this level is fundamental to building your temple within.

Nine—The Vase

The Vase represents our perception of love. What we love and how we love is basic to all human life, and love perhaps more than any other human characteristic comes from the deepest, sacred level of our beings. We can no more rationally choose a love partner than we can choose what we will dream tonight. We can *marry* for rational reasons—he's a good "catch," or his profession pleases her parents; she will be a good hostess and mother; or her beauty will enhance his business aims. But *love* is another matter. Love springs from within, from that deepest level of the soul, which knows what is right for us. The image of the Vase will tell you about love and your perception of it.

Whatever your image of the Vase, trust it to reveal your innermost secret feelings about what love means to you. If you fear or distrust love, or think it is difficult to find and keep, your Vase may be cracked or broken, old and dirty, or hidden away in a closet. In a dramatic rejection of what she found, one woman said vehemently, "I don't *want* that vase! It's chipped and ugly and I inherited it from my mother." We returned to the meditation and she smashed the old vase of her mother's interpretation of love and replaced it with a lovely new one of her own choosing, for her authentic self was a closet romantic who believed in love. Trying to love by her mother's standards was thwarting her fulfillment on both the personal and spiritual levels.

Another woman found a beautiful crystal Vase, but she was distressed because it was empty—never used. She went to the garden of the house and picked a bouquet of flowers to put in it. Upon contemplating both the image and her response to it, she discovered that her authentic self was a very loving person who had not allowed herself to fulfill her affectionate nature.

Ten—The Fence

The Fence represents our perception of death. Many people fear death or consider it an unfair intrusion into life. We all know rationally that death comes to all, that nobody lives forever, yet most of us consider death to be the enemy—to be conquered, coerced into going away, or, failing that, ignored. Yet, death is a much a part of life as is birth. Whether there is "life after death," in the sense of a continuance of *this* life, no one knows. I rather doubt it, but this does not mean that death is the end of everything. It is the end of a chapter, not the end of the book. Or, it is a sequel. Whatever you believe about death, it will come one day, and your perception of death, embedded as it is in your psyche, colors how you live. Fear of death is a great inhibitor of living your life fully. It prevents you from experiencing the sacred on a daily basis. The image of the Fence will reveal your issues about death. Facing it means looking at it from within your inner temple.

Having stared death in the face more than once, prior to experiencing this meditation myself I was convinced I was completely reconciled to my own demise. I was not bothered by the desire for an afterlife. However, my first view of the Fence was of a high brick wall close behind the house, and I was *furious* that my view was cut off. This sent me in search of deeper levels and eventually my Fence became a low stone wall far off in the distance, with grasses and wildflowers growing through the cracks in the masonry. Beyond it, I could glimpse the sea gently rolling in upon the shore.

An old man I knew experienced a weathered picket Fence, already lying flat on the ground. He saw himself stepping over it into a broad meadow filled with light and flowers. His life was almost over, and he was at peace with that.

Whatever your feelings about death, it remains for all of us a mystery. It's not death itself that's important—for it will come and others will come after us—but how we live that matters. Fear, anxiety, anger, and depression about death are only *thoughts*, and the sacred mind can choose what it wants to think. A positive relationship with the end of life makes the living of it more pleasurable and productive. Fear of death is a roadblock on the spiritual path. If you are angry or fearful about the Fence, you can confront the feeling safely and make necessary changes.

One man, raised with visions of eternal hellfire, saw a frightening vision of flames leaping beyond a high concrete wall, like that of a prison. He returned to the meditation with a fire hose and in drenching the hellish flames realized he had nothing to fear. Hell is a construction of the mind, not a real place. He had believed that he no longer was influenced by his parents' fundamentalist religion, but the fear implanted in him as a child was still active. Armed with that knowledge, he was finally able to shed the rigid and crippling notions of his past and free his authentic self. There are many images for the Fence. Contemplate yours for the information it can give you.

One of the major blocks to overcome on the way to accessing our ability to experience the sacred in our daily lives is *fear*. Fear holds us back from living fully, from experiencing fully, from a healthy ability to confront the inevitable challenges in our lives. When you emerged into this world from your mother's womb, you did not know fear. As a newborn, you came fearlessly into a world you did not yet know. Deep within everyone is a place of no fear. If fear—of death or any other fear—is preventing you from experiencing the fullness of the spiritual dimension, you can change that with the power of mental imaging. This is a meditation I created to assist my clients in overcoming their fears of all kinds.

Creating Your Place of No Fear

Find a time when you can be alone and undisturbed for at least half an hour. Create an atmosphere of absolute calm around you. Light a candle, play soft music, scent the air—whatever gives you a sense of serenity and peace. Make sure your clothing is loose and comfortable, then breathe deeply and exhale all negative feelings and fears.

Now, create in your imagination a lovely place where you can feel totally safe and free from all fear. It might be a secluded spot in a woods, or a cove on a deserted beach. This place is your sanctuary. When people are given "sanctuary," in a church or in an embassy, they are protected from all harm. As this picture emerges within you, let yourself be absorbed into its quiet, beauty, and sense of safety until you have an emotional response.

When you have created this feeling-toned picture, fill in all the details. Imagine the colors, smells, textures, sounds that such a place would have. Make this picture as complete as you possibly can. Remind yourself that no fear or threat can ever enter this space. Feel its protective vibrations.

When you feel totally comfortable in this space and have succeeded in creating a sense of safety here, look around and fix all the details in your memory. This is a place you can go whenever fear strikes to banish it from your psyche.

 Now, slowly breathe yourself back to normal waking consciousness and notice how refreshed you feel when you realize that you have nothing to fear but fear itself.

As you continue to build your inner temple, you will discover that life is more joyful, richer, and more satisfying on every level. You will get the sense of being *connected*—to your whole self and everything in the entire universe. You will feel "at-one-ment" and you will know your authentic self cannot fail. You'll have a wonderful feeling that everything's going your way.

part two
Sarced Ways, Sacred Days

In traditional medicine, health was defined to embrace virtually every aspect of human experience because the sages of East and West maintained that the body, mind, and spirit are a single unified whole . . . harmonized by an underlying . . . life force, a kind of spiritual energy that permeates the universe and manifests as individual beings . . . In the same way that the whole is greater than the sum of its parts . . . all your talents and abilities would be available to you to express as you desired. Such a state . . . brings with it the unity with the ultimate reality, a harmony with the creator of life itself.

Tom Monte
and the editors of EastWest Natural Health
World Medicine

chapter six
Wise Body

The life force is powerful. A tiny blade of grass, pushing up from a speck of a seed in the soil below, can crack open a cement sidewalk.

Your body was made by the same force that created the universe. It has been making life forms, including the human body, for eons. This force lives within you and it contains millions of years of wisdom. As the vehicle of life, the body possesses its own inner wisdom, which is at work within you all the time—repairing and replacing your cells, eliminating waste, nourishing tissues, fighting off germs, calming nerves, protecting from infection, balancing your hormones, and, when necessary, healing contusions and wounds. Each of your cells is a scientific genius, not only repairing itself, but with the capacity to renew and regenerate itself; in fact, every cell in your body replaces itself with a completely new cell every seven years. You literally produce a new body.

Your *unihipili*, your own personal elemental energy, has created many bodies over time, for that is its work, and it does innumerable things for you—breathes, digests food, eliminates waste, warns you of imminent danger, runs your internal chemical production, puts you to sleep, wakes you up, and more. Located in your solar plexus, your unihipili is the keeper of your personal archive, which is what the body is—the record of your life.

As Clarissa Pinkola Estes tells us in *Women who Run with the Wolves*:

> Like the Rosetta stone, for those who know how to read it, the body is a living record of life given, life taken, life hoped for, life healed. . . . To confine the beauty and value of the body to anything less than this magnificence is to force the body to live without its rightful spirit, its rightful form, its right to exultation. To be thought ugly or unacceptable because one's beauty is outside current fashion is deeply wounding to the natural joy that belongs to the wild nature.

Within your tissues are stored all of your experiences and memories. Becoming aware of your body and its needs and moods is the means to connect with your inner truth. Your inner truth is revealed by your instincts. Unfortunately, most of us have lost touch with the physical basis from which we derive. We ignore basic needs, override our natural drives with intellect or "willpower," allow ourselves to become emotionally stressed from a variety of causes—some minor, some major. Having lost respect for our basic instincts, which are always right, we fail to listen to our bodies. Writer Mark Gerzon tells us in *Listening to Midlife* that:

> Your body ultimately knows itself far better than any other person can. In its cells have been stored every experience that has ever happened to you since before you were born. It knows more about you than your own mother, more about you even than your mind. Our bodies will teach us more than we can imagine, if only we will listen.

It is sad that, in our science-oriented, technology-driven society, we have lost our natural connection with the deep levels of wisdom within our bodies, lost the knowledge that our cells are basic intelligence organized into patterns both visible in the flesh and invisible in the inner reaches of our SELF.

We must honor the body as sacred in order to grow into the spiritual beings we are. And to honor our bodies fully and respectfully, we must become *aware* of them and what they do on a daily basis. By following the path of awareness, we can reconnect to this inner knowing. Learn to heed the clues your body gives you and follow its directions no matter what the clock or anyone else tells you. Regaining communication with your body-self will enhance your sense of living a life that is sacred every day.

Buddhist meditation teacher Jack Kornfield makes this point in his essay, "Awakening a Sacred Presence," in *Nourishing the Soul.* He says that, realizing he "used [his] body but didn't really inhabit it," he became aware that he had to "come into my body as a spiritual practice," because, "Being aware of walking, eating, and moving is the ground of our awakening." He describes this awakening in detail:

> People speak of out-of-the-body experiences, but what we begin with in meditation is something more difficult: an in-the-body experience.
>
> To be attuned and fully present in our bodies can turn the simple activities of our lives into sacred practice. For example, we spend a lot of time buying food . . . bringing it home and putting it in the cabinets; taking it out, chopping, seasoning, and cooking it; placing it on the table; eating it . . . then cleaning up and putting all the things away. We do this two, three, four times a day. Yet we often do it on automatic pilot. It's as though we're sleepwalking. We do it, but we're not there. The quality of awakening, when brought to

111

our connection to food, first requires that we pay attention, that we notice the entire act of eating.

[In] the eating meditation in a monastery . . . you honor the sensation of hunger . . . you look at the food . . . you touch the food . . . you do a blessing of gratitude for all the labors of others, for the gifts of earth and rain that bring you this food.

Then you eat slowly and mindfully, with full presence. . . . The direct experience is always new and unique.

Even though we hear that "the body is the temple of the soul," we are taught conversely that the body is the repository of sin and the "sins of the flesh" are most horrible. Not only are we often ashamed of or embarrassed by our sexuality and our sensuous nature, but we hide our common bodily functions from view and do all we can to minimize their reality, subjecting ourselves to a multitude of anti-body agents, many of which are indeed a danger to both our physical and spiritual health.

The human body is like a blank canvas upon which our imaginations create images. Too many of us suffer from bad body images. Failing to appreciate that the body is the representative of the soul and thinking ourselves unacceptable as we are, we try to become something we are not to conform to some outside standard of fitness or beauty. And, when we do not because we cannot, we feel inferior; our self-esteem is damaged along with our soul. Though we may never resolve the debate about the precise time the soul enters the body, it is clear that the soul inhabits the body and when either soul or body is neglected or denigrated both suffer.

Ideas about the body vary with the times. Standards of beauty, health, and appropriateness concerning the body have fluctuated over the centuries, and even today different cultures have different bodily standards and views of the body, its nature and its use.

Artists have always been fascinated by the human body. In the attempt to convey its inner qualities through the outer experience of seeing it, they have employed a wide variety of methods and techniques—from the lush curves of Rubens' nudes to the harsh geometries of Picasso's cubism. Flesh tones perceived by painters have covered a wide spectrum, from natural skin colors to bizarre shades never seen in the flesh. These attempts to plumb the magic and mystery of the body express the artist's conception of what the body reveals of the inner person. The body is the visible expression of the soul.

To watch a human body at rest or in movement is to glimpse the soul of the person. Our souls are articulated in our gestures, movements, shapes, physiognomy, skin color, eye shine. Disturbances to the soul are expressed in bodily functions gone awry. Skin eruptions, impaired movement, disease, malfunctioning organs—all are symptoms of soul distress.

Swiss psychologist Carl G. Jung wrote that, "[It] is not only possible but fairly probable, even, that psyche and matter are two different aspects of one and the same thing." Jungian analyst Marion Woodman speaks of ". . . a transcendence through the body to a place where the soul resides." In her essay, "Sitting by the Well," in *Nourishing the Soul,* she says:

> Most of us think of transcendence as moving through spirit, taking us out of our bodies. Making space for the divine to enter through the vulnerability of our bodies is a very different experience. To open to our own humanness and our own humility—from *humus,* or the earth—is to accept our own deepest wounds. That is where the divine enters.

An excellent way to get in touch with your body and begin to honor it as a sacred precinct, as the house of your temple within, is through *touch.* We can "get in touch" by touching ourselves. Unfortunately, most of us have been taught that touching ourselves is narcissistic or, worse, sinful. The result is that we touch ourselves only perfunctorily—as in the performance of personal hygiene—or furtively, in an erotic manner. We need to learn the spiritual power of touch for it is one of the easiest and most effective means of contacting the soul.

Touching yourself in a loving way can be an extremely positive experience, and since tactile experience is so fundamental, self-touch can be a meditative experience, whether it is sexually neutral or erotic.

Touching other people and animals brings us "in touch with" their soul energies. Many people, however, are so blocked within that they are "touchy," or do not want to be touched. So negative has this simple, basic activity become, loaded as it is with taboos and connotations of incorrectness, that loving touch has become a rare experience in many lives.

Having had experience with hands-on healing of others, I encourage self-touch as a way of sensing the sacred dimension of which the body is a representative. Every mother uses the sacred power of touch whenever she kisses a child's small hurt "to make it better." And every loved child knows that mummy's kiss has tremendous power. Metaphorically speaking, you can kiss yourself. Below is a meditation I devised to help you learn to touch your body in a positive and loving way.

 ### *How to Use the Sacred Power of Touch*

To touch yourself positively, you must first let go of any feeling of embarrassment about putting your hands on your own body in a self-conscious manner.

To begin, wash your hands and face thoroughly with a sweet-smelling soap and dry them on a soft, warm towel. (Men should shave first.) You want to maximize the tactile experience in every way possible, and that means using your other senses as well. Next, put some lotion into your hands and rub them together until they are warm. Then, gently begin to stroke and caress your face saying either silently or out loud, *I love you, You're beautiful* or other words of affection and praise. Spend ten minutes stroking your face and then look in the mirror at the lovely glow.

One of my favorite forms of meditative self-touch can be done in the shower by consciously stroking any body part that is tense, in pain, or about which you feel negative, and speaking words of love and healing to it. Learning to cherish the totality of our bodies is a powerful way of realizing their sacredness every day. You can do this outside the shower as well—standing, sitting, or lying down. Before sleep is a good time to practice self-touch, especially if something hurts. Even if you can't reach the hurting part, such as your back, you can stroke the areas of your body that you can reach and allow the *intention* to heal to penetrate into the soul dimension. You will find this a very soothing experience and the more you use it the more effective it will become.

Use this technique especially to reunite yourself to parts of your body that you have denied or despised. Because we are fed manufactured, idealized images of beauty or masculinity, we learn to think our bodies are inadequate or inferior. Women especially are afflicted by this. Surveys show that even pre-teen girls already "hate" their hips, thighs, breasts. Until women develop the good sense to reject these idealized images—and to teach their daughters to reject them as well—the noxious fumes they exude will continue to permeate our psyches.

However, *right now* you can take steps to heal the pain you have suffered because your body didn't fit the image-makers' ideal. Touch any part of you that you consider imperfect or a problem and *give love to it*. It's the only body you have and it deserves your kind and loving care and concern.

Another way we can honor our bodies is by simply taking care of ourselves. One of the primary and most often neglected forms of self-care is *rest*. Are you tired all the time? If so, your numbers are legion. Why does true rest seem to elude us? We sleep—and wake tired. We vacation—and return home exhausted. Why is this?

Rest means giving yourself permission to be quiet, free of demands—your own or those of others. It is a place *within*. Although meditation can lead to rest or be an adjunct to it, it is not actually rest. When you are truly resting, you have no place to go, nothing to do, nothing to accomplish. You are utterly at peace within yourself—at rest. It is a state of calm emptiness. Life goes on all around us all the time, but we can withdraw into that center where all is still and unmoving and there gain our deserved rest.

Rest, though it refreshes us for what we must do, is not an interim to prepare you for another day's work. It is primarily a state of being. When you rest, you activate your inner sacred realm. It is a place where you reconnect with your SELF, with your deep internal rhythms, with your inner wisdom that knows how to heal you and balance you.

No, rest isn't a given. It's a commodity in increasingly short supply in our busy lives. Those "busy lives" are usually something we are quite proud of—as if overfilled hours, days, weeks, months, years, earned extra credit in heaven.

Recently, while attending a funeral, I heard one mourner say, "That's why I keep myself so busy—you never know when you'll die." Whereas the latter statement is true, the former may hasten its arrival. Those who cannot rest, or who refuse rest, set themselves up for all sorts of ailments. Rest requires both silence and solitude, two of our basic requirements for bringing forth the sacred in our everyday lives. Rest is natural, as natural as breathing, but just as many don't breathe deeply and fully, sipping the air instead of drinking it and thereby shorting themselves of the vital flow of oxygen. Many of us have lost the ability to rest, forfeited the knowledge of how rest is made. The very word *restful* has a soothing, calming sound to it. Think of a restful day and see what comes to mind.

Rest is the glue that holds body, mind, and soul together. You know that when you are tired you tend to "come apart." Tired children are fretful, prone to accidents and tears. Tired adults are grumpy, short-tempered, prone to argument and emotional upsets. When I'm tired I find I can't do simple things well. Though I am an experienced and accomplished cook, when tired I know that if I try to cook I'll cut or burn myself, so I don't do it. Many people think the need for rest is a weakness, a lower-level activity that must be endured in order to get back to work or other pursuits. Tired people make mistakes, injure themselves and others, and become ill. You've heard the saying, "I'm just bone tired." That is what happens when we fail to get proper rest. We are tired right down to the marrow of our bones. Lack of genuine rest is a major factor in stress-related illnesses, for our bodies (and minds and spirits) do not get the chance to recuperate fully from the daily wear and tear. Like a stretched-out rubber band, they lose the ability to "bounce back."

Many people confuse rest with laziness. "Doing nothing" is considered to be some kind of minor crime associated with a bad character. To the question, "What are you doing?" can you comfortably reply, "Nothing," or do you have to invent some activity in which you were supposedly engaged? In our Puritan-based culture, doing nothing is a dangerous condition, a situation not to be tolerated. We've all had "Idle hands are the devil's workshop," drummed into us when we were children.

Though as adults, we don't have anyone over us to perpetuate the notion that rest is somehow connected with evil, that it engenders "impure thoughts" or mischievous actions, we enforce the dictum on ourselves all the same. The busy housewife feels guilty if she collapses on the sofa for half an hour with her feet up and, if interrupted, is quick to assume a pose of industriousness. Office workers use their lunch time to go shopping or perform errands. Like the Red Queen, they feel they must run as fast as they can just to stay in one place. The idea of doing "nothing" seems to equate to the one of *being* nothing, as if, instead of "I think, therefore I am," the motto were, "I do, therefore I am."

That "nothing" is a valuable place, one you need to develop and protect. It is a refuge in times of stress, a sacred space within yourself, a source of strength, joy, and healing.

Only you can know what rests *you*. Rest means different things to different people. Your spiritual vibration can be a guide to what will give you authentic rest. It might be fishing on a lake, hiking up a mountain, petting your cat, or cooking a meal. Rest does not necessarily mean lack of activity, but must include some cessation of it. Perhaps after the hike up the mountain you sit quietly and contemplate the vast emptiness of a cloudless blue sky. Remember, rest is a profound place within yourself. You must find it and identify it and experience it on your own.

 ### *Restful Meditation*

> Here is a meditation I've devised to put you into a state of mind that can lead to real rest. To do this meditation—which is really not a meditation at all in any formal sense—recline or lie down comfortably when you can be alone and uninterrupted for an hour. Turn lights down or off and eliminate outside noises and distractions. Close your eyes and let yourself experience the silence around you and then move inward and find a place of silence inside. Affirm to yourself,

I now rest in the spirit where all is free and calm.
I now rest in solitude, comfort, and safety within.
Rest is my right and I embrace it with all my being.

Let yourself stay in this place as long as you feel comfortable. Begin to follow your breath without trying to alter it. Just feel the quiet rhythm of your SELF. As you do this, let your mind wander wherever it wants to go, like a puppy let outside for an airing. Follow it if you wish to see what interests it, but make no judgments. Think of your mind as a butterfly lighting now on one flower, now on another, gathering nectar. Don't push or move your mind in any particular direction. *Let it go where it wants.* That is the key here. So much meditation tries to harness the mind, tether it like a goat on a rope as bait for large game. Don't do that. As your mind is given the freedom to roam here and there, to *play* at will, it will lead you to your place of rest.

Opening to the vast possibilities inherent in your nature releases great spiritual power. Emotional openness to the sacred realm will bring you into alignment with your body.

Spiritual disorder can be symbolized through afflictions of the body. Some conditions, such as chronic stiffness, indicate something within that is restricted and needs to be released. Stomach cramps are often a result of fear and anxiety. Rheumatic stiffness symbolizes an unbending attitude.

What happens is that the inner disturbance works itself out bodily. One can often see this facially or in body language. For example, a pattern of dogmatic self-righteousness and emotional denial can concur with cardiac and circulatory malfunction, such as the aptly named "hardening of the arteries," which often precedes cardiac arrest.

119

The "lotus" meditation on page 84 is good for those suffering from what I call "spiritual constipation."

We have been taught to denigrate the body because we consider ourselves superior to the animals, and therefore to our own animal natures. This upside-down view causes us to glorify the intellect, or rational intelligence, which we believe puts us in a class above all other creatures on the earth. As a result, we deny, neglect, and repress our healthy animal instincts. But if we were *not* animals, we would not be here. It's as simple as that. The word *animal* has a bad connotation. We often use the word as a pejorative—"You're acting like an animal." We label some human behavior as "animal," when it is in fact something an animal would never do. Animals do not abuse themselves or their young. Animals do not litter their habitat. Animals do not rape, and they kill only for food.

It is not our animal natures that have got us into trouble, but the *denial* of them. If we behaved and thought more like animals, we would be better able to preserve ourselves and our environments. It is the denial of the animal in ourselves that has led to so much human conflict and unhappiness—and loss of soul. When we relegate our animal natures to the bottom of our life equation, we are in the underworld realm of Ereshkigal and, to become whole, we must make amends and change our ways.

The widespread alienation of people from their own bodies—a legacy of Réne Descartes's famous dictum, *I think, therefore I am*—has resulted in mass confusion about our bodies and why we have them. We neglect or abuse our own and other people's bodies, leading us to miss out on many physical pleasures which are a vital part of the sacred experience.

To realize your sacred relationship to yourself, and all else, you must admit your body and your basic human biology into your care and awareness. Ask yourself these questions:

🎋 Are you at peace with your body and your "animal" qualities or do you try to "rise above" them?

🎋 Do you acknowledge and treat respectfully your physical needs—for food, elimination, rest, recuperation, grooming—or do you try to hide from your own view and that of others the basic human reality of your animal self?

🎋 Are you proud and joyful to have a body that displays your connection to nature or are you riddled with shame and guilt about your body?

🎋 Do you believe fundamentally that your body is a place where "sin" resides, that you must be constantly on the alert to stamp out all bodily desires and needs?

🎋 Is your intellectual reasoning ability what you care most about, to the detriment of your biological self?

🎋 Do you feel that the unbidden urges and uncontrollable functions of your body are disgusting or shameful?

Your answers to these questions will indicate whether you experience yourself as a totality or have a one-sided view of yourself.

We must learn to incorporate our bodies and our animal natures into our spiritual practice, honoring this reality. Whenever we find ourselves denigrating the animal self, we must stop short and reflect that not only is there nothing to be ashamed about, there is much to be grateful for and to rejoice in. Minding our animal nature is a vital part of the living of the sacred every day. Here are some things you can do to honor your animal self to bring your body fully into relationship with your mind and spirit, to experience yourself as a single, unified being.

🎋 *Trust your instincts.* Learn to listen to your body. It has wisdom through and through. Never forget that your body is a wondrous thing, full of marvels. If you deny its perfection and circumvent its instincts, you will be unhappy with your body and blame it for not feeling good or not performing well. Learn that your body knows how to take care of itself if you will only allow it to guide you.

❧ *Realize that your body is much more than its functions.* It is not a machine but a living entity with intelligence and purpose. When you begin to relate to your body as having soul, you appreciate its unique beauty and expressiveness. Thomas Moore says that "the soul is involved in the perception of an intimacy between human personality and the world's communing body."

❧ *Learn to think with your heart as well as with your head.* Astrologically, the sign of Leo rules the Sun, which represents both our individual life purpose and the essence of human vitality. Leo the lion symbolizes the heart, the central pulse of one's being. The heart may be "just a muscle" to the surgeon doing a bypass, but to you it is the seat of love and courage. When we allow our hearts to be ignited by the all-fire of the Sun, we animate the central life energy of the Eternal Flame and glow with divine inspiration.

❧ *Pay attention to symptoms. Symptom* derives from the same root as *symbol.* Thus, symptoms are symbolic of a deeper process than mere physical discomfort. Ask yourself what it *means* when you become sick. Listen to the messages your body is sending you about what it needs.

❧ *Don't accept the idea that your body is in any way "disgusting."* Its normal functions are entirely natural and necessary. Unfortunately, we have been bludgeoned by the advertising industry to think that our necessary bodily activities, which keep us alive and healthy, are to be "corrected" by the use of some product or other. For example, since we produce odors, we must be deodorized. This conditioning produces anxiety and shame. These are toxic feelings.

🌣 *Refuse to accept anyone else's standards of how you should use your body.* Instead, pay close attention to your body and learn to live in harmony with it. You are one single entity—not a body *and* a brain/mind *and* a soul/spirit. You are all of these, but not separately. Without a body, your mind wouldn't be able to think and you would have nothing with which to develop spiritual consciousness.

🌣 *Learn to set your own pace for basic bodily needs like sleep, eating, exercising.* Do what is right for you rather than following the advice of "experts" whose data comes from experiments with laboratory rats. Eat when you are hungry. Sleep when you are tired. Exercise when you feel the need for movement. So many people feel they "should" follow somebody else's prescribed routine. We are inundated from all sides through the media with these "shoulds," to the point that we are confused about what is best for us. The plain truth is that your body already knows what is best for you. The sixteenth-century sage Paracelsus advised physicians to "speak of that which is invisible . . . [the doctor] becomes a physician only when he knows that which is unnamed, invisible, and immaterial . . . has its effect."

🌣 *Remember how you felt about your body as a child.* Think of some of the things you did then that felt good. Make a list of things you would like to do that you once did. Think back to how you felt about your body as you entered puberty—what messages did you get about it? Were they negative or positive? Remember what you felt about your body as a teenager. Was it a good or bad feeling? Are you still carrying those negative feelings around today? What did you feel about your body in young adulthood when you became sexually active? Were those feelings positive or negative? Do you need to correct a bad body image today? Write a short story with your body as the main character. Let it express its feelings directly in dialogue.

❧ *Find ways to enjoy your body and give yourself pleasure.* One might say that disease is a failure of the body to experience pleasure. Pleasure is a sacred pursuit, for it nourishes the soul. Too often we use our bodies in ways that are painful ("No pain, no gain.") because fundamentally we believe that our bodies are inherently *bad*. We must learn to treat our bodies with the compassion and understanding they deserve as the archives of our souls. Your memories are stored in the very tissues of your body—it is the visible record of your life. Think of your body as a library full of priceless historic information.

When we begin to truly care about our bodies—*to love them unconditionally*—we activate our SELF and begin to experience ourselves as whole persons, not fragments. I once asked a client if he had ever had an out-of-body experience, and he replied seriously: "I've never had an *in-the-body* experience." This man hated his body. To his mind, he was too thin, too weak, too tall, unattractive to women. For years, he had retreated into his intellectual work, becoming more and more withdrawn, living an arid life totally without bodily pleasure. In time, he learned to appreciate and love his body, to truly *care* about and for it. When we fully care for the whole of us, every part, no matter what erroneous notions we have absorbed in the past, we are on the way to bringing forth the sacred in ourselves and in our lives. Use these affirmations in your blessings:

I now truly care about all of myself.
I acknowledge that my body is beautiful and good.
I accept and love all my parts.
I affirm that I really care about them and their well
being in the totality of myself.
I bless myself and all my parts. I care about their success,
their happiness, and their good health.

Never mind if this seems hypocritical to you in the beginning. Pretend you are an actor "getting into the part." Soon you will believe, for it is the truth. Say the above affirmations different ways—with emphasis on one word or another. Repeat them softly; then loudly; then emphatically; then liltingly. Sing them if you like. After a while, you will realize that you actually do care about yourself, your whole self, and all your parts. This will make you understand that you have always cared about yourself deeply, but that you were prevented from showing this care outwardly because of previous conditioning.

Once you recognize that you are an integral whole—body and all its parts, mind and all its abilities, spirit/soul and all their potentials—you will bring a new and revivifying force into your life. As you begin to experience genuine caring for your body, you will discover that each part is in relationship to the total. Nothing operates independently. Discomfort or illness result when some part of the body withdraws from cooperative relationship with the rest because it does not feel recognized or loved. Recognize that each part of you is as important as every other part. For example, your colon may not seem as romantic or useful as your eyes or hands, but without its smooth and regular functioning you would become ill from toxic build-up.

Becoming conscious of your body, its needs and its relationships may seem a daunting task, but actually it is not difficult. You begin by regarding the whole, and then you become aware of any part that needs your conscious attention. By giving extra care to whatever is not working well, you will foster the process of integration. Once you begin to truly care, and let your body know you are committed to a caring relationship with it, it will advise you of areas that need attention. Perhaps you need more rest, or less food. Maybe you need more comfortable shoes or a warmer coat. Massage or body therapy may be indicated.

As you begin to care, a tremendous burden will fall from your shoulders, which may be tight from the tension of your not caring for a long time. Don't worry about being overwhelmed. Just do one thing at a time. Cultivate the habit of listening to your body without trying to drown out its communications with drugs, stimulants, or activity. As you progress, all your past social conditioning about your body and how imperfect or bad it is will drop away like magic. You will see that you are a unique, worthy, and *whole* person, fully deserving of all the care you can give yourself.

The **S**piritually **E**volving **L**ife **F**orce that you are is a caring force, born of love. It does not criticize you nor judge you for past mistakes. It waits patiently for you to recognize it and cooperate with it to create a harmonious balance. It is the most powerful force toward wholeness that exists, for life creates wholes, not parts. No human child or baby animal ever came into the world needing to be assembled, just as no flower had to go out and collect its individual petals before it could become a blossom. By doing what life does, by making it your intention to perfect every part within the whole, you will be swimming with life's natural current.

Here are some more things you can do to increase your awareness and appreciation of your body:

❧ In the privacy of your own room, at a comfortable temperature, undress and spend an hour communing with your naked self. Notice how you feel about being without clothing, register any feelings of discomfort, shame, or embarrassment. If you find yourself criticizing any of your body parts, stop and, instead of criticizing, send them love and appreciation. Thank your body for all it does for you.

🌿 Get some washable body paint and paint yourself. You can do this alone or with a friend. Pretend you are an aborigine living without any social constraints. What would you like to look like? Adorn your naked body with as much imagination and fantasy as you can and then dance around. Go a little wild and fanciful.

🌿 Write a short essay about how it felt to just hang out in your bare skin and how different it felt to "dress" in paint and feathers.

🌿 Imagine what you would think and how you would react if you had never before seen a human body. Observe all your moving parts and feel a sense of wonder at how the whole thing works together so marvelously. Consciously think of moving your finger or a toe and be amazed at how your body responds to your commands. Draw a picture of your body as you imagine it looks to others. Draw a picture of your body as it looks to you. Compare the two.

🌿 Imagine each of your organs separately and set up a dialogue with them. Ask your kidneys, your lungs, your heart, your spleen, your liver how they are and if they need anything. Thank them for the job they do so well. Pretend you are the boss giving out year-end bonuses for good performance. How would you rate each organ? Assign a color to each one and ask yourself what that color signifies.

🌿 Make three lists about your body. One about what you want to change. One about what you like as it is. And one about what you are grateful for.

❦ Over the course of a week, keep a notebook about the running commentary you make to yourself about your body. Pay attention to the circumstances in which you have negative thoughts about your body. Start to change the negative messages you send your body to positive ones. Write these down, converting the negative words you use into positive words. List all the positive things you can think of about your body and what it does for you.

❦ Ask yourself if you use your body as an excuse to prevent you from getting what you want out of life? If so, how? Or does your body help you to attain your goals? How?

❦ Set up a dialogue with your body and have a conversation with it every day.

Today, after many centuries of being indoctrinated in the concept that the body is the repository of sin, many of us are reclaiming our bodies as the holy vessels they are. We are tuning into the idea that the body is the original "church," or temple of the sacred. Traditional peoples have always used the body as part of sacred ritual, marking rites of passage by altering the body and undergoing physical trials. Some tribes use paints on themselves made of the substance of the earth and of their own bodies (blood or semen), or they scar their bodies in prescribed ways.

We paint ourselves, too, but unlike indigenous peoples, we adorn our bodies for non-spiritual reasons—to attract the opposite sex, to impress others, or, sadly, to disguise who we really are. Recently, teenagers have taken to piercing their bodies, getting tattooed, spiking and dying their hair bizarre colors, and dressing in a manner guaranteed to displease their elders. One reason for this adolescent behavior is their feeling that they are unregarded or invisible, but another explanation is that they are seeking new spiritual outlets. Tribal cultures around the world have used body marking and altering to show rank and membership, and to connect with spiritual totems. According to Rufus C. Camphausen, author of *Return to the Tribal*, the renaissance of interest in body adornment can be interpreted as a yearning to reconnect with our tribal beginnings in a world that has lost its sense of community.

Modern body misuse, or abuse of the body not done for sacred ceremonial reasons, results from misconceptions about the body and its importance in terms of the whole. Such acts indicate that the person is not really *in* the body at all but is considering it as an *object*, separate from the ego. An essential truth is that the body cannot become the sacred vessel for your spiritual life until you are affirmatively and positively *in* it. To create our temple within, we must heal the rift between body and mind and spirit by affirming ourselves for who we are, including the package we came in.

Our bodies are not constructed by the life force to fulfill the fashion industry's current notion of beauty or style. Bodies come in all sizes and shapes and colors, each one beautiful and unique. Some are "normal," while others are handicapped or deformed. There are many explanations given by metaphysics (e.g., karma, past lives) for this, but no one truly knows why the range of human bodies is so great. What we do know is that it *is*. And the acceptance of *what is* is a cornerstone of the structure of the inner temple. What is important is that each human body houses a human soul, and that each body takes that soul through its lifetime in one way or another, regardless of physical defects or anomalies.

You cannot revere the body as a temple at the same time you are criticizing it as "evil" "sinful" or "dirty." Nor can you polarize the body between the extremes of asceticism and debauchery, which too many of us tend to do. It's the old yo-yo syndrome. Pig out on chocolates today, starve tomorrow. Or, work hard and stay sober all week, get falling-down drunk on

Saturday night. The secret to bringing forth the sacred through our bodies is *balance.*

Our bodies are the vehicles through which we experience spiritual ecstasy. Pleasure experienced in and through the body is a genuine aspect of the sacred. For example, in the writings of mystics, which appear in all religious traditions, the saints describe physical conditions. In his book, *The Occult,* Colin Wilson tells in great detail the story of St. Joseph of Copertino, the "flying monk," born Giuseppe Desa in Apulia, Italy, in 1603. Apparently Joseph sailed through the air when in a state of high excitement, or ecstasy, what the Hindus call *samadhi.* His levitations often took him atop the high altar, amid the burning candles, but he was agile as a cat and never knocked anything over.

At the end of this fascinating account, Wilson states, ". . . Fr. Joseph flew. There can be no possible doubt about that . . . Fr. Joseph's flights undoubtedly proceeded from his own powers." According to Wilson, his "feats are well attested by many witnesses."

Difficult as it may be to believe that a man can sail through the air on a current of pure spiritual joy, that Fr. Joseph performed his amazing feats under his own power seems indisputable. There can be no doubt he was in his body!

✸ *Love Is a Many-Splendored Body*

Here is an exercise that will enable you to commune with your own inner self, through the body, its vehicle. The goal of this technique is to reconnect our *whole* selves with the body, to re-establish that link we had with our physical selves when we first entered this earth plane and were separated from our mother's umbilical cord, taking our first breath. We didn't hate ourselves then, and for quite a time thereafter we enjoyed exploring our bodies and, through them, our world. The aim is to dissolve bodily tensions, originating in lack of love, and free our energies for healing and purposeful living.

Choose a period of time—an hour or more—when you can be alone and undisturbed by others or outside distractions. First, take a warm bath scented with oil or salts. Gently wrap yourself in heated towels or a soft garment. Take a comfortable reclining position. Close your eyes. Breathe several minutes concentrating on the breath.

Focus your mind on your toes, sending them love. Feel your toes as living tissue and think of all they do for you. If images of imperfect toes arise in your mind, bless them and remind yourself that your toes are perfect in Spirit. Bask in the experience of your toes being alive and pulsing with the life-giving blood coming from your heart. Say to your toes, "I love you. I thank you for what you do for me. I promise in future to treat you with love and respect."

Move on to your feet, ankles, calves, thighs, hips, genitals, reproductive organs, buttocks, repeating the exercise. As you do this, check to see if there is discomfort in any part of your body and send it not only love but healing energy. Repeat "I love you. I thank you for what you do for me" to each part of your body as you proceed.

Continue on upward, to your abdomen, chest, heart, lungs, shoulders, arms, hands. As you do this, experience a new feeling of aliveness in your body. Determine that you are going to be on intimate terms with your body, more intimate than you have ever been with another person.

Slowly, proceed to your throat, face, head, eyes, mouth, tongue, teeth, scalp, giving love to each in turn, thanking them for what they do for you. You will be amazed at how much your body does for you all the time without being given a whit of praise. Love and praise yourself, part by part, and then see the whole of yourself as being in perfect health, residing in perfect love you give yourself. Repeat this exercise frequently, especially at times when you are feeling down on yourself. Correct the balance as quickly as you can, re-establishing yourself as the giver of love to your body and to your inner self.

chapter seven
Honoring the Goddess

oddess religions invest nature and the body with spiritual meaning and value. The earliest known cultures were based on the worship of the Great Goddess, which underlies the beginnings of all civilizations. Artifacts and clay figurines representing the Goddess date back to prehistoric times and have been found all over the world. One of the first written accounts we have is *The Golden Ass of Apuleius* in which the Goddess herself speaks:

> I am she that is the natural mother of all things, mistress and governess of all the elements, the initial progeny of worlds, chief of the powers divine, queen of all . . . manifested alone and under one form in all the gods and goddesses . . . my name, my divinity is adored throughout the world, in divers manners, in variable customs, and by many names.
>
> (W. Adlington translation—The Modern Library)

In her seminal book, *When God Was a Woman,* Merlin Stone notes that she "found the development of the religion of the female deity [in the Near and Middle East, where Judaism, Christianity, and Islam all were born] was intertwined with the earliest beginnings of religion so far discovered anywhere on earth." There are accounts of a female Creator of all existence—of not only people but heaven and earth and all its creatures—in Sumer, Babylon, Africa, Australia, India, and China.

In Egypt, some five thousand years ago, the Goddess was known in many forms—Hathor, the celestial cow, who carries the sun between the horns of the moon on her head, is the great progenitor figure, maternal and all-providing, nourishing the earth with her milky rain; Nut, the goddess of rebirth, is not the earth but the sky, rising as the vault of heaven over the earth, represented by the male deity Geb, as the feminine principle identical with the generational power of the sun; Isis, from whom Pharaoh derived his power, was Queen but also the *throne*, a sacral symbol of the Great Mother, which term, originating in matriarchal symbolism, has played a significant role in succeeding centuries. Bast, represented as a cat, as the goddess of love and beauty, fertility and harmony, was everywhere revered, with temples containing thousands of statuettes of cats proffered as offerings by those seeking her blessings; Neith, the Lady of the West and twin sister of Isis, is "one of the oldest and most widely distributed Egyptian deities, going back to the predynastic era," according to Erich Neumann, who writes in *The Great Mother*: "She is the goddess of Sais, of whom Plutarch wrote: "I am all that has been, and is, and shall be, and my robe no mortal has yet uncovered."

In Babylonia She was Queen Inanna; in Mesopotamia, Ishtar was called Directress of People and Lady of Vision; the Greeks knew Her as Demeter; to the Romans She was Ceres; Celtic tribes acknowledged Cerridwen as the Goddess of intelligence and knowledge; to the pre-Greeks, as Gaia She provided the wisdom of divine revelation.

In Minoan Crete, c. 2500 B.C.E, where the last known High Priestess of the Great Goddess, Ariadne, daughter of the legendary King Minos, lived, the great temple at Knossos was crowned by a pair of horns representing the Moon. Sacred dancers consecrated to the Goddess performed the daring "bull leaping," which is preserved in the pictorial remains at the palace of Knossos on Crete. Hymns were sung in Her praise, their composition being one of the functions of the colleges of the holy isles of the Mediterranean. In Greece, at Eleusis, Her mysteries were celebrated by the famous initiation ceremonies. Though little documentation exists, we do know that some of the finest minds of Greece's "golden age" were initiates at Eleusis.

The Goddess is also earth. Says feminist writer Starhawk. She is:

> Mother Earth, who sustains all growing things, who is the body, our bones and cells. She is air—the winds that move in the trees and over the waves, breath. She is the fire of the hearth, of the blazing bonfire and the fuming volcano; the power of transformation and change. And she is water—the sea, original source of life; the rivers, streams, lakes and wells; the blood that flows in the rivers of our veins. She is mare, cow, cat, owl, crane, flower, tree, apple, seed, lion, sow, stone, woman. She is found in the world around us, in the cycles and seasons of nature, and in mind, body, spirit, and emotions within each of us. Thou are Goddess. I am Goddess. All that lives (and all that is, lives), all that serves life, is Goddess.

Everywhere She was revered as wise counselor and prophetess, as lawgiver and sage dispenser of righteous justice. She was the "personification of the eternal female principle of life which was self-sustaining and self-existent and was secret and unknown and all-pervading," says the British archaeologist Sir E.A. Wallis Budge.

The Goddess is said to have given humanity the arts of writing, agriculture, the preservation of fire, the domestication of animals, and pottery making. Her priestesses discovered and researched the healing arts, learning the characteristics and powers of herbs, and, through their "simples," secrets of the human body and mind that allowed them to relieve pain and ease childbirth, to heal wounds and cure diseases. (Unfortunately, in the later medieval Christian era these talents caused them to be accused of witchcraft.) Their women's arts led them to profound knowledge of nature that enabled them to tame wild animals, propagate wild grasses and weeds into foodstuffs, distinguish between poisonous and edible plants, and make and fire ceramics for pottery.

According to Neumann, "The sacral relation of the woman to the pot originates . . . in the symbolic significance of the material from which the pot is made, namely, clay, for clay belongs to the earth, which stands in a relation of *participation* with the Feminine."

Over the centuries of the development of civilization, Neumann tells us, even the most abstract matriarchal symbols preserve their relation to the vessel-body of the Feminine.

> Wisdom becomes the milk of wisdom, and thus retains . . . its character as food and its connection with creative birth through the Feminine. Similarly, the elixir . . . appears as herb or fruit of immortality [or] as diamond or pearl, as flower or kernel.
>
> Finally, the world of the spirit as something born, as a product of creative nature itself, has as its most abstract symbol in the form that leads from mouth to

breath, and from breath to word, the logos, the spiritual symbol. . . .

If we survey the whole of the symbolic sphere determined by the . . . Feminine as "creative principle" encompasses the whole world. This is the totality of nature in its original unity, from which all life arises and unfolds, assuming, in its highest transformation, the form of the spirit.

In civilizations where the Goddess reigned supreme, from Her came all things, and to Her all things returned. She both gave life and "ate back" the dead. The Goddess as Mother was carved on the walls of Paleolithic caves, painted in the shrines of the earliest known cities, on the Anatolian plateau. The great stone circles—known as *henges*—in the British Isles were raised in Her honor, as were the later *dolmens* and *cromlechs* of the Celtic peoples. These great centers—in Anatolia, Malta, Iberia, Brittany, and Sumeria—are ruins now, silent stones attesting to the worship of the Great Mother as the progenitor of all things. Gone too are the records of Eleusis, of which we have only literary clues, as is the great library of Alexandria, whose curator was a woman, Hypatia, which contained thousands of early books of literature and science and was destroyed by murderous mobs of the "new religion."

Nonetheless, the tradition of Goddess-centered worship lives on in the hearts and psyches of people everywhere, tracing its roots back to the time before the ascendance of patriarchy. As Merlin Stone says in *When God Was a Woman:*

For people raised and programmed on the patriarchal religions of today, religions that affect us in even the most secular aspects of our society, perhaps there remains a lingering, almost innate memory of sacred shrines and temples tended by priestesses who served in the religion of the

137

original supreme deity. In the beginning, people prayed to the Creatress of Life, the Mistress of Heaven. At the very dawn of religion, God was a woman. Do you remember?

Among the Iroquois, a council of women chose the tribal chiefs, and they had the power to replace him. In his book *Shape Shifting*, John Perkins reports a conversation with a Mayan wise man Viejo Itza:

> This world is basically feminine, you know. It's what allows survival. Not "survival of the fittest"—that's just a male concept. Survival is all about nurturing, loving, sustaining—the feminine aspects. Without them, where would we be? Our early history was predominantly one that honored these qualities; like your Iroquois, women decided all the important issues. My culture here worshiped the goddess, as did people all over the world—all over *Mother* Earth—until recent history, a few thousand years ago, perhaps a couple of thousand years before Christ.

To recognize, experience, and celebrate the sacred in our daily lives, we must realize that, as Starhawk says in her essay "Witchcraft and Women's Culture," in *Nourishing the Soul*:

> The Goddess is manifest in the world; she brings life into being, *is* nature, *is* flesh. Union is not sought outside the world in some heavenly sphere or through dissolution of the self into the void beyond the senses. Spiritual union is found in life, within nature, passion, sensuality—through being fully human, fully one's self.

And, Starhawk reminds us, in the Goddess "There is no dichotomy between spirit and flesh, no split between Godhead and the world."

Our society, and by extension our approach to what we consider to be sacred or holy, is conditioned by patriarchal domination, which includes the mechanistic scientific view that Nature is soulless, a mere machine designed to produce animals and plants for the benefit of humans, to whom a patriarchal God gave "dominion" over all other life forms, many of them now extinct, others seriously endangered, as a by-product of that worldview. The result is a philosophy that denigrates the feminine principle as it has been expressed from time immemorial.

The Goddess is Mother, and She is Earth. Upon Her bosom we rest, upon Her sod we tread, from Her fructifying womb come all living things and within Her sacred body lie all those precious resources that enrich the lives and the pocketbooks of humans. But because She has been declared dead and inert by the high priests of the most recent religion, Science, we take from Her without thought or consideration for the consequences. Though some of us express concern for "the environment," few of us see that *we* are part of that environment, that humanity itself is an endangered species. No legislation can solve or eradicate the problem. Only we ourselves as individuals, and in our communities, can do that. And we will do it by honoring the Goddess first in ourselves, and then in our world at large.

Our patriarchal society is based on certain unstated assumptions about the nature of the universe and all in it. We can reject that system of thought, or revise it to suit ourselves and our needs. After centuries of mostly unthinking acceptance of what we have been told is right and correct in terms of how we live our lives and approach or experience the sacred realm, we now have the tools at our disposal to make far-reaching changes—in ourselves and in our world.

Patriarchy is neither ordained by divine revelation nor proclaimed biologically, though it claims and acts as if it were both. Merely a system of thought, it can be changed, no matter how deeply ingrained. However, in order for it to be changed, it must first be challenged. Feminist theologians are doing this, but it is the job of all of us who wish to live lives authenticated by the SELF. In *The Changing of the Gods,* Naomi R. Goldenberg asks, "If a woman comes to the conclusion that the patriarchal religions of Western culture do not help her in her life and, in fact may very well hinder her sense of well-being, what can she do?"

Goldenberg's answer is that there are two options: one is to withdraw all energy from spiritual concerns; the other is to give energy to the formulating of spiritual concepts that allow a religious view apart from the oppressive forms prescribed by traditional religions through the use of "the spiritual processes at work in [women's] psyches independent of religious processes endorsed by contemporary religion."

These female theologians are concerned about the need for holistic vision and for getting in touch with our bodies and nature, realizing that, as Mary Daly says, "This becoming of *whole* human beings will affect the values of our society, for it will involve a change in the fabric of human consciousness."

Can we succeed at this daunting task? The answer ultimately will depend not on who the prevailing culture says we are but on who we determine ourselves to be, and why.

Although the Great Mother Goddess preceded male gods by thousands of years and was once venerated as the sole deity in all corners of the Earth, her displacement by the patriarchal system was all but complete. The good news is that She is making a return. The Goddess, banished and seemingly lost through the past millennia, is once again making Her presence felt in an epiphany in modern consciousness. According to theologian Nelle Morton:

> We have experienced the death of the stereotyped
> images, the breaking of them from within so that self
> can be affirmed and potentialized. No one can take
> this journey . . . but [those] who are involved. . . . It

may be that the most authentic celebration is not that which can be structured from above . . . Maybe the most authentic celebration begins with rejoicing in that which is breaking up from down under."

Echoing this, Sheila Collins says: "Without being fully conscious of it, women today are recovering or rediscovering the pre-Judeo-Christian understanding of themselves. . . ." By beginning to understand and incorporate the deep psychic meanings inherent in a Goddess-centered view of the world, which have been continually suppressed in Western culture, they are preparing to go to a new synthesis. Collins further says, "Goddesses are being resurrected and are demonstrating that their transformative and integrative powers are equal to that of the Christian Christ."

The era of the Great Goddess for thousands of years provided support and comfort to all humanity. We can, through honoring the Goddess, reconnect to inner wholeness.

Our concept of the feminine resulting from centuries of mythological representation—and misrepresentation—reaches deep into the fabric of our society, and into the fiber of our beings. Recent developments in psychology and science—including the new explorations into the realms of intuition, ESP, global harmony, and the relationship of mind to matter—have shown that our currently impaired concept of the feminine is wreaking havoc in our world. In 1955, psychologist Erich Neumann said prophetically:

The investigation of . . . the feminine psyche is one of the most necessary and important tasks [for] the creative health and development of the individual. [It] has equal importance for the psychologist of culture, who recognizes that the peril of present-day mankind springs in large part from the one-sidedly patriarchal development of the male intellectual consciousness, which is no longer kept in balance by the matriarchal world of the psyche. In this sense the exposition of the Feminine is also a contribution to a future therapy of culture.

To foster "the creative health and development of the individual," we must all, men and women alike, escape the patriarchy's powerful enmeshment. Overcoming the attitudes inherent in such a social structure requires embarking on another type of hero journey—not the outward one of the traditional male hero, but the feminine-oriented inward quest whose positive outcome is *a shift of emphasis within*. If we are to change our lives with lasting significance, we must examine and understand our point of view *toward* the feminine, and also the *inward processes of identifying the feminine principle*, which operates in everyone, male and female alike. The goal of such an inner journey is not to change the world; it is to change ourselves, thereby contributing to a "future therapy of culture."

Who we are within, and how we proceed out of our inner selves, cannot exist without conscious knowledge of the options available from which to choose.

Traditional religion, abetted by science, has sold us a cheap bill of goods—a shoddy half-life around the masculine power structure. Both stem from the same patriarchal root, and both are ultimately responsible for the current deplorable state of affairs described thusly by David Korten, author of *When Corporations Rule the World*:

> . . . we are creating dysfunctional societies that are breeding pathological behavior—violence, extreme competitiveness, suicide, drug abuse, greed, and environmental degradation. . . . Such behavior is an inevitable consequence when a society fails to meet

the needs of its members for social bonding, trust, affection, and a shared sacred meaning.

This tradition, exemplified by a God who lived in a distant realm separate from Earth and who revealed His will and wisdom through male prophets, is proclaimed superior by the sword, as Joseph Campbell notes in *Occidental Mythology*:

> When the Goddess had been venerated as the giver and supporter of life as well as consumer of the dead, women as Her representatives had been accorded a paramount position in society as well as in cult . . . opposed to such, without quarter, is the order of the Patriarchy, with an ardor of righteous eloquence and a fury of fire and sword.

Clearly our perception of the Feminine, which is revealed by the way women view themselves and the way they are perceived by men—as lawmakers and politicians as well as husbands, lovers, and sons—is one of the most important and potent forces at work in the world today. To integrate the divine Feminine is to be in harmony with the inner person, not merely fulfilling the socially accepted and politically ordained "roles" assigned to both women and men.

One of the most effective means of doing this is through an understanding of the symbols that affect us so deeply. By reorienting ourselves to the symbols of the divine Feminine, we heal the inner split that came about in the human psyche when the Great Mother Goddess was replaced entirely by the Father God with the result that one-sidedness has riven Western culture ever since.

Symbol is myth's vehicle, the chariot by which legend and story, and myth's higher form, religion, are drawn through the heart and mind, and through time, the pages of history. Symbols express underlying patterns of thought and feeling stemming from the mythological roots that still affect us in a very real way.

The great symbol for the Goddess is the moon, whose three aspects represent the three faces of the Great Triple Goddess: as the newborn crescent, the Moon is Maiden, the Virgin—not chaste, but belonging to herself alone, not bound to any man. She is associated with Artemis, the "Lady of the Beasts," and all in nature that is wild, free, and untamed. At the full Moon, She is the mature woman, sexual and maternal, giver of life. In this phase, She is associated with the great grain Goddesses—Demeter, Ceres, Isis, and also with Aphrodite, the Goddess of love and beauty. At the end of her cycle, the waning Moon about to turn dark is representative of the wise old woman whose years have ripened into wisdom. Here, as prophetess, diviner, inspirer, she is associated with the powerful Goddesses Hecate, Ceridwen, and Kali.

Symbolically, the Moon serves to illuminate the non-conscious side of human life, and in that diffuse light we can often see more clearly than in the glare of the noonday Sun. The light of the Sun enables us to see the world around us—what is *outside ourselves*. But the Moon allows us to shine light into our inner spiritual world, to illuminate what springs naturally from *inside ourselves*. In moonlight we perceive the reality of our inner spiritual selves more clearly, we are more aware of the shadings and nuances of feelings and inner perceptions, we tune in more accurately to the spiritual vibrations of others, and our SELF is more in tune with the information universe.

This is because during the hours of night our subtle senses are more open and receptive to our inner spiritual harmony. The Moon has been called the "soul of life." Without it, we would have only the mechanical, an endless solar efficiency, which, in the end, is soulless. Without the Moon we would have no poetry, literature, art, music, dance, or dreams. Artists are notorious for being "dreamy," and it is at night when the Moon reigns that we dream.

Astrologically the Moon represents the Soul, which is the link between Spirit (Sun) and Matter (Earth). Your *lunar self* is the channel for the flow of the divine Goddess energy. One of the legacies of the patriarchal era is that in our society we give far much more weight to the Sun, or masculine-rational, functions of ourselves than we do to the Moon, or creative-nonrational. What is valued most are the traditional *masculine* traits of action and rational, linear thinking. Although the feminine lunar traits are vital to our well-being—such crucial issues as dependency and nurturing, our sense of security and safety, and the ability to relate emotionally are the Moon's domain—they are not highly valued by our dominantly solar culture. It's the hustling salesman, the profit-driven executive, the hard-nosed lawyer, the tough politician, the professional athlete who get the attention, the money, and the applause.

When we become too involved with our Sun energy, we tend to neglect or deny our Moon energy and throw ourselves out of balance. Men especially are out of touch with their lunar selves. Culturally, in our very race to reach it, we have abandoned the Moon! Many people are disconnected from their lunar selves because of pressures to conform to the solar world around them.

The Moon passes through all twelve of the zodiacal signs every twenty-eight days, coinciding with the female menstrual cycle. Thus, each person is said to have the Moon in a particular sign. (For information about determining your Moon sign, see Apendix.) Knowledge of your Moon and how it operates will give you the key to rebalancing your lunar and solar energies, to restoring the Feminine to your life. Here's how the individual signs relate to the Feminine principle:

Aries

With your Moon in the independent sign of Aries, you belong to the realm of Artemis, patroness of all that is wild and free. As "Lady of the Beasts" and Goddess of the Hunt, Artemis as Goddess of the Moon confers an independent spirit. Your spiritual path is one you choose yourself without regard to tradition.

Taurus

With your Moon in the sign of Taurus, where the Moon is astrologically considered to be exalted or "in honor," you are in the realm of the Great Cow Goddess, Hathor, who wears the horns of the Moon. She is the quintessential representative of nurturance. Your spiritual path will involve nurturing others and the Earth itself.

Gemini

With the Moon in Gemini, you are in the sphere of Neith, who mediates all things. Often represented with wings spread, She claims kinship to the Moon. She is male-female and represents the eternal feminine principle that is self-sustaining and all-pervading. Your spiritual path is to reunite your feminine and masculine.

Cancer

With the Moon in Cancer, you are in the realm of the Great Mother Goddess, Demeter, the quintessential representative of the maternal principle. Whether you express this through having children or through providing nurturing for others, your spiritual path is through the Feminine maternal element personified by the Goddess.

Leo

With the Moon in Leo, you are in the territory of Bast, the cat Goddess who symbolized fire to the Egyptians. Through her kinship with the Moon, She belongs to the unitary world of the Feminine accented by the power of Fire. As Goddess of the east, she represents birth and what is new. Your spiritual path lies through love and creativity.

Virgo

With the Moon in Virgo, you are in tune with Hestia, the Goddess of the eternal flame that burns in temple and home alike. Hestia represents order and the care of the everyday and ordinary. She makes home a sacred place and the attending to small chores a holy endeavor. Your spiritual path is to concentrate on your inner, subjective experience.

Libra

With the Moon in Libra, you relate to Hera, Goddess of marriage. Libra is the sign of relationships, and Hera represents the relationship of marriage. She is the Goddess who personifies wife. She is also the Goddess who tests the hero—Her name is the feminine form of *hero*. With Hera, your spiritual path is through relationships and balance.

Scorpio

With the Moon in Scorpio, you are in the realm of great Hecate, Goddess of the underworld. Mistress of magic, She is the spinner of human life and of darkness as well as light. She rules the West Gate, the entrance to the underworld and as such represents the ultimate mysteries of life and death. Your spiritual path is through the journey into your own depths to inner transformation.

Sagittarius

With the Moon in Sagittarius, you are in the arms of Athena, the Goddess of wisdom, representative of the highest feminine intelligence. As protectoress, she carries a spear, while in the other hand she has a spindle, symbol of Her as spinner of human destinies. Your spiritual path is through the acquisition of wisdom and the practice of valor.

Capricorn

With the Moon in Capricorn, you are consonant with Isis, the "enthroned Goddess," upon whose lap the ruler sits. She is the Mountain Mother, and it is Capricorn's nature to climb mountains. She is the Goddess who has her seat on the earth. Your spiritual path lies through proper use of the material world as you ascend the mountain of self-development.

Aquarius

With the Moon in Aquarius, your patroness is Maat, the Egyptian Goddess of justice. Her chief function is to test souls and Her symbol is the Feather of Truth, which She uses to weigh against them. Her primary characteristic is impartiality. Your spiritual path is to seek yourself through impartially serving humanity.

Pisces

With the Moon in Pisces, you relate to Persephone who spent half the year in the upper world and half in the underworld. Through Her annual return from the underworld, celebrated in the Eleusinian Mysteries, the Greeks experienced renewal. Your spiritual path is to renew yourself and others by inhabiting two different worlds, the seen and the unseen.

Another way we can "tune in" to our inner spiritual dimension of the Feminine is through the recently developed science of neurolinguistic programming, which provides us with tools to reconnect ourselves to inner archetypal energy, such as the Feminine. In their book *Changing Your Destiny*, Mary Orser and Richard Zarro have provided "attunements," expressed in the first person, which could be considered as an *invocation*.

Moon Attunement

I am the Moon,
Ruler of Blue shadows and moist silence in
The Bowl of Heaven.
I give form to creative force.
I am Fertile Matter which sustains and nourishes
Seeds of solar life.
I absorb the solar currents
By being passive, feminine, and receptive.
I am the sentient substance
Of instincts, memories, and desires
Waiting to be impregnated
By the light, heat, and power of the Sun's rays.
I am the Great Mother.
The ancient ones called me
One thousand names of mystery.
I am the Celestial Midwife
Cherishing the Child of Divine Seed.
Sister of the Sun, the caress of The Mother,
I am the breast of Life,
Lover of Lovers,
The Wisdom of the waters,
Of instinct and ancestral experience,
Of nature and spirit, Fate and the motion of Time.
I harbor the secret knowledge and power of Love,
Of the subconscious, of immortality,
Of inspiration and instinctive desire.
Mother of Enchantresses and Magicians,
I rule the function and form of matter,
Rhythms of the body and fate of the soul,
Where one has been and what one has yet to face.
I am the Captor and Reflector.

To help my clients harmonize their lunar selves with their solar selves, I devised the following meditation as part of my AstroVision^{TM} series.

Sun/Moon In-tune-ment

Prepare for this exercise by first walking about and taking a good long stretch to loosen your muscles and ready yourself for an inner experience. Then, sit or recline in a comfortable position you can hold for ten or fifteen minutes. Loosen or remove any tight clothing and close your eyes. First, pay total attention to your breath, without making any changes; simply observe the breath coming in and going out for several minutes until you feel a sense of relaxation and unwinding as you proceed to your inner SELF.

Now, imagine yourself holding your Sun in one hand and your Moon in the other. You may want to do this with your hands outstretched, or in your lap, or whatever feels comfortable. Allow yourself to feel the weight of each of the "lights" you are holding, as if you were trying to discover the differences between them. Choose one and put the other down. Then, with both hands, turn your chosen light about in your hands as you would an object that is new to you. Feel the size, texture, weight of it. See if it has any other characteristics such as smell or sound or color.

Spend a few minutes, or as long as you feel comfortable with the first light, making friends with it as you might with a new puppy or kitten, and then put it down and take up the second light in your hands, repeating the procedure.

After familiarizing yourself with the two lights on an individual basis, feel intuitively how they relate to each other. See if you want to say anything to either or both. You may want to ask questions, find out the best way to use the energies, or see what each needs of you. You can ask both Sun and Moon if it feels fulfilled or if you can bring more of its energy into focus in your life. Ask how to do this. Do this procedure with both lights.

Then, take them both up together, one in each hand, and see what happens—you may feel that they want to dialogue, or that they have something to give each other, or work out together. Give them equal time.

The more often you do this exercise, the more you will be in balance with both your inner Moon and your inner Sun.

You can also observe the phases of the moon to feel your own inner tides. The Moon's cyclical and ever-changing nature is analogous to the great flux and flow of life itself, regular and rhythmical as the ocean tides she rules, and of our inner spiritual lives. The Moon reveals our inner contours to us. Try this experiment to prove this to yourself:

Choose an hour of the day—say, from three to four—and sit quietly in a room by yourself with no distractions. See what comes to your mind, how you feel, what you think, where your awareness goes. Afterward, that same hour in the night, repeat the procedure. Notice any differences. If you let yourself be in tune with the cosmos, you will *feel* the Moon's energies, not only "out there," but in you.

Another way to tune into the Moon's energies is to pay attention to the phases of the Moon. From the nights in which we observe the newborn Moon's slim shining crescent to those when her full and glowing face illuminates all, and back again to the opposite-facing sliver, she is passing through what are known as *lunar phases*.

To do this Moon work, you will need a lunar calendar which shows the phases of the moon. Often, these are listed in the newspaper. Pay close attention to each one.

The *waxing*, or increasing, Moon brings an energy of expansion. This is a positive influence. It is the best time to concentrate on issues of growth or a new beginning of any kind. Whatever is seeded now will grow into fruition.

When the Moon is *full* the energy moves toward the completion of what was previously set in motion. The lunar energy is at its strongest and most powerful. You can focus this by using the appropriate meditation and affirmations. The light of the full Moon eliminates shadows, so this is an especially good time to work on clarity in your spiritual concerns.

During the period of the *waning* Moon, the energy moves toward decreasing and, finally, at the dark Moon, eliminating. This phase is ideal for dealing with negative issues you want to eliminate from your life. Now is the time to practice releasing and letting go. Use the waning phase of the Moon to help you discharge all negativity from your life. Release it and let it go.

The energies of the Moon change slowly, seguing from one phase into the next. After the night of the dark Moon, for example, the energy of the new Moon slowly increases into the expansive growth phase that will culminate in the full Moon. The energy of the full Moon begins to build two days before the total fullness is achieved, and it continues in effect for another two days afterward, only somewhat diminished in power as the waning phase takes over. The energy of the waning Moon fades slowly as its visible area decreases.

You can increase your sensitivity to the Moon and your lunar self by making direct contact. To do this, sit facing the direction of the visible Moon. If you cannot see her, acknowledge her by closing your eyes and imagining the beautiful silver crescent or disk in the dark sky. If possible, position yourself in front of a window or go outside where the rays of the Moon can shine on you. Sit quietly for several minutes until you can feel the Moon's energy contacting you. Imagine her luminosity entering your body, connecting your soul to her as the soul of our planetary system. Feel the magnetic pull of the Moon on your sensitivities and allow yourself to be touched within by her softly glowing light. Let it illuminate your "dark night of the soul," inspiring and uplifting you.

By connecting to the universal divine Feminine and consciously reclaiming the power of the Goddess, we can take back responsibility for our lives and reweave the torn fabric of our self-image and self-esteem. Remember that the Goddess is the weaver. And, although this task must fall squarely on the shoulders of each individual, it is only through the collective that we can transform our dominant belief systems and values, thereby making the institutions of our societies responsive and responsible to ourselves, our planet, and everything on it.

As we learn to honor the Goddess and to relate to Her symbols, new—mayhap startling—connections may be perceived, insights gained. Ours is a time of transition. The old patriarchal structure affects the entire planetary society, but it is evident to all who see clearly that this is no longer a viable way for conducting life on Planet Earth. As Rosemary Radford Reuther says, ". . . nature and society are giving clear warning signals that the usefulness of this spirituality is about to end." Though these attitudes, emanating from the male mythologies, have worked their way into the minds and hearts of our entire society, a new tide is rising, an inner shift that will not be denied. It is issuing out of the deep mythological wells that feed the psyche: all pressures are not social; some come from within.

It is my hope that a new appreciation of the Feminine will lead us all to reject misconceptions and outdated stereotypes and reveal what is valid and still usable, what can be built on in a future shaping of a new spirituality, positive and free, which will benefit not only today's women and men but reach out and influence future generations.

A spiritual quest is a deeply personal intimate journey. No two are alike. There is a Way, but each individual sets their own footprints on it in a special and induplicable manner. Each finds a spiritual framework that is unique. Yet, as all roads up a mountain lead to the top, the end result is the same. It is a *process of transformation*, and the product of that process is renewal and rebirth, a spiritual healing into wholeness. The most eloquent statement of this urgent need I know is that from Edward C. Whitmont, who says, in *The Return of the Goddess*:

> . . . the ancient Goddess is arising. She demands recognition and homage. If we refuse to acknowledge her, she may unleash forces of destruction. If we grant the Goddess her due, she may compassionately guide us toward transformation. . . . This critical point in time marks the turn of the tide again.

chapter eight
Creating Ritual

itual is an art form whose aim is to connect us to the spiritual. Its use is a way of making what is internal manifest in the external world; the external practice serves to make us more receptive to and aware of our thoughts, feelings, and actions. When we use ritual, we *sanctify*. And with sanctification we bring our lives closer to the sacred. It's said that you can light a candle because you need the light, or because it symbolizes the light you need.

The ancient Egyptians performed elaborate rituals to serve a variety of ends. These followed a precise order—any deviation would spoil the intended result. Magic, to which ritual is closely related, depends on each step in the proceeding being carried out exactly as prescribed.

In Egypt, ritual and ritual magic served to connect the entire society. Special ceremonies of purification were performed prior to the rite itself. Priests bathed and removed their body hair before dressing in clean white linen robes kept for each separate ritual. Pharaoh, who was the representative of the gods as well as ruler of the land, was the center of many rituals that were performed annually or seasonally. Since he was

155

responsible for the spiritual health of his people, he was required to maintain the connection with the divine.

Isis, the Egyptian Great Mother Goddess, upon whose lap the king sits, and from whose divinity he derives his power, both temporal and divine, was also the focus of regular rituals.

As a society that was so closely bound to the land, and whose food supply was dependent on the annual flooding of the great Nile River, Egyptian rituals often related to planting and harvesting, as well as to celestial events such as the phases of the moon and the appearances of the planets.

In times when life-sustaining fire was precious, and therefore sacred, the live coals were transported with ceremony, protected in a vessel lined with moss, carried by a select elite, and welcomed with pomp and circumstance. The ritual of fire gave each person a heightened awareness of its value to their lives. Blowing on the embers to keep them alive was a privilege. Today, though we depend on it no less, fire is a commonplace. Try to remember the last time you experienced a power outage and had to light candles against the sudden dark. You will discover that you unwittingly fell into the ritual of fire. Whatever you did, wherever you placed your candles, you did so with a renewed awareness of fire's light and warmth, and of the danger that lurks when it goes out.

Whether elaborate and formal or simple and informal, ritual brings us into the presence of the sacred. When I was a child, the Catholic mass was still said in Latin. The priest's intonement and the congregation's response in this formal "dead" language, along with the complex pattern of sitting, standing, and kneeling, the rustling of the richly embroidered silken robes of the prelate, the wafting of incense, the sprinkling of holy water, and the tinkling of a little bell to signal a spoken response from the worshippers provoked in me an altered state of consciousness that often lasted all day. Conversely, the simple blessing of a meal, or the taking of a glass of wine in praise of the Goddess, can be a significant ritual if done with sacred intent.

Rituals have great power to influence the mind and emotions. Whether we are believers of a specific tradition or not, we all need ritual. It seems to fill a basic need in the human psyche.

In today's busy world, we have all but lost the connection to meaningful ritual. As we have become disconnected from them, traditional forms have faded in importance. Often they no longer serve any meaningful purpose in our modern lives. However, we can successfully create rituals to serve our own purposes. By so doing, we reconnect to the sacred in our everyday lives. You may have already done this without quite knowing it—certain routines of our lives attain the importance of ritual, even becoming somewhat formalized, such as family gatherings that are marked by special food and drink and an order in which things occur. Children naturally both create and respond to ritual—such as that of getting ready for bed—and can be upset if the precise sequence isn't followed. "No, no. I get in bed *first* and *then* you bring Teddy Bear."

Ask yourself these questions:

- 🌱 What rituals do I use for ordinary everyday life? These may include how you prepare yourself for bed, for work, for dinner, for play or recreation.
- 🌱 What rituals do I observe as part of my spiritual practice? These may include churchgoing or any worshipful practice carried on through an outside or public forum, or purely private activity such as doing yoga, meditating, or praying.
- 🌱 Do I enjoy these public observations?
- 🌱 Am I fully aware of my private rituals?
- 🌱 How can I bring more awareness into my use of ritual?
- 🌱 What do the rituals I use mean to me?

- ❧ What connections do I make through ritual?
- ❧ Do I want to include more ritual in my everyday activities?
- ❧ Does ritual satisfy a need in me?
- ❧ Would I enjoy designing my own rituals for myself and my family?

Here are some suggestions for incorporating ritual into your daily life:

- ❧ Create a welcoming ritual for any new possession, especially an important one. In Japan, any new piece of equipment in a factory is formally blessed by a priest before it is used.
- ❧ Japanese Buddhists observe "Needle Memorial Day," to honor all the needles that have been "killed in action," or worn out during the year. You can create a disposing ritual to "bury the dead" things in your household.
- ❧ Make a ritual to prepare you for each day's work. Bless your computer, or drawing board, or whatever tools you use, before starting work. Thank them for helping you.
- ❧ Go on a pilgrimage. It could be to a sacred site within a tradition you like, to a childhood home, or to a national memorial place.
- ❧ Invite others to participate with you in creating a ritual to honor common space, such as a park or playground.
- ❧ Make an Earth ritual to celebrate the advent of each season. Perform this on the Spring and Fall equinoxes and on the Summer and Winter solstices.
- ❧ Ritually honor the Moon at each New and Full Moon.
- ❧ Discover your own Moon sign and prepare a simple ritual to perform on the day the Moon enters the sign it occupied when you were born. This is your *lunar return*.
- ❧ If you have school-age children, plan a ritual for the first

day of school each year; bless the past summer for its gifts and give thanks for the new year and all that will be learned during it.

🎋 Make a ritual around any activity that you want to "spiritualize," from household chores to shopping trips.

🎋 If you can, take a daily nap as a mini-ritual.

🎋 Take a "spiritual break" every day and get off by yourself to appreciate something in your life.

🎋 If you keep a spiritual journal, create a ritual around that.

🎋 Listmaking is a fine ritual. Make lists of how you can sanctify your life and the things you do. List all the things you'd like to do to make your life more meaningful and read them over weekly. Remember, "Images the mind makes work into life."

🎋 Turn your personal hygiene and grooming into a ritual to honor your body. Consider the actions you perform as devotional acts in praise of your physical reality.

🎋 If you know someone who is lonely or shut in, make a ritual of telephoning them periodically, or send a special card or note on a particular date each month, such as the day of birth, i.e., if a person was born on March 7, send a card on the seventh day of every month.

🎋 Make a ritual around your time of silence. You could always wear a specific garment, or add a scarf or piece of jewelry for that purpose.

🎋 Do a movement ritual. Make spontaneous movements that please you and perform them daily. This kind of homemade Tai Chi will center you in your body.

In addition, you can make a ritual out of any activity you perform daily, such as washing dishes or vacuuming the rugs. In *Care of the Soul*, Thomas Moore comments on the value of "ritualizing" everyday activities. He says:

> The ordinary arts we practice every day at home are of more importance to the soul than their simplicity might suggest. For example, I can't explain it, but I enjoy doing dishes. I've had an automatic dishwasher in my home for over a year, and I have never used it. What appeals to me . . . is the reverie induced by going through the ritual of washing, rinsing, and drying.

Moore goes on to say that Marie-Louise von Franz, the Swiss Jungian author, observes that "weaving and knitting, too, are particularly good for the soul because they encourage reflection and reverie."

When I lived in a rented house in the Catskills in New York, I had a black rug on the living room floor. Of course, it picked up every piece of lint within miles and had to be vacuumed daily. In order to see all the tiny specks, I had to get down on my knees and crawl around on the floor with the nozzle. One day a friend surprised me at this task and asked: "What are you doing, a vacuum-cleaner meditation?" And I realized I had been doing just that . . . on my knees! Thereafter, my daily vacuuming became a pleasurable ritual and my battleground of the black rug became holy ground.

Ritual connects us to *mystery*, and awareness of mystery is what opens the heart to the sacred dimension. Mystery can never be explained—life is not an Agatha Christie novel. Mystery shimmers and beckons. Like magic, mystery draws us to the center of our being, it takes us to the core SELF. Mystery, magic, and ritual—these give us heightened senses, they activate our *subtle* senses, taking us onward and upward into the etheric realm. Ritual shines a powerful beam of sacred light into our ordinary lives, brightens up the drab and the dull, polishes the patina of the soul. It opens us to that sense of wonder—so that what we have lost is found in common moments. Ritual is the gateway through which we walk from the commonplace and into the rare, following the footsteps of angels.

Handmaiden to ritual is sacred space. Throughout history, people have created sacred spaces where they performed their rituals, from elaborate temples to simple groves of trees. And these geographical locations have come to be considered as "power points"—Stonehenge in England, the Ganges river in India, the Western Wall in Jerusalem, Ayers Rock in Australia, the Temple of Delphi in Greece, St. Peter's Basilica in Rome, Mecca in Saudi Arabia, to mention the most famous of these sites. If you have the opportunity to visit one of these, or another sacred site, by all means do what so many who are seeking personal transformation have done.

However, you do not have to travel to be on sacred ground. The place where you are standing now is holy ground. Or, as Black Elk said, when he was sitting on top of his mountain, "This is the center of the Earth. Where you are is the center of the Earth. The center of the Earth is everywhere."

You can create sacred space just where you are, in your home, office, or on your property. Anyplace on Earth can be read for spiritual significance. However we regard the origin of the species, whatever spiritual journey we choose must take place here on Earth. The starting point is wherever you happen to be at the moment. Joseph Campbell points out that in India a sacred place might consist of a red circle drawn around a stone, creating a metaphor. He says, "When you look at that stone, you see it as a manifestation of Brahma, a manifestation of the mystery." In *The Power of Myth*, Campbell says:

> You must have a room or a certain hour of the day or so where you do not know what was in the morning paper, where you do not know who your friends are, you don't know what you owe anybody, or what they owe you—but a place where you can simply experience and bring forth who

161

you are, and what you might be. . . . At first you may find nothing's happening. . . . But if you have a sacred place and use it, take advantage of it, something will happen.

Your sacred space is also space for silence and solitude. It should be carefully prepared and tended. Remember that contemplative silence is necessary for the spiritual journey. If you choose, you can include an altar in your sacred space. Here are some guidelines:

❧ Set aside a space in your home that you will designate as sacred.

❧ Make this space a place where you can practice silence and solitude.

❧ Make your sacred space comfortable and calm, and advise family members that when you are in your sanctuary you are not to be disturbed.

❧ Treat your sacred space with respect. Keep out anything that will profane your intentions there.

❧ Collect objects that help you to feel your spiritual energy, that connect you to SELF.

❧ These objects can be "found" items or ones you have acquired specifically for the purpose. They might include rocks and crystals, flowers, driftwood, twigs or tree branches, pine cones, candles, incense, essential oil, and a special chair, pillow, or floormat.

In addition to preparing yourself physically and emotionally (or psychologically) for entering your sacred space, you want to have a calm and serene mind. Below is a meditation for achieving this.

Mind-Calming Visualization

Begin by following the instructions for preparing for a relaxation exercise. After relaxing, let your mind take you to a beautiful natural setting. It can be a place you love to visit, or a place you have seen in a magazine picture or a TV travelogue, or an imaginary place.

You might take a walk through snowy woods, hike up a mountain pass, have a leisurely sit-down by the side of a cool lake, or go to the beach at whatever time of year you like best. The idea is to pick something you find calming and soothing.

For example, try imagining sitting by a lake in spring when the wildflowers are just beginning to bloom. Visualize yourself walking down a country road to the shore of the lake, enjoying the cool-yet-warm spring air with its breeze that hints of nature's renewal. Allow yourself to feel invigorated yet relaxed. Feel the warmth of the spring sun on your shoulders. You might take off your jacket and turn up your face to its gentle warmth.

When you reach the lake's shore, find a comfortable spot to sit and relax—enjoy the feel of the grass beneath you, smell the scent of the wildflowers, watch the lake waters' gentle swell, listen to the birds chirping, see the myriad forms of life all about you exhibiting nature's annual renewal of herself.

Take off your shoes and dabble your feet in the water, feeling its refreshing coolness. Perhaps a small fish nibbles at your bare toes and tickles you. Watch a pair of mating ducks land on the lake and see the water birds soaring overhead in the clear blue sky. Feel at one with the scene. Notice how the water catches the sun's light and see the reflection of a passing cloud on its placid surface.

Take your time to enjoy this place, letting all your worries and tensions slip away until you feel utterly calm.

Once you have done this meditation, you can return here whenever you like. With practice and the use of a symbol to represent this calm and peaceful place, you can evoke it in only a few minutes. You can change or vary the scene at will. For example, I have a special place I go, perched on a mountainside. It is the retreat of a Buddhist monk I call Genji. I have been going there for several years, at all seasons, in all weathers, at all times of the day and night. The place changes with the hour, the month, the season. In winter, I enjoy the mountain's stark beauty, softened by snow at times, and I watch the play of moonlight on the glistening white snow cover, which enhances the silence. In spring, I thrill at all the little new shoots and buds coming out and eagerly look for the emerging growth. Summer brings things to full bloom, and produces brilliant colors in the garden. In autumn, when things are beginning to withdraw into their dormant state, comes the harvest and the sunsets are of a particularly spectacular beauty. I never tire of this ever-changing place which always puts me into a state of deep and serene calm.

❧ Preparing Sacred Space

To prepare a sacred space, choose where you want it to be. If you have the luxury of a separate room, that is ideal, but any space you can spare will do. It could be an alcove, a niche, or just a corner of a room you use regularly. The important thing is your intention to keep your space sacred. Though most people will want a space in their homes, your sacred space does not have to be indoors. For centuries people worshipped in the open—in grottos or caves, in groves of trees that were sacred to the Goddess, or on mountaintops. Once you have chosen the space, mark it out mentally (or walk around it) and with your arms outstretched, palms downward, say, "I now declare this space to be sacred." Your sacred space can contain an altar if you like, and a chair or cushion. Some people mark out their sacred space by using a small rug to define the area. A table or shelf can serve as altar space on which you can put items of significance to you, such as pictures or photographs, and one or more candles, crystals or other objects, a plant or fresh flowers. A container of water is thought to draw off negative spirits and must be emptied after each use and set out fresh every time you use the space. Native Americans "cleanse" the air by burning the herb sage. You can place a few leaves or a pinch of the powdered form in a shell or other flameproof dish and scent the air with its pleasant odor.

It's important to have a sense of reverence about your sacred space. Do not enter it unless you have properly prepared yourself. Do not permit others to enter it without your permission and the correct attitude. If you consistently treat it as *sacred*, it will become imbued with a sense of holiness.

After you have chosen and prepared your sacred space, create a meaningful ritual to use before you assume it. You can have a bath or shower, soothing yourself with scented oil afterward, change into fresh clean loose-fitting clothes made of natural fabrics (silk, linen, cotton, wool, rayon) that you reserve for this use. Afterward, do the mind-clearing visualization and then state your intent for the use you will make of your sacred space. Remember that *"where intention goes, energy flows."* Allow profound silence to develop and—*wait*.

To create a ritual to use before entering your sacred space, or for any other purpose, you need only perform a few actions in a certain order. It could be something as simple as removing your shoes and outer clothing, washing your hands, and lighting the candles. Or it could be something more elaborate such as taking a bath in scented water, putting on a special garment for the purpose (priests in all cultures have always worn ceremonial robes), arranging a few fresh flowers in the vase you always use, having a ceremonial drink of wine, tea, or water. Whatever actions you pick should represent what is meaningful to you.

They should have the effect of making you feel you are entering your sacred space *within* preparatory to entering the sacred precinct without. In temples and shrines of old, there was an outer precinct through which one had to pass—often guarded by fierce-looking figures—in order to enter the inner holy of holies. By performing a ritual and putting oneself in the right inner space, one readies for contact with the Higher Power. Once you enter your sacred space, you should have a form to follow. Perhaps you sit on your cushion or chair and breathe quietly for a few moments and then begin your prayer. I like to hold a large, smooth rose quartz crystal. As you work with creating ritual, you will find what suits you best. Feel free to make changes that seem appropriate until you find what resonates with your SELF.

chapter nine
Keeping a Spiritual Journal

All travellers are advised to keep a record of their journey. A spiritual journey is no exception. In fact, keeping a journal can in and of itself *be* a spiritual practice. A spiritual journal not only will tell you where you have been, it will show you the form of where you are going. It can a serve as a channel into your higher self. The spiritual quest can seem like a lonely trek through an unknown and unpopulated wilderness. A journal is a wonderful companion, for it is truly a friend. Often people say to me, when they learn that I write books, "You should write about *me*. My life would make a great book." And it is true. Everyone's life is a book, and everyone should write the book of their own life. Publication is not a requirement for a book to be written. Honoring the SELF is sufficient criteria.

Think of your journal as the *Book of My Life* as well as a friend who will always be there to hear your woes and celebrate your triumphs. Going back to pages you have written in the past can be an illuminating experience. You may wonder if the person who wrote those lines a few years ago was really you. Journal-keeping was something that came to me late in life, but

167

now I produce several hundred pages a year, easily the length of this book. And how I wish I had kept a copious journal during the years when I did no personal writing!

A journal is a marvellous tool for just about any purpose you want it to serve—companionship, a place to spill your thoughts and feelings, a friend who will keep your secrets, a factual record, the telling of your inner life. It can be used to communicate with the many layers of yourself, to experiment with forms of expression, to mirror your many facets. As an exploratory vehicle, a journal is superb—writing about your life's experiences, both inward and outward, can bring fascinating insights and be full of delightful surprises, as well as connect you with your darker, hidden side.

An example of this is a personal journal-keeping experience of mine. A few years ago while on an extended trip to Italy, an emergency required my travelling companion to return home two weeks early and miss the last leg of our planned trip, a visit to Florence. At the time we were on an extensive exploration of the Amalfi Coast and had already spent several weeks in Italy, including some delightful days and romantic nights in Rome—climbing the Spanish Steps, throwing pennies into the famous Fontana de Trevi, lingering at the Piazza Navonne with its old Roman chariot race-track and its Bernini fountain, dining *al fresco* in Trastevere across the Tiber River, seeking out *trattorias* frequented by the natives.

I had lived in Italy before but as it was his first trip, there had been much pleasure for me in being his tour guide. From the island of Capri we traveled back to Rome, where I accompanied my friend to the airport to say goodbye. It was an emotional parting. The joys of travelling with someone with whom one is in close rapport are many, and I felt sad to be going on alone. As a compensation for his being deprived both of Florence and my company, he exacted a promise from me to keep a written record of my experiences in his absence.

Returning to Rome on the airport bus, I found myself tearfully lonely. Grey skies and a dismal rain echoed my state of mind. Yet I was glad to be leaving for Florence, which as yet held no memories for me, there to experience some of the greatest art the world has ever known. I was eager to relive the Renaissance firsthand—stand in awe before Michelangelo's *David*, gaze at the world-famous *Duomo*, touch the magnificent Brunelleschi doors, see close–up the pristine sculptures of della Robia, stroll through the splendid Uffizi galleries, and walk the corridors of the imposing palace of Cosimo de Medici, the Renaissance prince and patron of the arts, who befriended Michelangelo when he was only a boy. Just the idea of walking the cobblestones where such feet had trod five hundred years ago was a thrill. *Florence*—to breathe its rarefied and hallowed air would be a privilege.

I boarded the train at the hectic and crowded Rome station. A few hours later—standing up all the way as in the turmoil I had neglected to make a seat reservation—the train pulled into Florence—and I stepped out into another world, distant from Rome in more than mileage.

Remembering my promise, and already full of excitement about writing my thoughts and experiences to later share with my friend, I stopped at a tobacconist's shop and bought a couple of cheap notebooks of the sort school children use for their lessons. After checking into my *pensione* and getting settled, I bathed and dressed for dinner. Coming upon a lovely restaurant near the pensione, I enjoyed a marvellous dinner of Florentine cuisine, which is very different from that of Southern Italy. The waiters were kind and solicitous, but I was uncomfortable being the only person dining alone, especially as ladies without escorts at night are a rarity in Italy. To occupy myself between courses, I took out one of the little notebooks and began to write about what had happened to me since leaving Rome.

Daily thereafter, finding that being a lone woman with no one to talk to over afternoon tea or evening meals was faintly depressing, the little notebooks became my constant companions. Despite its magnificence, the great art of the past wasn't much company; I had failed to "pick up" the vibrations of the Renaissance. What I sought wasn't there—I felt I was in a museum, not a living city. Further, the constant stream of Italian being spoken around me was an impenetrable blur that cut me off from my surroundings. One afternoon while having tea, I began a stream-of-consciousness writing in what had started out as a letter to my friend. Becoming so absorbed in writing that I forgot the time entirely, I was startled when the waiter came to tell me the café was closing. I was amazed to discover that the sun was down and dusk was falling.

After that, I no longer felt awkward sitting alone in a café or restaurant. In fact, I eagerly looked forward to my time to write. My afternoon break became a new and fulfilling pleasure as I wrote down my impressions of the art I was daily viewing, my reactions to it, and what I felt about what I saw that had nothing to do with art.

For example, I spent an entire afternoon observing a man in the piazza, which was full of pigeons. They apparently knew him well, as he was covered from head to foot with the birds. They flew in and landed on his shoulders and his head and circled all about him as he scattered breadcrumbs. I was fascinated with this performance and enjoyed describing it for my friend. Now, I know that I was experiencing the sacred right before my eyes (in sight of the great Duomo!) in this simple man's love for pigeons and their response to him. Maybe he was a reincarnation of St. Francis of Assisi.

Carrying my little notebooks with me everywhere, I wrote copiously, sometimes attracting attention with my intense absorption in the act. The *maître de hotel* in an elegant restaurant politely questioned me about what I wrote: a love letter? No longer a letter, by then it had become an intensely personal exploration of some issues that went very deep with me. As I wrote, I discovered. And as I experienced each day— and for eight hours a day I tramped the streets of Florence in search of that fifteenth-century Renaissance I was determined to find in the twentieth century—I became more and more connected to my own deep spiritual levels. I began to understand that my quest to experience the Renaissance art I had been taught to revere was actually a mission to discover myself as an artist. Overlaid as this had been by miseducation, it was now struggling to find itself. I was reminded of, and wrote, these remembered lines from a famous poem, which I memorized in high school and which perfectly expressed the inner reality of what was happening to me, floated into my mind and went into my notebook.

> *And what is so rare as a day in June?*
> *Then if ever come perfect days.*
> *Then Heaven tries Earth if it be in tune,*
> *And over it softly Her warm ear lays.*
> *Every clod feels a stir of might*
> *An instinct within it that reaches and towers*
> *And groping blindly above it for light,*
> *Climbs to a soul in grass and in flowers.*

What was happening was that I was being thrust out of my usual self and into a new dimension, activated and nurtured by my journal–writing. That can often happen—when we are without our regular routine, or forced to use our own inner resources to cope with strange and unfamiliar surroundings, we find new depths in ourselves. Journal-keeping is the best adjunct to this process that I know.

I filled up not only the first two little booklets, but another five of them as well, acquiring something of a reputation as an eccentric. Who was the American lady always writing in a child's booklet? What was she writing? And why? The *signora* who owned the pensione looked askance at me because instead of yammering away with my fellow tourists at breakfast, I wrote, and the man who ran the paper shop could not understand why a "rich" American was buying cheap schoolchild's notebooks instead of the beautiful papers for which Florence is so justly famous.

The waiters in the café near the Duomo where I went for coffee and *gelato* every afternoon talked about me (I understood enough to know what they were saying) in perplexed tones. That's not how Americans behave in Florence. And the maître at the restaurant where I regularly had lunch, being Italian, was charmingly insistent that I was writing a love letter and wanted to know all about my absent lover. He clucked over me like a hen with one chick, peeking at the words he couldn't read and giving me complicitous smiles and winks as if he *knew*. It was wonderfully amusing and I let the romantic soul think I was pining for my beloved. The aura he imputed to me got me the best service and a complimentary lunch on my last day.

All as a result of a bit of writing. But the waiters, the maître, the paper seller, the mistress of the pensione, fellow tourists who stared at me, the pigeon man, even the dead artists whose souls I could not contact—all were part of my spiritual journey and it wouldn't have been the same without them. And, whereas when I first arrived in Florence I was hoping to meet people with whom I could converse, I ended up avoiding all English-speaking people so that I could better be alone with my journal. I knew enough Italian to get by in a conversation if I were concentrating fully on listening and speaking, but when I wasn't paying particular attention the language of Dante merely flowed over and around me, like a stream of gentle water.

By the time I left Florence, I had resolved some extremely important issues that were standing in the way of my making any further progress, creatively or spiritually. I had reached a rapport, not with another person, but with *myself.*

You don't have to visit a foreign country alone to become involved in journal–writing. No grand tour of the continent is required. Just a simple beginning—a pen and some paper. You don't need a grand send–off for this new adventure, or a reservation at the captain's table—you are the captain of your own spiritual ship and, once underway, you are responsible for staying on course.

A spiritual journey, and the record of it, is not something we must go off into a wilderness and fast to experience. These so-called "vision quests" can be wonderfully illuminating and a thrilling adventure, but the real core of spirituality is tucked away in the corners of everyday life. It comes when we are diapering the baby, washing the car, taking a shower, vacuuming the rug, building a shelf, raking the lawn, or grocery shopping. It is there when we stand in line at the bank, make a travel reservation, eat at a restaurant, or spend the day lounging around at home. It is the commingling of the inner, private self with the details of life's commonplaces. We may go on a vision quest, like a two-week vacation to an exotic clime, but every day we commute to work and in a year log more miles travelled than on our airline trip to romantic places. Life's like that, and it is in the living of our lives every day that we find the spiritual. This is real soul food—it nourishes us.

Whatever you are doing now, wherever you are in your life, you are on a spiritual quest. You may call it something else—a search for meaning, "finding yourself," or "getting in touch" with what you really want to do in life. Labels are unimportant. The spiritual quest *is* life, and life is a spiritual quest. It is that center out of which all else comes.

The words "journal" and "journey" are both derived from the Latin word *diuranlis* which also gives us "diurnal," or day.

One meaning of journal is "itinerary," and another is "a day's journey." Thus are journal and journey connected to each other and to day, and journey can mean not only travel or a trip but simply whatever is done on a given day. Each day then *is* a journey, and—Sunday, Monday, or Friday, rain or shine, cold or warm,—all days are sacred in their happening and in their detail. Our days are even named after gods—Monday is Moon Day, the province of the Great Mother Goddess; Thursday belongs to Thor, the Scandinavian name for Zeus of the thunderbolts; Sunday, of course, is the day of the Sun, the grand and flaming chariot of Apollo. And so on.

The charm of journal writing is that it is entirely private. You can think of this activity as the exteriorzation of your inner being, a way of manifesting into concrete reality all the thought forms and feelings that float around inside you. No matter where you are in your life—at the beginning, in the middle, or near the end—I would encourage you to begin to keep a journal if you do not already do so. If you once kept a journal, but let it lapse, go back and read over some of your entries. You will become sufficiently intrigued to continue the practice.

A journal is somewhat like a butterfly net—we can use it to catch beautiful specimens and then preserve them for future study and pleasure. In writing a journal, you interface with your own experience, thus apprehending the spiritual in the ordinary. Writing is also like map-making. It's a way of describing the territory you have traversed, of identifying and marking out the significant landmarks.

Journal writing when fully experienced has a *liminal* quality—it provokes a glow from within. I often imagine what it must have been like for Howard Carter when, after years of searching and digging in the inhospitable desert, he peered through the rubble outside into the gold-filled tomb of Tut-Ankh-Amon and stood stunned and speechless at the wondrous sight of wall-to-wall gold and bejeweled riches beyond comparison. Metaphorically speaking, this is the experience waiting for you as you proceed with what I call "soul excavation," and begin to unearth your own inner treasures. After all that hard and patient digging, you see it: GOLD. Not the common gold of the market-place, not even the polished gold of great treasure, but the gold of the soul, the *lapis philosophorum*, or philosopher's stone, which the alchemists sought.

The lapis was the end product of the alchemists' process of transformation, meant to purify both the substance and the one who performed the work. What was sought was not ordinary gold, but, to quote Joseph Campbell, "gold . . . such as only art bestows, through its transfiguration of the world as commonly known." Our spiritual journal, and the keeping of a record of it, is a transformational process not unlike that the artist undergoes as he works on the material that forms his product while simultaneously working on his inner artistry. By following our soul-directedness—what I call the "internal imperative"—we keep on the course that will fulfill who we truly are, without the societal and personal traumatic overlays that have obscured the gold of our authentic selves.

There is a well-known mythological symbol of two birds sitting in a tree—one is eating, the other is watching the one who eats. The symbol represents the two sides of our selves: the doer and the watcher. These might also be thought of as the *actor* and the *recorder*. The actor represents your outward existence, your struggles and achievements, your movements toward others, your *participation*.

The recorder represents your inward life, your thoughts, feelings, attitudes, beliefs, hopes, dreams. This self is the watcher, the one who reflects on what the actor is doing. It is *contemplative*.

Jung called these inner expressive powers *archetypes*, but we can think of them as vibrations to which we resonate at many different levels of our SELF.

Together, the actor and the recorder create *consciousness*. Just as thought without action is invalid, action without thought is mere movement. Both are necessary to create a being conscious of itself and its actions. Do you remember your first conscious moment? There is a time when we first open our eyes to the world around us and see ourselves as both participating in it and separate from it. Child specialists debate just when this happens in terms of age, but I see it as a continuous process attendant upon the spiral ascent. At each further turn of the spiral, we gain more consciousness, we become more conscious of our own consciousness. And we do this through the interaction of our actor and our recorder. In the words of Gershen Kaufman and Lev Raphael in *The Dynamics of Power*:

> We learn to live consciously through becoming aware of inner and outer events *as they are happening*. Building a conscious self means becoming increasingly aware of inner events, bodily events and interpersonal events. A conscious self is able to experience in full awareness all the distinctly different components of the self, including feelings, needs, drives, and values. A conscious self lives consciously.

Consciousness is our most precious possession. Without it, we are mere robots, only going through the motions of life, not really *living*. In the ability to think, reflect, and wonder we possess treasures greater than found in all the tombs of Egypt, or the immense riches of the Orient, or the vast diamond mines of South Africa. Without consciousness, we do not know who we are and cannot find out. This greatest of gifts should be guarded carefully and used wisely. The human mind can observe itself thinking—subject and object simultaneously. We can "see" ourselves doing what we do. Consciousness is the inner companion who never goes away. It is even attested that some surgical patients emerge from under anesthesia with memories of what was happening in the operating room. Doctors, assuming they were "unconscious," can't figure this out. The reason is simple: consciousness is *always there*, at some level.

We have a confusion about "conscience" and "conscious." Conscience is supposed to guide us in matters moral and ethical, but without consciousness of exactly what the meaning of our actions is, we cannot judge them. This is where consciousness comes in. It is our ability to *be aware* that makes the difference. When we become conscious of some behavior or thought pattern, we are in a position to change it for the better. The pilgrim on a spiritual journey is actually on a consciousness-raising mission. As we progress along the Way, consciousness emerges into the light of spirituality and we become aware, not only of our true selves but also of the fact that others possess true selves, and we want to know *those* selves, not the false ones we are most often presented with. Consciousness emerging is like peeling away the layers of an onion—with each layer removed you get closer to the center.

It takes consciousness of "all the distinctly different components of the self," to make us aware of the whisperings of inner guidance. So often our inner guidance is drowned out by the noise—both external and internal—with which we surround ourselves. Consciousness thrives in the silence of reflection.

The information about what is going on may reach us merely as a vague sensation, either mental or emotional. It can be a tension or a sense that something is about to happen. Consciousness may register no more than an ephemeral state of being, like the feeling that one has forgot something important but cannot for the life of one remember what it is. Things working themselves out from the implicate to the explicate order may be expressed as *feelings*, or we may find ourselves undergoing a change in values as the result of a crisis. Here is a journal entry I made in 1991 during such a crisis, both my own personal one and a national one, the Gulf War.

The past few days, since the Middle East war started, my psyche is going through so many revolutions per minute that I can't keep up with myself at all.

I have been in a terrible state mentally and emotionally. The first two days, I was glued to the TV and then had to limit the news radically as it was too upsetting. I just want to crawl away from the world and all its senseless cruelties, mostly the result of what is called "religion." The last two days I suffered the worst psychic pain *ever*. This was so intense that all I could do was sit very still for long hours and meditate and pray, with no possibility of work or even thinking clearly. I have been doing a lot of praying, but I can't say it really comforts me much. This morning I realized, after a dream in which I was talking to my friend Joan, that I am in a *spiritual crisis*. And I had no idea, absolutely none, that such a thing even existed! The "crisis" seems to be a combination of the war, or my reaction to the war, and my own creative problems. I find I am recoiling from any interaction with the world at large. I am not sure I want to write more, but feel compelled to do so.

I feel a need, a real craving, for *depth*, and it seems that this depth can only be found in what we term "God." It is very hard to explain. I have even considered the idea of entering a yogic order. What irony if, having started life in a convent I should finish it in an ashram in flight from the realities of "the marketplace."

At the root of all this is a very deep sense of *dissatisfaction*, for which I can find no cure. There are, of course, real problems, but I don't think these elements are the root cause. I think it is something *in* me. Rather like I carry a time-bomb that was set to go off at a particular time, only I did not know it was there until it started ticking away. All of the anxiety, all of the general *Sturm und Drang* of the past months MAY be only symptomatic of the deeper need, and not in themselves the reasons. One simply *must* find something *worthwhile* to do with one's talent and energies.

The above entry was made shortly before a major life change. Writing about the intimate details and relating them to what was going on in the world at large helped me to gain perspective and to understand that my crisis was not *caused* by the national crisis, but was a reflection of it.

When we listen and pay attention to "the still small voice," we find inner guidance is available. The directions we need most often come from within, yet they can be mirrored by what is happening without. The question is: how can we sort through our multiplicity of feelings, sensations, intuitions, thoughts, reactions to get to the spiritual core of the matter?

Many people are plagued with self-consciousness when confronted with a blank page. They feel shy as if meeting a powerful stranger for the first time. Worries about "how to do it" rise up and inhibit the mind from transmitting to the hand what needs to be written. But it need not be so. A journal is a private place and should be guarded from intrusion. We need not worry about how good our grammar is, for there is no one to correct it. We only need start the flow and it will continue of itself, creating a bridge between the inner and outer worlds, connecting our acting with our reflecting.

The nineteenth-century American writer Willa Cather spoke of "the furniture of the mind," and said, "Miracles seem to rest . . . upon our perceptions being made finer so that for a moment our eyes can see and our ears can hear that which is about us always."

We can furnish our minds with our conscious observations of what is about and inside us. A renaissance of personal writing is going on all around—people are writing their histories, probing their parents and grandparents for personal recollections; autobiography, which was once considered naive in academic writing courses, is again popular. Even self-help books are based upon personal interviews and the life stories of ordinary people living ordinary lives. True, there is a segment of the population that craves intimate details of the lives of international celebrities, but they wallow in this gossip and tabloid journalism to the detriment of their own personal life stories. Of course, a pop rock singer or a Hollywood mega-movie star leads a more interesting life than does a John or Jane Doe—but that is only because John and Jane haven't investigated their own lives fully and deeply.

Writing is a sorting process. It is also a great teacher. A dialogue with the self is never dull nor uninteresting. Once you get to know yourself at your deeper levels, you will find you are a fascinating person. And you have the ultimate reward of actually experiencing your own life first–hand, not just living vicariously through TV and newspaper accounts of famous people, who in person may prove to be very dull indeed. If you could be a fly on the wall in the brain of some glitzy glamour gal or lad, you might find yourself surprisingly bored by all the egocentric chatter going on. *How do I look?* and *What will they think?* would likely be what you'd hear.

So, please lay aside your fears that somehow you won't get it right. There's no *right* or *wrong*. It doesn't matter if you have terrible handwriting or are a master at calligraphy. You can be a high-school dropout or possess a Ph.D. in literature. Whether you can parse a sentence or hardly know how to construct one is immaterial. And, if you are lacking in writing skills, what better way to improve them than by writing? A famous author was once a visiting lecturer at a college writing class. This awesome man, full of presence, marched into a room full of eager wannabe writers who, with pencils poised, were eagerly waiting for pearls of wisdom to drop from the great man's mouth. Taking a firm stance behind the lectern, he barked: "How many of you want to be writers?"

Seventy enthusiastically hopeful young arms shot up into the air simultaneously, waving like sea anemones. The Master surveyed his class and then said softly,

"Then get the hell home and *write*! Don't waste your time in writing classes."

With that, he turned on his heel and strode from the classroom leaving seventy young mouths gaping in his wake, for they realized they had heard Truth.

Write. That's all. And don't worry about the details. Just put them down as you see fit. You can also draw, doodle, paste in cutouts, or anything else that pleases you. If you like structure, be neat and orderly. If you don't, scribble any old way (so long as you can read it later).

I'm often asked, "How can I remember?" or "How do I know what to write about?" Reaching into our intuitive realm can help to put us in touch with what we need to know. My monitoring technique can help with this.

 ### The Monitoring Technique

As we go about our daily lives, we usually are in a blur of automatic, preprogrammed thoughts and activities. Our mental processes most of the time are like a slightly out-of-focus photograph. We ordinarily only go into sharp focus in times of crisis and emergency. As a result, we are often bored and "not there." So much of our everyday life is such a blur of routine that we miss what is going on at the deeper levels of our SELF. To combat this tendency, I have developed and teach a technique I call *monitoring*, which is a way of consciously focusing on the day's input, either as it is happening or during brief periods of reflection.

If the idea of learning to monitor your thoughts and feelings at first seems daunting, do not let that prevent you from attempting it. Like learning to ride a bicycle, it at first seems clumsy and impossible and then, suddenly—*bingo!*—you are off and away with astonished ease.

Begin by *consciously* storing in memory your thoughts, feelings, and reactions to the events of the day, especially those preceding or during an illness. For example, if you feel a cold coming on go over the events leading up to the sensation of a congested head or a sore throat.

If you have trouble remembering, train yourself to take brief notes during the day at or following significant events, especially negative ones. Note the particulars of the situation along with your reactions. A few words will do—you will develop a kind of shorthand in time. The purpose is to give your memory a jog later and enable you to recall the entire event with its "feeling tone."

When thoughts and feelings arise from the inner self, do not ignore them or push them away; record them either mentally or physically so that they do not vanish in the well of forgetfulness. During the day, whenever you have a spot of unoccupied time— waiting for a bus, sitting on a train, standing in line— review what you have noted to fix it firmly for later evaluation.

At the end of the day, set aside a few minutes' time to examine the entire day's input for insights about your inner workings, clues to your implicit order. The more you are aware of these constantly

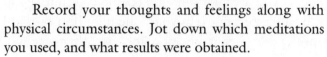

ongoing processes, the better equipped you are to use your consciousness to its best advantage.

Record your thoughts and feelings along with physical circumstances. Jot down which meditations you used, and what results were obtained.

In time, you will perceive patterns of meaning—your life is not an accidental or random event, it has meaning and purpose. Keeping a spiritual journal will help you to discover this.

If you are already a journal keeper, keeping a spiritual journal will be no problem. If you are new to journal keeping, you may need some time to acclimate yourself to writing about your spiritual experiences on a regular basis. Whatever you do, make it an *enjoyable* experience. One friend makes it a habit to write down a self-created affirmation, a sort of ode to her spiritual journey, each day.

Use any form you please—I find a bound notebook is best as I tend to lose separate pieces of paper. A simple spiral notebook is inexpensive and widely available, or you may prefer something grander like a cloth-bound book with blank pages.

Rereading what you have written the next day or a year later can be an illuminating experience. For one thing, you may be little aware of your progress until you see where you were this time last year. *Enjoy* your journal—think of it as a dear friend with whom you spend intimate time.

How much time you spend with your spiritual journal is up to you. During a six-month period when I was undergoing an intense healing after a plunge into the pit of depression, I wrote many pages every day. In fact, keeping my journal became for that period of time my life work. Many of those experiences are here reflected. Had I not written it all down, I might have forgotten much of the lessons I learned, lost the details of my journey, or even had the whole experience fade away like last summer's flowers.

Write when and for how long or how much as suits you each time. If you are a person who responds well to a scheduled activity, by all means put it in your schedule. If not—and I think this is preferable—let it be spontaneous. Whatever works for you at the time is best.

Your spiritual journal can also be a way to help yourself lessen stress and handle anxiety or depression. Whatever your goal, making a commitment to writing on a regular basis is the key to success.

Here are some tips for journal-keeping:

❧ Decide if you will write by hand or keyboard.
❧ If by hand, select loose-leaf paper or a bound book.
❧ Choose a book that opens flat.
❧ Do you prefer lined paper or unlined?
❧ The writing implement you use should be one that is permanent and does not smear. You may want to keep a special pen or pencil just for the purpose.
❧ If using a keyboard, you can use paper that is three-hole punched and keep your pages in a ring binder.
❧ Browse in a stationery store for an assortment of pens, markers, and colored pencils and use them for varieties of moods and experiences. One client writes all her dreams in purple.

Here are some exercises to get you started:

❧ Practice "flow writing." To do this, simply write anything that comes to mind for fifteen minutes.
❧ Write an outline of the major turning points of your life for later elaboration.
❧ Ask yourself where you are *now* and write about it.
❧ Write a short essay on why you are keeping a journal.

🌿 Create a piece of artwork for your journal.

🌿 Go back to the image of your Path and draw the scene.

🌿 Write about how you felt about the Fence.

🌿 Choose any of the other experiences in the fantasy and write about them. Note what you want to change.

🌿 Meditate upon a symbol that expresses your life's work and write about it or draw it.

🌿 Find some pictures that express spirituality to you and make a collage of them.

🌿 Write a description of your solar actor self.

🌿 Write a description of your lunar reflector self.

🌿 Write a dialogue between them.

🌿 Write a letter to yourself about why you are keeping this journal, what you intend to accomplish.

🌿 Write a letter to your guardian angel and invite him or her to be a participant.

🌿 Write a letter to God or the Goddess.

A spiritual journal can itself be a spiritual practice, or it can be an adjunct to whatever else you practice. In it you keep a *private* record of your spiritual growth. You record your thoughts and feelings, even the physical circumstances in which the experience occurred. In time, you will see meaningful patterns. Your life is not an accidental happening—it has meaning and purpose, and journal-keeping is an excellent method for coming to understand your individual pilgrimage on this Earth. In it, you will be having the adventure of your life—the discovery of your authentic self, and of your SELF.

If you respond to the idea of keeping a spiritual journal with the common disclaimer, "But when will I find the *time?*," my answer is what it always is: *We find the time for what we feel is important to us.*

You have the time to watch TV, see movies, visit with friends, go on outings and vacations, shop, and pursue a myriad of other pleasurable activities. Keeping a spiritual journal is meant to be another pleasure, not a chore. If at first it seems an unwelcome task or a burden, take heart and keep at it. This is a rewarding facet of your overall spiritual development.

When should you write in your spiritual journal? There is no "right" time—occasionally you may give it more time; frequently, less time. You are following your own rhythm—let the journal "speak" to you when it wants your attention. I do recommend writing as frequently as you can manage—daily if possible. Some of my clients like to use the end of the day, in the quiet period just before bedtime, as the time they turn to their journal. This time of pre-sleep can influence your dreams. It's also good to combine journal writing with your relaxation and meditation periods. The time just after waking is excellent—I like to use this time to fit together the experiences of the previous day and the night's dreams. Whenever you write, for however long, you will be enhancing your consciousness.

What are the ideal conditions for writing? Like timing, conditions will vary for each person depending on their personal conditions of space and privacy. To my mind, the ideal situation is to have a quiet, regular spot—whether it is your study or the kitchen table—that is entirely private, at least for the time you are writing. As with doing relaxations and meditations (and journal-keeping is a form of meditation), using the same place all the time is conducive to the activity. When your spirit senses that you are in your writing spot and ready to make contact, it will shift into the right gear automatically. I sometimes sit at my word processor and simply stare out the window at my garden for a few minutes until the flow begins of itself.

However, I also know people who can placidly write in the middle of a traffic jam. One man carries his notebook in his glove compartment just for that purpose. He says writing in his journal while all about him are losing it keeps him calm and collected. Others comfortably write while commuting on a train or bus. As with all the other exercises in this book, it's up to you and your needs.

Often I'm asked, "How much should I write?" Well, how long is a piece of string? This is a question that can only be answered by you and your personality. Write what you want, where you want, for how long you want is my only advice. If you feel you have nothing to say to yourself, don't write at all. You may write copiously or sparsely, and do either or both at different times in your life. There's no minimum and no maximum. Sometimes I jot down a few words; at other times, I write several pages. For those accustomed to taking notes, jotting a few lines in their own brand of shorthand suffices to jog their memories when they want to reread. For others, there is an outpouring of immense detail.

If at first you feel shy or have difficulty, don't worry. It's only stage fright and you will get over it. Remember, this is your *personal* spiritual journal and no one else ever need see it. Practice "flow writing," as described above, or do a relaxation exercise before writing, if you feel uptight or restricted. Remind yourself that you are doing this for *you*. It's not schoolwork, a business report, or a test. It's an artwork.

Make a covenant with your spiritual journal. Think for a few minutes about why you are doing this and why you are willing to make a commitment to writing regularly in your journal. Then put this into words. Study what you have written for a few minutes and see if you are satisfied with your purpose. You may want to make changes. Your statement of purpose might go something like this:

> I'm keeping my Spiritual Journal for the purpose of getting in touch with my Higher Self, my intuition, and with the aim of generating more consciousness. My goal is to become more aware messages from my sacred mind and to act on this information for my spiritual growth and development. I believe that keeping this journal will aid this

process by providing me with a framework in which I can record and reflect upon my experiences and wherein I can chart my progress.

When you are satisfied with your written statement of purpose, write out a contract that you are making with yourself. It might go something like this:

[Statement of purpose.] Therefore, I make a covenant with myself to pursue this effort on a regular basis. I promise to write in this journal _____.

Here, you will fill in the blanks. You might say, ". . . every day for fifteen minutes," or ". . . every day," or ". . . at least twice a week for half an hour," or ". . . for no less than one hour per week," or ". . . a total of X hours per month."

You are making this agreement with yourself, and it is up to you to keep to the terms you make. Trust your SELF to keep up its half of the bargain.

Let your spiritual journal be a gift you give yourself. You might think of it as a hobby. Rereading what you have written is a pleasant way to remind yourself of how much progress you have made. Like looking at a photo album of a vacation trip, it will bring back the memories.

Think of your journal as a friend and companion, one to which you can turn whenever you need a boost or someone to talk to. Enjoy it as you would enjoy spending time with any dear friend who is genuinely interested in you, your problems, your daily life, your successes, your setbacks, your dreams, your goals. Your journal is someone you can "tell your day" to without worrying about lack of interest.

Consider the time you spend with it as time spent with your Higher Self, or the Source, or God, whichever term fits your personal belief system.

part three
The Invisible Support

The journeyer is at home while under way, at home on the road itself, the road being understood not as a connection between two definite points on the Earth's surface, but as a particular world. It is the ancient world of the path. . . . He who moves about familiarly in this world-of-the road has Hermes for his god . . . he is also called *angelos* . . . the messenger of the Gods. . . . there is also an experience of the world that rests on the basic assumption that a man stands in the world alone. . . . No such assumption exists, however, when it comes to that other experience of the world which the antique statements correlate with Hermes.

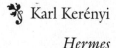 Karl Kerényi

Hermes

chapter ten
An Anthem of Angels

The many books being written about angels today attest to a renewed and burgeoning interest in them. Angels have a long tradition. We don't know if they appeared to prehistoric man, but when history begins to be recorded we find images of them in many cultures around the world. These suggest that the notion of angels is embedded in our psyches.

From the city of Ur, in the Euphrates valley, c. 4000 B.C.E.–2500 B.C.E. comes a *stele* depicting a wingéd figure, who has descended from one of the seven heavens, pouring the water of life from an overflowing jar. In Mesopotamia there were giant wingéd creatures, part human, part animal, known as "griffins." And in Egypt the twin sister of the goddess Isis, Nepthys, is shown in paintings and reliefs enfolding the dead in her beautiful wings. Angels appear all over Asia Minor, in different cultures, and westward into Greece and Italy. Iris, "the rainbow of Zeus," and Hermes, messenger of the Greek gods and guide of souls, both wear wings and serve angelic functions, carrying messages and giving humans aid. The Greek "Winged Victory" was a precursor to the Italian representation of wingéd angels in the form with which we are today familiar.

Angels have many names and are arranged in a hierarchy radiating downward from God or heaven. One of these is *cherubim* (a plural noun), from the Assyrian *karibu*, which means "one who prays" or "one who communicates." The Islamic form is *el-karrubiyan*, meaning "brought near to Allah." Cherubim praise God unceasingly night and day.

In Assyrian art, cherubim are the figures we call griffins—with wings and human or lion faces and with bodies of eagles, bulls, or sphinxes. Highly symbolic, these griffins combined in one body each of the four signs of the zodiac that marked the solstices and equinoxes in the earliest period of Mesopotamian astronomy: the bull (Taurus, or the spring equinox and eastern quarter); the lion (Leo, or the summer solstice and southern quarter); the Eagle (Scorpio, or the autumn equinox and western quarter); and the Water Carrier (Aquarius, or the winter solstice and northern quarter).

These figures often carried little pouches, symbolic of the elixir of immortal life. They were guardians, as were the angels who, in the Biblical account, stood at the gates of the Garden of Eden with flaming swords after the expulsion of Adam and Eve, to prevent them from returning to eat the fruit of the Tree of Immortal Life. However, the more ancient angels do not prevent humans from enjoying the Tree but foster its care. A cylinder seal (eighth–seventh century B.C.E) in the Morgan Library in New York City depicts two wingéd figures, or *genii*, fertilizing the Tree of Immortal Life from the elixir in their pouches.

Are angels real, or a figment of our imaginations? In *The Reenchantment of Everyday Life*, Thomas Moore describes his little daughter's matter-of-fact question to her parents. "Do you see those angels over there?" the child asks, pointing to the opposite side of the lake. "They're dressed all in white," the girl continues as if giving a report. Moore goes on to say that he has "no doubt that my daughter saw angels and that angels are as real as anything else."

When I was a child, I held conversations with angels on a regular basis, finding the experience neither odd nor disturbing—as matter-of-fact as Moore's daughter did. Angels were my friends. Today, sadly, I have no exact memories of what the angels said to me, nor what I said to them, but in one way or another angels have kept me company for most of my life.

Why are angels such a popular topic now? In pondering this phenomenon, I can only surmise that the angels have decided to come out of the closet, as it were. My feeling is that they are manifesting to our consciousness in response to many heartfelt prayers, not always directed to the conventional gods of the formal organized religions, who have failed us so often.

What are angels? No one knows for sure, but I believe that they are celestial intelligences—some say beings of pure light— who vibrate at a very high rate, which makes them invisible to us. However, unlike ourselves they have the ability to change their vibrations at will and assume material form. When they lower their vibrations to the approximate rate of humans, they become visible to us. Also, they can assume other forms and appear as people or even as thoughts and experiences. My own first clear memory of an angel interfacing with my life came at the age of nineteen.

At the time I was sharing a house with two other girls. The living room was graced by a piano and a Persian rug. One fall afternoon I was alone in the house with nothing to occupy me. I lay down on the living room rug in front of the piano for no particular reason, except that I liked the feel of the rug. I wasn't accustomed to lying on the floor, and I wasn't sleepy. What happened was extraordinary, but, perhaps due to my earlier experience with angels, it did not seem so to me.

First, I heard music as if someone were softly playing the piano, or as if the piano were playing itself—which my logical mind knew to be impossible. Next, I had what today would be described as an out-of-body experience. I had the sensation of being lifted up—up, up, and away I flew out into the stratosphere, carried by an angel who held me upside down by the feet. I knew nothing of symbolism then, but the feet are related to Pisces, which is ruled by Neptune, the planet of Higher Love and mystical experience.

The angel told me I was about to see my future. We soared on until we reached outer space. The Milky Way was so close I could have reached out and touched it, like a thick carpet of shining stars. From my vantage position upheld by the angel, I could see all the stars and planets, and—believe it or not—I saw Earth exactly as it was later photographed by the astronauts. I distinctly remember the shock of recognition when years later I first saw the actual pictures of our beautiful blue-and-white planet photographed from space. *I knew I had already seen it—* just as it appeared in the NASA photographs! This experience would be called déjà vu, or a sense that one has been somewhere one could not logically have been before.

Who sees angels? There are many factors in who does or who does not see angels. The old virtue of "purity of heart" may be the deciding factor, but there are stories of evildoers who, confronted by an angel, gave up their wrongful ways. Certainly children can see angels, and this may be simply because they have not been taught that angels are mere superstition. A child's eyes are open wide to the wonders of life on Earth until adult admonitions and restrictive "teachings" cause them to close tight against the miraculous.

What do angels look like? Whatever pleases them or suits their purpose. They seem to take a form that the person who is receiving their message can relate to. No angel speaks English to someone whose native and only tongue is French or Spanish. Sometimes angels appear without form, as a sense of being given unerring direction. Angels can manifest as a thought in your mind, an urge of your body, or a surge of intuition. Rick Fields says in *Chop Wood, Carry Water*:

> The source of [the still small voice within] . . . may be without sound, and yet is heard—is called by many different names: the inner guide, guardian angel, spirit guide, the collective unconscious, or just plain intuition. Actually all of us hear the whisperings of this voice every single day of our lives, but many ignore it.

And in *Care of the Soul*, Thomas Moore says:

> When a summer breeze blows through the open window as we sit reading in a rare half-hour of quiet, we might recall one of the hundreds of annunciations painters have given us, reminding us that it is the habit of angels to visit in moments of silent reading.

This variability of angelic presences may account for the ease with which skeptics dismiss angel "sightings" or other evidences of these messengers contacting us humans. As if consistency of form were an appropriate characteristic for a divine messenger! We tend to see our angels as we have had them represented to us through our culture, which is actually as much a form of language as the tongue we speak. And just as languages are modified by dialect, so do angels fit their appearances to the circumstances involved.

An example of this is a story told by Hope MacDonald, a writer. A young girl, homeward bound on a bus, found herself being followed by a suspicious-looking man. Terrified, she began to pray. When the bus drew up to her stop, there stood a large white dog, a Great Pyrenees, waiting for her to disembark. As she stepped down, the huge dog put its head under her hand and together they walked the distance to her house. The stalker, apparently wary of the dog's size and presence, took another route. When the girl reached her own door, the dog disappeared. Commenting on this, in *A Book of Angels*, Sophie Burnham says:

> To people who live close to the earth, spirits live everywhere—in rocks and stones and trees and rivers and desert scrub. Divinity shines forth everywhere, so why shouldn't guardians walk beside us too? And why shouldn't simple nomads, innocent as children, trust their own senses?

On three separate occasions, angels have saved my life. Twice through the agency of other human beings, once through an eerily compelling experience I can only describe as miraculous.

The first time an angel intervened directly on my behalf (that I know of) occurred when I was nineteen, less than a year after I was flown through space. At that time, I suffered from severe black depressive moods that came and went unexpectedly—from the heights of gaiety I could plunge into the depths of despair. Too young to understand that these extreme mood swings were a result of the abuse I suffered in childhood, and unable to afford therapy, I lived with my affliction as best I could, never asking for help from any human agency.

One night, after partying with two friends, a man and a woman, the three of us went to my apartment for a nightcap. We had drinks and laughed and talked animatedly until midnight when my guests left. Alone, the unheralded despair hit me like a ton of bricks. Suicidal thoughts had been a frequent visitor to me since my teen years, when I daily had to fend off my father's abuse. In the wake of my friends' departure, suddenly everything seemed bleak and hopeless. Why go on? With seeming mental clarity about the logic of the thing, I turned on the gas jets of the stove, stuffed towels in the cracks under the doors and windows, and lay down to die.

The next thing I knew I was in my front yard with a man bending over me forcing air into my lungs. It was my friend who had left me but an hour before. Returning, he had smelled the telltale odor of gas, smashed a window, and climbed in to pull me unconscious out into the night air.

When I had recovered, I wondered what on earth he was doing there. Why had he come back? He said that he and my girlfriend, who lived on the other side of town and whom he was escorting home by following her car with his, had decided to stop off at a bar near her house for a last drink. But inside the place he began to feel extremely uncomfortable about me, without knowing why. The logical thing would have been to telephone, but further logic said that a telephone call would wake me up, assuming I had gone to sleep shortly after they left my apartment.

The sense of urgency would not leave him, and to combat it—for he felt silly—he stepped out for a breath of fresh air. There, hovering near his car, he saw a faint light. Walking over to investigate, he heard a voice in his head say, "M.J. needs you. Go back *now*."

Without further debate with himself, he rushed inside to say he was leaving, speeded back across town, and rescued me. Though a lapsed Catholic, R. was privately a deeply religious man, and he never doubted an angel had appeared to him to announce my need of his ministrations.

Perhaps you have angel stories of your own.

As this example shows, angelic presences, or spirits, do not necessarily exist separately from the humans around us. How often to we say to a child, "You little angel!" or to a lover, "What an angel you are!" How are we to approach angels if they are so variable and mysterious? The answer is *with belief and total trust* as did the great painters of the past who have left us with so many representations of angels—with wings and without, grand

and small, fierce or benign, male and female, adult and child, serene or active, speaking, singing, flying, standing, enfolding, defending, praying, announcing, and playing a variety of musical instruments from harps to trumpets. We must take their reality and their powers seriously and with respect to invoke it in our lives. Thomas Moore says, "Angels . . . are all we have left in our desire to connect with ultimacy and divinity. Without the flutter of their wings in the background of experience, we have only the grinding and purring of machines or the white noise and hum of our own ceaseless thought."

My second encounter with an angel was dramatic. It occurred on my twenty-first birthday. I was living in Houston, and my housemate, Nancy, had arranged a surprise birthday party for me aboard a Holland-America Lines ship, which was docked in the Houston ship channel. This was a major treat as no one was allowed aboard cargo ships without an invitation from the captain. As it happened, Nancy was friends with the local manager of the shipping line, who did the honors.

When we started out in our car with Nancy driving, I had no idea where we were going. I'd never seen the dock area, which was ugly and very different from the beautifully manicured part of town where I lived, off Houston's broad and tree-lined Main Street. We stopped at a dockworkers' bar and there met the manager and his wife, who then led the way along a bleak stretch of industrial road to the dock itself. The way was complex and dark.

The long, confusing trip was well worth taking, however, as aboard ship we were placed in the lap of festive luxury. The Scandinavian captain and his officers were all in brass-buttoned, gold-braided dress-blue uniforms, a resplendent sight. First, we were entertained with cocktails and exquisitely prepared hors d'oeuvres in the salon. I thought this was the entire party until a steward announced that dinner was served.

We were escorted into a formal dining room, the table set with snowy double cloths and an array of silverware that foretold many courses to come. Never before nor since have I seen such a display of elegant food. The manager had instructed us in the customs of the country—you did not drink the *aquavit*, which was on the table at all times, until the captain stood and raised his glass in a toast, at which point you downed the contents of your aquavit glass in one gulp, followed by a beer chaser. A steward stood behind each chair making sure the aquavit glasses were kept full at all times. The captain made frequent toasts, and after a few of them I was more than tipsy. But that was not the extent of the libations. Different wines accompanied each course and, at the end, after cheeses were served, a huge sparkling glass bowl of fresh strawberries (in January!) was presented with Champagne, followed by coffee and Cognac in the salon.

It was a marvellous evening. No girl could wish for a more splendid twenty-first birthday celebration. We disembarked clutching an assortment of gifts, including a five-pound wheel of French Roquefort cheese the captain had insisted I take because I appreciated it so much. Navigating the narrow, swaying gangplank over the dark harbor water below, I lost my balance and nearly dropped my treasure in the oil-slicked water. To say that Nancy and I were both "four sheets to the wind" would be an understatement, but we were young and foolish.

Our guides lived off in another direction and, assuming we could find our way, left us to our own devices to get home. As we climbed into our second-hand car, the sky was lightening slightly from the ink-dark of night to the pale gray of pre-dawn. Nancy took the wheel but, as the old car had an unreliable starter, she had trouble getting the engine going. Finally, it sputtered to life and I hoped it would not stall on us. When it did, which was often, it usually took twenty minutes to get it started again.

Shortly after we began the long and unfamiliar drive along deserted roads, I promptly passed out in the passenger seat. Suddenly, I woke—and found myself in an unmoving car that sat astride a railroad track. Nancy was slumped over the wheel. As I took in the situation, I saw the glaring eye of an oncoming train. Immediately cold sober and with no aftereffects from the night's imbibing, I assessed my options with lightning speed and utter clarity, as if some directing force had taken over my brain. There was no time for me to get out of the car, run around it, open the door, shove her into the passenger seat, get back in, and try to start the car. Also, Nancy was a tall girl, heavier than I, and I knew I could not move her body nor drag her to safety. The only possible solution was to get the car started *immediately*. But *how?*

Despite the gravity of the circumstances, I remained absolutely calm and coolly collected. With the train bearing down, only minutes away, I knew precisely what to do. Shoving the double seat back as far as it would go, I climbed into Nancy's lap, turned the ignition key and prayed—*and the car started*. The sudden infusion of fuel kicked the engine into operation just long enough for the car to roll down the incline to safety before coming to a halt. The train went thundering past our backs. I could feel the ground shaking in the shuddering wake of several tons of steel moving at sixty miles per hour.

At the bottom of the incline, only a few feet from what might have been the disaster scene, I looked back—and saw a glowing light hovering about the track.

After twenty minutes of pushing and shoving the still-unconscious Nancy, I finally got her onto the passenger side and climbed into the driver's seat. At this point I realized I hadn't the faintest idea where we were, nor any idea of how to get home. The pale pink rim of dawn was staining the horizon by the time I got the car started. Then I became as a homing pigeon. I drove unerringly through a maze of unknown territory—in the bleak, deserted industrial dock district—for more than an hour without once getting lost or having to retrack, until I reached familiar ground. Somehow I just *knew* the correct route, and I am known for my lack of a sense of direction. Friends used to say I could get lost in a phone booth. Angels, apparently, can function like global positioning satellites.

As has been said, angels can appear in many different forms, visible and invisible. Mostly the Christian West associates angels with white-robed, winged, humanlike figures. However, this popular conception of the angel rarely appears to our perception. Often, angels come in human or animal form, or they operate through the agency of a real human, as was the case in my rescue from a suicide attempt told above.

There is still another way the angelic realm interfaces with us. This is when a celestial energy superimposes itself on someone, who then *acts in the angel's stead*, without knowing the person being helped, nor why he or she came to be there. When this happens, a person is unwittingly called upon to render assistance and does so as a matter of course, just being "the right person in the right place at the right time." Such an occurrence marked yet a third life-saving rescue mission undertaken for me.

It was on a sailing excursion when I was twenty-two. I couldn't swim, but I liked being on and in the water, and I was a skilled sailor. My friend Harry, divorced and with a little boy, owned a lovely boat with a ketch rig and liked to use it for weekend parties with me serving as hostess. As he didn't like to be bothered with the details of getting a party together, he left it all up to me—which guests to invite, what food to prepare and bring. One Sunday, I invited a couple who asked if they could bring their houseguest, a single man. None of these three knew how to sail, and Harry liked to have extra crew on board, so I also invited a man named John who was an experienced boat person. A stranger showed up at the last minute to take John's place.

When my hostess chores were finished, I wanted to get in the water and be towed by the boat. Harry indulged me by tying a twenty-foot line around my wrist so I could play porpoise in the sea. I was shallow diving and enjoying the *whoosh* of being pulled through the water when the rope slipped from my wrist and I found myself suddenly untethered in the open ocean. The boat shot forward at an alarming speed when relieved of the drag of my weight, and I watched helplessly as it grew smaller and almost disappeared. I remember little else, except that under the water I was very happy, even ecstatic. I saw visions of light and could communicate with the fish and other marine animals. This underwater world seemed a wondrous place. All was beauty and serenity, with a wonderful luminosity.

The next thing I knew I was flat on my back on the deck being given artificial respiration by strong arms and vomiting up a lot of sea water. Harry, at the tiller, had known immediately that I was no longer tethered to the boat, but, under full sail and with a brisk wind, it had traveled a considerable distance before the crew could tack, come about, and return under power. But, in the open sea, with no markers, how had they managed to find the precise spot where I had vanished?

The extra man brought by the couple was a strong swimmer, as was Gary, who had replaced John. These two dived into the water and—miraculously—found me. When we returned to the Houston Yacht Club's dock and disembarked, Gary took me aside while the others went into the clubhouse.

He was older—mid-thirties or so—and he looked at me intently. I can still remember the clear green color of his eyes, like peridot flecked with spots of amber. Taking my hand in his strong, tanned one, he said gravely,

"You lead a charmed life. Did you know that?"

Not understanding what he meant, I shook my head in the negative, but his tone impressed me with its seriousness.

Oddly—or perhaps not, given my history—the incident had not seemed to me particularly extraordinary. Being close to death had not made much of an impression on me. Looking into my eyes penetratingly, he continued,

"I was the one who found you. And I wasn't supposed to be on this boat today. I'm supposed to be in San Francisco right now. I don't even know Harry. I only came because my flight was canceled and John wasn't feeling well. And I'm the *only* other friend John has who knows how to sail. I came because of *you*."

Without understanding this, I accepted it as fact because of the way he said it with total conviction. I never saw Gary again and he never sailed with Harry again. Later, John told me Gary was a professional diver who traveled all over the world guiding searches for lost treasure.

Although he did not say it in so many words, I sensed that uncanny guidance had led this man to be on the boat and to find me in the sea. Considering the time-lag and the open ocean, he knew the odds were against them finding me alive, or at all. Clearly the experience had impressed him deeply. I also sensed that he was a man of extraordinary sensibilities. Perhaps spending so much time under the water does that to a person.

The question also arises: why didn't I drown? Why didn't I sink? I can only say that while I was under water I felt buoyed up by a force of light, like resting on an air mattress. That I floated was a major factor in the rescue. Did an angel hold me up until the men found me? Did an angel cause Gary—just the person needed—to be on the scene? Was there some lesson for me in the near-death experience? The answer for me is "yes" to all three questions.

Angels are less often seen than they are *felt*—as presences, as thoughts, as ideas, as guidance. Often when I am searching for a reference that is I know not where, a book I wasn't looking for will catch my eye and when I pick it up it will fall open to precisely the information I need. Many writers have commented on this phenomenon, referring to "the Library Angel."

There are many ways you can tell if an angel is around. Sometimes there are sweet smells like flowers, or there can be a slight breeze. I have a hanging Tiffany glass lamp that sometimes sways gently back and forth when all the windows are closed and the air is entirely still. It's a signal that an angel is visiting me. Bodily sensations can also be caused by angels—in the form of heightened senses, or in the relaxation into an altered state of consciousness that is conducive to the receiving of messages. Some people hear sounds—bells, chimes, or trumpets. It has been speculated that the sound of trumpets is actually the angels crashing through the sound barrier as they break into our dimension by lowering their vibrations. Light is another angelic form of announcement, as with the train story, and the feeling of being suffused with love is another, as in the following example.

The word *angelos* in the original Greek means "messenger," and in this respect angels may be related to the function of Mercury, or Hermes, one of whose daughters is called "angel" by Pindar. A daughter of Zeus, Iris, is also described as an angel by the writer Hesiod. These terms suggest that an angel is a special carrier of messages from the gods, as was the case of the angel Gabriel announcing to the Virgin Mary that she was to become impregnated by the Holy Spirit. In paintings, angels with such messages often ride a beam of light.

Early in the beginning of my discovery of and devotion to my spiritual journey and the contact with the "invisible world" that resulted, I was visited by a soft pink light, very diffuse but compellingly powerful. It entered through a window like a rose-colored fog and slowly filled my entire apartment. A feeling of holy awe overcame me and I spontaneously dropped to my knees beside the bed, like a child in prayer.

The light communicated that it had traveled far, from the stars, and it was there to approve of the course on which I was about to embark, which included the study of astrology, and, later, psychic and healing work. There is no way for me adequately to describe the sense of peace and happiness I received from this pink glow, which gave me the feeling of being loved completely and of being totally cared for and supported. I think it might be the way a baby feels when, bathed and powdered, dry and cuddled, it drinks its mother's milk at her warm breast. I felt loved.

Angels can also appear in dreams. Though I have dreamed of angels frequently, one dream stands out from all the others, titled *Dream of the Angelo*. To explicate the fascinating interweaving of the dream process, I should also note that when I lived in Italy I was close to a man named Raphaelle (a form of Raphael), who was a Caprese. It happens that the people who live on the Italian island of Capri are genetically closer to their forebears than are others in Italy, and one finds there faces that are startlingly similar to the faces seen in the art of the Renaissance. For example, I took a photograph of a Caprese child who looked as he had just stepped from a painting by one of the great Italian masters. My friend Raphaelle had such a fifteenth-century face and could have posed for a portrait by his famous namesake.

> *Dream of the Angelo*: I am asleep in my own bed when I am awakened abruptly by a loud knocking at the door to my apartment, which alarms me as it is the middle of the night. I call out, "Who's there?" and I am answered by a rough, gangster-type voice that says, "Angelo!" in a preemptory manner, commanding and demanding. As I know no one named Angelo, and as the voice was threatening—I thought of the "mob"—I didn't answer. The knocking grew louder and more insistent, as if to say, "Open up or else."

I call out, "What do you want?" and the answer is unintelligible, like rapidly spoken dialect, which bears little resemblance to the language from which it derives. (Capri, where I lived for a year, has such a dialect, and even those who speak Italian fluently cannot understand these variations.)

I do not answer the door, and the man finally goes away. The dream progresses to evening, and I am giving a party. My friend Raphaelle suddenly appears on the little balcony outside my living room window, sitting cross-legged like an elf. He is handsome and smiling as I remember him. As I go to the window to welcome him and invite him inside, I wonder how he got up three flights to perch on my balcony. Inside, he guides me through the throng of partygoers and out into the hall, where he says he has something to tell me. We sit on the steps above my landing and he relates a fascinating story to me about my ancestry, disclosing the history of four generations, about whom in real life I know virtually nothing. He says that each generation has written a book about itself. This history was, however, incomplete because I was not included—I was, he said, "a missing character."

The stories he told me about four generations of my family were absolutely fascinating, and I longed to read these books. I asked about the book of my own generation, and he replied, "It is already written. It only needs for *you* to make it complete."

Sitting with him in the dimly-lit hall with the noise of the party in the background was cozy and comforting, and I was mesmerized by the family story he related. My thought was: How *I* would like to write such a fascinating book! But, the books—all of them—were already written. So how did I fit in? I wondered. How could I get myself into the books so they could be complete? I didn't know and he didn't tell me.

Finally, he said he had to leave and I was sad to see him go. I woke from this dream feeling he had actually been there and it took several minutes for me to realize it had been a dream. Though I could not remember what was in the books, I woke with the same thought I had had in the dream: that I would dearly love to write such a book as he had described to me.

My interpretation of this dream is that "Angelo," unable to gain entry through the front door, a symbol for the conscious mind, had transformed himself into a figure with which I was familiar and could therefore accept. Raphael is, of course, the name of one of the archangels, who have immense powers; "Angelo" had scared me with his power. The message was clear: I do have ancestors and though they are unknown to me, I am not unknown to them. The angel has come to tell me that "I" am missing—that is, that I have a book to write which will put me in the family archives. For a long time I had wanted to research both the maternal and paternal sides of my family, and to write an autobiographical book about my search for my roots. The angel's message was not only that the time to write the book had come, but that *the book is already written*, as indeed all books are already written in the divine mind. One has only to set one's fingers to the keyboard or take pen to paper and allow the doors of the great cosmic repository to open and present their treasures.

Angels are *there*. You might not see them, but you can always sense them, and when you begin to have contact with your SELF you are likely to have contact with higher beings and infinite energies. The more alert and open you are to these extraordinary experiences, the more likely it is you will find them in your life at some time or other. *Expect a miracle.* And

be prepared to recognize one when it occurs. Be on the alert—
if you feel the presence of an angel become still and wait for a
message. As you become more and more aware of their
presence when they visit, you will draw them closer and experience them more often. Many of them are coming closer to
the human realm in this period of the ending of an old,
outworn millennium and the birth of a new age. They are
coming to serve as a bridge to the ultimate cosmic consciousness which is ready to manifest in all who are ready to
receive its energy and message of love and peace to all everywhere. Listen with your ears, eyes, mind, emotions, body,
and—above all—with your heart.

❧ Invoking the Angels

To call forth an angel or a spirit, you can practice this invocation. First, enter your sacred space and sit in silence and
stillness. Center yourself and open to what images will come.
Then ask the spirits to come forth. As you say the words,
imagine that you see a beautiful white angel with its wings
spread protectively.

Angels have long been associated with the "four corners,"
or the four directions, or the four elements. As you speak the
invocations, stand facing the direction indicated.

 Spirits of Fire
(West)
I call upon the angels of Fire to bring love, protection, and safety. May the warmth of the lifegiving
Fire come into my being and guide me. May the
strength of the Sun come to me and illuminate me
on my Way.

Spirits of Earth
(North)

I call upon the angels of Earth to bring love, protection, and safety. May the regenerative and restorative power of the Earth ground me and guide my Way. May the renewing power of the Moon come to me and light my path.

Spirits of Air
(East)

I call upon the angels of Air to bring love, protection, and safety. May the gentle winds of heaven blow always and imbue me with their airborne energies. May the communication power of Mercury come to me and guide my Way.

Spirits of Water
(South)

I call upon the angels of Water to bring love, protection, and safety. May the waters of heaven cleanse and purify me. May the flowing and regenerative powers of Water come to me and guide my Way.

You can also write letters to angels using the above formulations, choosing which is most suitable to your purpose. Angels of Fire would be for bringing more active love energy, to protect outdoor adventures, and to make safe courses of action. Angels of Earth would be for bringing more stable love energy, to protect the home and family, and to make safe the hearth, childbirth, or feminine concerns. Angels of Air would be for bringing more variable love energy, to protect intellectual pursuits, and to make safe enterprises having to do with air, such as flying. Angels of Water would be for bringing more spiritual love, to protect creative pursuits, and to make safe anything having to do with water, such as boating or taking a cruise.

Unity minister Catharine Ponder identifies seven types of angels to whom one can write for specific purposes related to *other people*. These are:

1. The angel of *Ephesus*, for those who are appealing but hard to reach.
2. The angel of *Smyrna*, for those who are lovers of beauty and adornment or who tend to get into financial trouble.
3. The angel of *Pergamum*, for those who are closely knit in family or business relationships or wary of strangers, new friends, and new ideas.
4. The angel of *Thyatira*, for those who are idealistic but have trouble producing actual results.
5. The angel of *Sardis*, for those who are timid, apprehensive, fearful, indecisive, hypochondriac.
6. The angel of *Philadelphia*, for organizations that espouse brotherly love but don't practice love.
7. The angel of *Laodicea*, for unstable, unsettled, changeable wanderers seeking new doctrines, new places.

For a full exposition of "angel-writing techniques," case histories, and examples of letters to the seven types of angels, see Ponder's book *The Prospering Power of Love*

Angels, then, come in many forms. In her book *Sacred Space*, Denise Linn says:

> Right now angels are bridging our physical reality with their pure spiritual energy. Like a leaf falling softly on the still pool of our consciousness, we recognize their presence. As we trust in them, they will pour their blessings on us. . . . And as you become aware of angels they will be more and more drawn into your life.

210

chapter eleven
The Grace of Guides

To embark upon the spiritual journey is to invite unseen forces to interact with us. These creative energies manifest in many ways, a principal one of which is as guides. Guides bring us into grace and show the way. To encounter a guide—and they come in many guises—is to enter another realm, a place of great powers and, sometimes, of great secrets. This realm belongs to the invisible world, although its denizens can, like angels, come in human or animal form. To interface with this world is to be impacted in a way that is life-changing. With guides, we enter a world of supreme power—not the power of the material world but of the invisible order that supports and nourishes our world and our lives here. It is the realm of the sacred.

Marsha Sinetar in *Ordinary People as Monks and Mystics*, says:

> The true mystic is not merely involved in esoteric thoughts or beautiful images of God in heaven. He is totally absorbed in a life movement, a journey in which his essential self—his real self—comes into life with and in God. This "coming to God," as it has been called, is the journey.

211

And, when one goes on a journey into unfamiliar territory, it is best to have a knowledgeable guide who knows the terrain, speaks the language, and is familiar with the customs. Classical Greek Hermes, the "guide of souls," is emblematic of such guides. The classical scholar Karl Kerényi speaks of the "activity of Hermes" as referring to "alternatives of life, to the dissolution of fatal opposites, to clandestine violations of boundaries and laws." In other words, the overturning of the rational-mind-dictated world and the discovery of the magical powers of the inner world.

Hermes was called Mercury by the Romans, and the deeper expression of Hermes-Mercury's role as messenger of the gods is that which mediates, or delivers messages between the conscious mind and the unconscious realm, which I have called the "sacred mind." This is a more subtle meaning than is usually encountered, but it is one of the most important factors in understanding how guides operate. In answer to the question, "What appeared to the Greeks as Hermes?" Kerényi states:

> . . . he is the supra-individual source of a particular world-experience and world configuration [that] is open to the possibility of a transcendent guide and leader who is also able to provide impressions of consciousness, but of a different kind: impressions that are palpable and manifest, that in no way contradict the observations and conclusions of natural science, and yet extend beyond the attitude which is the common one today. . . . The sum total of pathways as Hermes' playground; the accidental "falling into your lap" as the Hermetic material; its transformation through finding. . . . They are the world and they are *one* world, namely, *that* world which Hermes opens to us.

A guide is actually a symbol for our own deepest Wisdom, which resides in the SELF and connects us to all the other SELF-entities everywhere, to non-human life, to non-organic life, to the cosmos itself.

During my life, I have encountered many guides. You, too, will have more than one guide during your lifetime. You can call upon guides at any time you feel you need guidance.

A guide may present as an "archetype"—an Old Man or a Wise Woman, a human figure you may or may not recognize, such as a grandparent or an idealized teacher, an animal that talks or communicates telepathically, a spiritual entity such as an "intelligence" from another dimension, or even as a rock or body of water. These symbols are likely to shift and change over time and with the subject for which you are asking guidance. For example, asking for guidance with healing may produce a figure consonant with your idea of a healer. Accept what comes, for it arises from your deepest SELF.

About fifteen years ago, I encountered a group of guides who first appeared to me in an exceptionally vivid dream.

Dream of Green Fire. I am in a large house in a wooded area with a young woman friend. Outside, there is a blizzard. I hear my name called. I cannot imagine who would be calling my name late at night with a storm raging, but I know I must go and find out if someone in trouble needs my help.

Bundling up, I forge out into the blowing snow, in the direction of the voice calling my name. Going through a dense woods, I come upon a clearing, surrounded by a ring of green fire. Inside the ring of green fire there is no storm—all is quiet, placid, peaceful, and warm. Nine men robed and hooded like monks, in long woolen olive-brown gowns, tied at the waist with knotted golden ropes, sit in a circle inside the ring of green fire. In the center of the circle formed by their bodies there is a small bonfire that glows with the same emerald green light as the fire ring.

By gesture, they invite me to enter the circle. From the maelstrom of the raging storm I step into this center of absolute calm, safety, and warmth. A great sense of peace descends over me, as if I have at long last come home. Beneath their hoods I can see their faces—all are very old and wizened with deep, dark eyes like pools of unfathomable wisdom. I feel a sense of protection coming from them.

One rises and steps toward me and I see that he has my cat, Fuzz, cradled in his arms. I realize that the voice I heard calling my name was that of my precious Fuzz, who was lost in the terrible storm and needed rescuing. He is handed to me ceremoniously, like a gift on an important occasion. I can tell he is perfectly all right and has suffered no injuries from the traumatic experience of being lost in the cold and snow. Taking him from the monk's wrinkled old hands, I feel a sense of complete and utter peace and safety.

When I woke, I pondered the symbolism—and the answer came immediately: Fuzz was my heart. They had told me something very important, that my *heart*—most fearfully broken more than once, in essence *lost* in the dark cold—had been rescued and kept safe. Now it was returned to me intact and healed.

The nine men appeared to me several different times over the next several years, always accompanied by ice and snow, to which they were immune and within which they created a warm center. Though they appeared to be human, I knew they were other-worldly. Once they called me to a remote mountain top, covered with snow. I could drive to the bottom of the mountain, but to reach the summit I had to climb on foot. I was frightened and I refused to go up through the dark, snowy woods covering the slopes. Turning back, I went home.

In another experience, they give me a large book made of parchment sheaves, ancient and yellowed but not fragile, the pages covered with a mysterious writing I cannot decipher but which I understand to be important esoteric knowledge. Then I realize that the nine men are great magicians—sages from the world of no-time.

I came to call them "The Council of Nine." Later, I wrote a poem about my encounters with this strange and powerful group.

The Return

There came to a certain place
Men, nine in number, with a
Task, or chore, to perform.
Unknown, unheralded, they came,
And uninvited as well.

Speak to me of them, I said—
Knowing not what I said, for
I was All-unknowing, virgin.
And answer I did not hear.
For answer there was not.

Later I was called upon a
Mountain, in dark and snow,
Invited, then, to participate.
But fear drove me away from
Them, whom I knew not. But
Had met many times, secretly.

When I returned from the Journey
Into their realm, I was changed,
But I knew not how nor why—nor
If there were a reason for the—
Transformation. Of my mind, of
My soul, of my shall I say psyche?

So, now, here and not there, I wish
For more. They are not generous—
Nor parsimonious. They Speak when
They will. And say what they may.
Emotion is not something they know,
Though they understand we have this.

Return. I often ask them to return,
But asking serves no purpose for they
Are their own masters and do not do
What they do for our purposes, but
For theirs—mysterious, but benign.
I think they mean us no harm, yet I
Believe we must monitor them and make
Our own decisions about these matters.
And They agree, for They are learning,
Too—of what is unknown to them. Our
World. Without end. Amen.

When I read Betty Eadie's book *Embraced by the Light*, I was astonished to find that one chapter was entitled "The Council of Men." In her vision, she met twelve men seated around a kidney-shaped table who radiated "absolute love" to her. She also learned from this council of men many fascinating things about herself and her life. In addition, she describes three men who meet her at the beginning of her near-death experience. The numbers twelve, nine, and three are all related, each being divisible by the core number *three*. Three represents the trinity, or the triangle, of mind-body-spirit and the threefold nature of divinity, of great symbolic importance and spiritual significance. *Nine* is the number of completion, of humanitarianism and universal compassion. *Twelve*, which is the number of the signs of the zodiac, reduces back to three using the numerological formula $12 = 1 + 2 = 3$.

The description Eadie gives of the council of men she met is eerily like that of my own Council of Nine:

> They wore beautiful, light-brown robes . . . a hood on the back. . . . Each wore a gold-braided belt that was tied about the waist with the ends hanging down. A kind of glow emanated from them, but not unusually bright. [They] appeared to be about seventy or eighty years old, but I knew somehow that they were on a time scale different from the earth's. The impression came to me that they were much older than seventy or eighty years old—that they were ancient. I sensed in them great spirituality, knowledge, and wisdom. . . . I began to think of them as monks—mostly because of the robes—and I knew I could trust them.

I am not suggesting that Betty Eadie's council and mine are the same group of guides. What I do think, however, is that we are all capable of experiencing contact with our own deeper dimensions symbolically. It is through the use of symbols that we can connect with what cannot be seen, heard, touched, tasted, or smelled. Whatever symbolic form your guides and teachers will take will depend on what forms are palatable to you, to which forms you are most open and able to respond. In my case, these often have to do with art and books, such as this significant dream.

> *Dream of the Great Library.* I am visiting the house of a man who goes by the nickname "Winnie," possibly a pun on the word win. He tells me that if I will forgo getting my Ph.D., he will teach me everything contained in the books in his library. He shows me a magnificent collection of ancient texts on papyrus, handwritten tomes from antiquity, illuminated manuscripts, medieval books on herbalist lore, mysterious alchemical texts, books of magic spells, esoteric teachings of all kinds and from all ages. The books seem to

glow with magical power. I ask him, "What will I accomplish if I learn all this?" and he replies, "Nothing."

The message as I interpreted it was that I must relinquish my conventional thinking, exemplified by the Ph.D. degree and our society's obsession with academic credentialing as the only path to a successful life, and take in its place the powerful ancient tradition, which is far superior to dry, academic "book learning" that places all value on the rational-linear mode of thought and what can be proven in a laboratory. However, learning the ancient wisdom will not "accomplish" anything in the usual sense of our limited thinking about what accomplishment *means*. That is not the purpose of esoteric knowledge. Though it can be used on the mundane plane, i.e., to enrich one's self in a material way, its true purpose is for the development of the spiritual life.

The teachings we receive from the "other side" may not be remembered after the particular altered state of consciousness in which we experience them is gone, but they nevertheless make an impact as do unremembered dreams. There was a lot you learned at school that you "forgot"—who can recall their high-school algebra or Latin? But somehow those subjects sunk in as part of an overall pattern of learning to *think*.

Some fortunate people are able to regularly receive lessons while in an altered or dream state, and remember everything and record it. Viola Petitt Neal, who wrote *Through the Curtain*, reports how she attended "night classes," which she dictated to Ms. Shafica Karagulla while in the altered state. In this book, the authors speak of a "Council of Seven" (a number which combines three with four, the number of the four directions; the seven also represents the spiritual path and is often diagramatically represented as a triangle enclosed within a square, symbolizing the trinity and the four directions). So it would seem the symbol of a council is a common one.

Others, most notably the late Jane Roberts, can receive the teachings of a guide through the medium of a trance state. Over a period of many years Jane Roberts dictated the words of "Seth" to her husband, Robert, producing several thick volumes which make fascinating and illuminating reading.

It's even possible for one person to receive guidance from another person's guide. I had such an experience when I first began to practice astrology professionally. My friend, the late Josephine Corado, a blind psychic, had invited me to spend the weekend at her home on Long Island and had arranged for me to read the charts of several of her clients. I arrived on a Friday afternoon carrying some astrology books. At that time, I was accustomed to spending three or four hours of preparation time on each chart, and although I had prepared most of the charts I was to read over the weekend, one remained undone.

That evening as we sat chatting in Jo's living room—she in the recliner from which she did her readings, me on the couch—she suddenly burst out laughing.

"What's so funny?" I asked in puzzlement.

"Akenaton," she replied. "He's standing right in front of you."

I knew Akenaton was what she called her guide, but there was nothing in front of me but the coffee table.

"Where?" I asked, looking around.

"Right *there*," she pointed a finger to my tummy.

"What does he want with me?" I asked perplexedly.

"I haven't the faintest idea," was her unhelpful reply.

Shortly after this conversation, she announced that she was going to bed early because she didn't feel well. I reminded her that I had a chart to prepare the next morning before my first reading at noon, and she promised to get me up by nine A.M. It was about ten P.M. when she retired, and as I'm a late-night person I was at loose ends to occupy myself. Since Jo was blind,

219

there were no books and no TV. We'd had wine with dinner, and I wasn't in the mood to study astrology, the only books I had. I lay on the couch to meditate.

As I lay there, wide awake but very relaxed, a curious thing happened. My entire body began to vibrate as if someone had plugged me into an electric socket. It was very intense, though not actually uncomfortable. The source of the sensation seemed to be the center of my forehead (where the "third eye" is located). I didn't understand at all what was happening to me, but as I was in what I knew to be a psychically saturated atmosphere, I made no effort to get up. The room was not dark; there was a streetlight just outside the uncurtained window. I looked about myself, but I saw nothing out of the ordinary.

The sensation finally stopped—*three hours later*. As unexpectedly and inexplicably as it had started, it stopped, like the switching off of a light. Whatever circuit I had been connected to went dead. I felt none the worse for the experience, and I got up and went to bed. In the morning as promised, Jo woke me and I sat at her dining-room table to prepare the chart. I worked away, consulting my books only occasionally, and when I had finished, I asked Jo, who had a talking watch, for the time. "It's nine forty-five," she told me.

I knew this could not be right, for I had finished with three hours' worth of work and I had not started until a bit after nine. "That's impossible," I said. "Could you check your watch again?" She came over to me and held out her wrist and I heard a little mechanical voice say, "Nine forty-six." How could that be? I wondered. I had not felt any sense of time speeded up, had worked at my usual slow and thorough pace, or so I thought, and yet I was done. To make sure, I called the time service. Then I remembered the previous evening's strange experience and Jo's having told me her guide was standing in front of me. Could there be a connection?

In the weeks that followed, it became evident to me that I had a far greater understanding and knowledge of astrology than before I went to Long Island that weekend. At a conference where I was a lecturer, a thoroughly seasoned astrologer who had been practicing for twenty years came up to me and said that I was the "best technical astrologer" she knew. Amazed, I understood that I had received a powerful teaching that night, like an intracranial injection straight into the brain. Since then, my readings have risen to a level of comprehension that still amazes me, for I know that I didn't earn the knowledge I have—it was a gift.

Guides and teachers are a very personal, sometimes profound, experience. There is no way any of us can pass on information about them except by relating our own experiences. Here is one more of mine, the most dramatic of all so far.

In 1986 I had reached a point in my practice of psychotherapy where I was working intensively with clients rather than doing the usual fifty-minute hour once a week. Several of my clients responded especially well to this intensive method of working several hours a day for one or more days successively. To facilitate this way of working, I rented a house in the country where the client could live on the premises and we would be able to work with her dreams in the morning when recall of them was fresh. It was also a place to hold seminars.

I took possession of the house over the Labor Day weekend, a friend having come along to help out with the transport of gear. He stayed a couple of days, and then I was left alone in the house for the first time well after midnight on Sunday. I was sitting on the porch having a stargaze when I distinctly heard the crunch of brush underfoot. The house was in a copse of pine trees and cut off on all sides by bushy growth. Who could be out walking in the woods at this time of night? Suddenly, I *knew*!

A dark figure appeared out of the woods about ten yards from where I sat. I could "see" him clearly. A Native American man, about forty years old, six feet tall, lean, muscular, he wore unadorned fringed buckskins the color of blueberries. His dusky-looking skin had a bluish undertone and his long straight hair was blue-black, like ink. He wore no headdress nor beading. He simply stood at the edge of the copse of trees and stared at me, rather as if *he* owned the place. I thought: if I stay out here one more minute, he is going to walk over here and speak to me and I can't handle that.

Scaredy-cat that I was, I went inside the darkened house and turned on all the lights. Recently I read that blue is the color of wisdom, but at the time I was unaware of this.

The next week, a young woman arrived for an intensive session of several days' duration. A Pisces who had suffered abuse as a child, she was a "sensitive," someone who easily contacts the invisible world. Her efforts to escape from harsh reality had resulted in drug addiction, and she had come to me for help in "kicking the habit."

During the first afternoon, I was taking her through a guided meditation when to my consternation I saw her slip away into a trance state. I sat quietly watching over her until she returned and then asked her what had happened. She reported matter-of-factly that she had been "with the Indians." And she described the same man I had seen on my first night in the house! As I had told no one about my experience, I didn't know what to make of this startling revelation, but the hairs on the back of my neck stood up. Upon further examination, she revealed that the entire tribe had said prayers over her and that she had been given some herbal concoction to drink.

The following afternoon, while I prepared our lunch, she went outside to have a cigarette. Suddenly she burst into the kitchen and said excitedly, "He's out there!" To my question of

"Who?"—although I well knew the answer—she replied, "That Indian I saw last night. He's coming out of the woods now."

It seemed we were perilously close to something very powerful and mysterious.

During the ensuing days, we both experienced his presence daily. During meditations, she was "taken" several times for "treatments," given more herbal drinks, and met the women of the tribe, who treated her as a daughter, and performed healing rituals to cure her of her addiction. When she left, she told me she felt strong and whole for the first time in her life and that she would never use drugs again. I wish I could credit my skills as a psychotherapist for her complete recovery, but I know who was really responsible for what seemed to be a "miracle cure."

Later that fall, during a weekend mask-making seminar, the Woodstock shaman, as I came to call him, manifested in a way that allowed a photograph to be taken. The workshop attendees were decorating their masks using paints and glue and glitter. One participant spilled an open vial of blue glitter all over the black rug. After the seminar was over, I moved her chair to vacuum and there on the rug in clear outline was a strong face all in blue—bits of different colored glitter had fallen in such a way as to furnish the details of the portrait. Oddly, one person had gone out of her way to bring a camera to photograph the finished masks, driving extra miles on a Sunday to purchase film. Thus were we able to photograph the Woodstock shaman for posterity.

On New Year's Eve, a friend came to spend the holiday with me, but she had caught a terrible cold and had to go to bed early. It was extremely cold, and the guest room heater was not working properly, so after giving her an aspirin and some hot tea, I tucked her into my bed at nine o'clock and closed the door to await the New Year alone. At ten, I peeked in and she was soundly asleep. After quietly celebrating in utter and peaceful silence, I joined her. As I crawled into the bed beside her, she woke saying she had to go to the bathroom, which was across the large studio that formed the main part of the house. Scooting out into the now cooling big room, she returned a few minutes later, hugging herself against the cold. As she climbed back into the warm bed, she said,

"Say, who are all those Indians out there? That big guy—he's really good-looking."

Before I could respond to this extraordinary remark, she was asleep again, but I lay awake pondering. What was going on? I slept, and dreamed of an Indian village presided over by a tribal council who seemed to be in session. The next day I asked her if she remembered what she saw, and she described "a bunch of Indians sitting in a circle" in the studio, silent and motionless, as if they were sitting in council in their own meeting room. The "big guy" was the Woodstock shaman as I had first perceived him and as my client had described him.

During the time that I worked and lived in that house, I experienced the shaman frequently, as did others who visited. My own experiences always took place at night. Once I woke from sleep as if a hand had touched me on the shoulder, and I was instantly alert in the thick dark of a winter's night. I felt all my senses were sharpened, and into my mind came the following passage, which I wrote down verbatim immediately afterward:

> *Magic is constructed on the mental plane. [Learn to] create such structures on the mental plane in order to work magic power. Magic is SYSTEM. Not hocus-pocus. ORDER. Not mental (intellectual) order as in logic or an orderly thought process but on the mental plane. Not in the mind but OF MIND. Understand difference between MIND and mental or thinking.*

I understood MIND, called *manas* by the ancient Egyptians, to mean Universal Intelligence.

Over time, the shaman told me the story of his life and work. How did he "tell" me? Obviously not in ordinary conversation— I suppose it was a form of telepathy. The thoughts simply arrived in my mind, and I knew they were from him. I was able to record much of the "conversations" in verbatim notes.

He was an advanced practitioner for his time, which a trance medium later told me was before Europeans arrived on these shores, the same time period as the Renaissance. He was developing what he called "spiritual technology," which involved deliberately invoked out-of-body immersion of himself with other life forms and the elements. He conducted this work alone and in secret, as any true shaman must, going to an old burial ground for the purpose. (I later discovered my house had been built over such a place.) As a shaman, he knew how to use psychotropic plants (like psychedelic mushrooms or peyote) as an adjunct to out-of-body travels into other dimensions of reality. He would have believed he could absorb animal and vegetal powers into himself, and he would have had training for this.

But he was adventurous and wanted to know more, to experience more, to "push the envelope" as we say. So he took risks. With each success, his confidence grew, and he became careless, taking greater risks than were prudent, for such ventures are extremely dangerous. As he always worked alone, there was no one to back him up, hold on to him, so to speak. Finally, one black night of the dark moon he felt he was on the verge of great discovery, of accessing more power than anyone had ever thought possible. He went too far away from his body, and could not return. He died. He said he would groom me to carry on his work, but my stay in the house was truncated by circumstances and I moved away a few months later.

On my last night in the house, feeling sad about leaving a place that had provided me with such rich spiritual experiences, I was packed and ready to go when my friend who was driving me back to the city called to say he would be a couple of hours late. There was nothing to do in the empty-feeling house, so I lay down on the bed to meditate and pass the time that way. I must have dozed off. I saw bright light, like that of the full moon, and I roused to go and look at the moon shining on the new snow, a scene I love. But when I got up I discovered the moon wasn't full, or even visible in the clouded-over sky. The room was in darkness. Puzzled, I lay down again. Then, I felt the shaman's presence more strongly than ever before. Touching me gently, he told me he was going to give me a healing treatment. For more than an hour, I felt a gentle pulsing going through my body, felt connected to parts of myself that had long been outside of my awareness. My legs, which had been damaged by childhood polio, felt alive for the first time I could remember. I felt myself open like a flower under the beneficence of this healing vibration. It was a parting gift from the Woodstock shaman.

It is not necessary to perceive an actual *figure* as a guide, though this seems to be the most usual form in which guides appear to us. However, one can simply *sense or feel* guidance, or the presence of a particular guide. Jane Roberts, in the Seth books, often comments prior to going into trance, "I can feel him around now" or "He's about to come through."

Guides of different qualities have manifested to me. For example, during one period when I was intensively studying the Tarot, I received information and guidance through specific *sounds*. I identified three different "energies," as I call them, one of which was a thin, high-pitched tone, barely audible but piercing nonetheless. The second was lower, but still in the high range, and seemed to cover a slightly wider band of the sound spectrum. The third sound was much lower, almost a bass, and broader. Each of these sounds conveyed a different type of information. For example, when I heard the highest note, I knew it was time to sit quietly and meditate, that a "message" was coming in through this vibration. These sounds occurred at all times of the day and night and in places other than my home as well. They seemed to follow me around. So, be aware that you can receive guidance and teaching in many guises.

Here is a method for making contact with a guide/teacher. Remember that you can do this any time you feel the need. You may meet a guide who will stay with you for a long or a short time. You may meet different guides along your Way. There is no right or wrong way to contact a guide, although some do appear spontaneously without your asking, as did the Woodstock shaman. Others respond to your call.

By making the effort to meet and dialogue with your guide, you will be setting a precedent for getting help on a regular, sometimes unasked-for basis. Your guide can warn you of incipient problems in advance; it can provide you with penetrating insight; it can reveal subtle nuances of meaning that are imbedded in your everyday experience.

To prepare yourself to meet a guide whom you can trust and rely on, do the following:

1. Articulate a question you wish to ask your guide. State the question as clearly and succinctly as you can. Vague questions beget vague answers. The more specific the question, the more specific the answer will be.
2. Do not ask a question that can be answered by a simple *yes* or *no*. The purpose of the first effort to contact a guide is for you to get to know this realm of your inside being.
3. Stick to your present situation and avoid broad generalities.
4. Do not ask a question requiring a prediction. This is usually interpreted as trying to "test" the guide. Simply asking for guidance is always good. State the subject about which you wish guidance.

5. Be willing to trust your guide and to take whatever form appears to you. If you draw a blank, try again later when you are more relaxed.

6. When a guide appears, pay attention to the appearance. Ask your guide for a name or a symbol by which you can recognize him in the future.

 ### *Meeting Your Guide*

After you have prepared yourself for your encounter with your guide, find the time to be alone and undisturbed for half an hour. Using any of the breathing and/or relaxation methods already given, relax yourself completely and let go of the day's tensions and cares.

Mentally take yourself to a place somewhere in nature—a forest, the seaside, a flower-filled meadow, a lake shore, a cove, a woods—whatever appeals to you. See in front of you in this pleasant place a veiled object, full of mystery. A puff of wind comes along and blows away the covering and your guide is revealed to you. Take whatever image comes and begin to dialogue with it. Ask your question and wait for an answer. If one doesn't come at once, be patient. The answer may come in words, through intuition or telepathically, as an image, even a snatch of song or an instruction to read a book or magazine article.

In these guided meditations, the specifics are not as important as making the contact. Whatever springs into your mind is the right answer, because you are using a process to contact your own inner wisdom. Your guides are within the realm of the deepest part of your being, which is connected to all reality everywhere at all times and places.

When you have met your guide, introduced yourself, and asked your question, notice the details of the place so that you can return here whenever you like. Fix it in your memory. When you get the answer to your question, thank your guide and say you will look forward to further dialogue in the future.

If you do not get an answer, or if the answer seems to make no sense, accept that also and try again later. Remember you are learning a new skill.

Before leaving, make an appointment to meet with your guide again at a set time in the future and follow through on this with another meditation.

Spirit guides come in many forms and can manifest in many ways. In his book *Shape Shifting*, John Perkins tells of a shaman he knew who transformed himself into a bat and then disappeared as a human being. Later, he saw a bat flying around in his backyard and felt strongly that the shaman was visiting him. Then, while he was attempting to help a sick woman to heal, a bat appeared to him in a vision and drained the fluid out of her chest. She recovered completely, a "miracle" cure officially recorded by the Mayo Clinic.

The above story is an example of the deeply mysterious region of the invisible world, which includes guides of all sorts. I have been asked, "What is the difference between an angel and a guide?" and quite honestly I do not know. There may not be a difference. Angels and guides may be different forms of the same basic energy. Since all of life is energy, and since energy has the ability to take any form, there is no certain way of knowing.

As stated by the contemporary native shaman Medicine Grizzlybear Lake, in his book *Native Healer*:

The Creator can and does talk to you through anything if he or she so chooses, a rain cloud, a burning bush, a whirlwind, or a high mountain. He talks to our Native American medicine people the same way it has been from the beginning, for all races. He sometimes talks to us through dreams, visions, an eagle, hawk, raven, wolf, coyote, deer, buffalo, snake, rock, bear, lightning, and thunder.

When we venture into the invisible world, we encounter *mystery*, for there exist no neat categories of "this and that" such as divide our rational world into recognizable events and objects. In the invisible world, all is shifting and changing, like a dream. So, when you open yourself up to Hermes' world, do not be surprised at what may happen. I myself have had many fantastic and surprising adventures in this most wonderful and mysterious realm of the invisible world. Now I close this book by telling you one of the most compelling of all, one that had a direct influence on the writing of this book.

❦ A New Year Visitation

On New Year's Eve, as the year 1987 was turning into 1988, at approximately midnight, I had a stunningly extraordinary experience which ultimately proved to be the catalyst for the writing of this book.

It occurred during a period of intense growth on many levels, a personal transformation of far-reaching import. Though I had already undergone many strange and unprecedented events, nothing had even remotely prepared me for this occurrence.

At that time, I was seeking new direction for my life and work, and I was embarked on a refurbishing of my home—a physical manifestation of an internal new beginning. In the midst of the resultant temporary chaos I had settled into bed before the New Year's celebratory noise-making began.

Suddenly, as if a hand had been placed over my eyes, everything went dark. A profound blackness descended—as if someone had put a hood over my head. There was not a particle of light anywhere in this thick dark, the epitome of night most mysterious. I had an inkling of what it must have been like long ago, in the time before electricity, to be under a moonless sky— when only the brave or the desperate went abroad after nightfall.

Then, *cold*—a cold so penetrating as to seem bloodless. Yet, this abysmal chill had a living quality to it. As it slowly permeated the room, I had the sense of a presence entering my space, bringing with it the dark and cold, an absence of light and warmth that was absolute. Terror rose up in me—what power, possibly evil, could suck all heat and light out of a living environment? Why was it here and what were its intentions? I felt in mortal danger, as if some support that holds this world in place had fallen, some barrier that protects us from the fearsome unknown had been breached.

Terrified as I was, with no recourse against whatever was now clearly moving about my apartment, I began a series of frantic affirmations, but I didn't believe pallid words could affect the awesome power prowling about. Reverting—as they say we all do in extreme stress—to the religion of my childhood, I began to implore the saints. As if in miraculous answer, a life-sized image of a saint, such as one sees in medieval paintings, appeared in full color on my newly painted wall, like a giant slide projection.

This image was of my childhood favorite, Saint Anthony, and I cried out "Oh, Saint Anthony! I'm so glad you have come," but the image faded, to be replaced by another, more imposing, august figure, a personage unknown to me. I gazed in awe at the commanding figure of this saintly being and blurted out, *"Who are you?"*

"Saint Jude," came the stern answer. Remembering that he was the patron of lost causes and impossible situations, I figured I was in serious trouble. His image, too, faded, leaving the room as cold and dark as before. I now knew that I had to face whatever it was alone.

Moments later, two whitish figures floated out of the darkness toward me, clearly a man and a woman, hovering in midair near my bed. Though I remained in awe, the abject terror had abated. I waited.

They began to speak to me—not in audible words, but by projecting word-thoughts into my mind. They told me they had been travelling *through time*—which I understood to be a different measure than ordinary time as the living experience it. I asked from whence they came, and the answer was,

"2500 B.C."

Pictures began appearing in my mind, including diagrams and floor plans, some of which I recognized or half-remembered from archaeological studies.

As these thought images continued to flow, the apparitions became clearer and I could discern that they were small-boned people. He was taller and broad-shouldered with narrow hips; she was wasp-waisted and high-bosomed. I had seen pictures of such people, but in my muddled state I could not remember where. I asked *why* they had come.

They explained that they were my parents, and that they had abandoned me when I was a baby. Their position as members of a royal household, not permitted to marry each other, had meant that a child born to them would spell both social and political disaster. The birth had been concealed; the baby given to foster parents. This original abandonment of me, they elucidated, had generated lifetimes of repetitions of the experience of being abandoned. I asked what they wanted of me. The answer was,

"Forgiveness."

Without a moment's hesitation, for there was palpable pain emanating from them, I proffered unconditional forgiveness.

232

Then, as if to present me with a parting gift, they projected into my mind a series of diagrams and images related to mental magic, or spiritual "technology"—the art of manifesting thought into reality—telling me these "powers" were my rightful heritage. One image was a huge green crystal so real it seemed palpable—I understood clearly it was an organized thought pattern capable of becoming manifest in the material world.

After this, they gradually withdrew, and in their departing wake normal light and warmth returned to the atmosphere. I later regretted I had not had the presence of mind to ask more questions, but other than the sheer thrill of the theatricality of it all, I did not know what to make of the experience.

If I believed the story literally, I was squarely in neurotic territory. Legends abound of the hero of royal parentage who is raised by surrogates, and who, after many trials, regains his rightful inheritance. In examining these, the psychologist Dr. Otto Rank, in his monograph *Myth of the Birth of the Hero*, had asserted that the mythic pattern of the hero who has a noble, divine, or higher birth; infant exile or exposure; adoption by a family of lower rank; and the prospect of return to his "true" estate is typical of a "certain type of neurotic daydream." Interestingly, however, the hero who suffers such a fate is always male. Also, the difference between me and the neurotic personality Rank describes is that this was not a made-up fantasy but an unpremeditated vision.

If I looked at the experience from a purely psychological point of view—that my own unconscious had thrown up this entire episode for the purpose of bringing to my attention an inner state vis-à-vis the issue of abandonment in order for it to be integrated into consciousness—I was not only stuck with the unnecessarily complicated presentation, but was in any case already well aware of themes of abandonment in my life. Though perhaps I had not dealt with them as completely as possible, that they existed as part of my personal psychological fabric was not exactly breaking news.

Another possibility existed—to consider the matter from a metaphysical or metaphoric perspective. *Metaphysical* actually means nothing more esoteric than "beyond the physical," which is exactly what we mean when we speak of the spiritual dimension.

Joseph Campbell suggests that Dr. Rank may have missed the point, saying that,

> [His analysis] underestimates the force of the actual derivation of the formula from a cosmological myth. The whole series cited falls well within the range of the world-diffusion of the arts and rites of agrarian life, and consequently cannot be treated as a mere congeries of daydreams independently produced from a certain type of individual state of mind. Indeed, it might be asked whether the state of mind is not a function of the legend rather than its cause; for, as it stands, the legend represents a descent from the cosmological plane to an individual reference.

Viewed thusly, and if, as I believe, the entire universe—past, present, and future—is one great continuum, then could I not view the experience, inclusive of content and presentation, as in some way *purposeful?*

What did the Christian saints have to do with it all? As they were characteristically medieval in appearance, it seemed likely that to contact the deeper mythic level I had to pass through the overlay of Christianity with which I had been reared. The psyche, it occurs to me, is very like an excavation site—there are many strata to be dug through before one reaches the bedrock on which the first foundation is laid.

234

After writing everything down, and making drawings of the plans and images, I filed this occurrence away with notes of other, less spectacular, events wherein the veil between the worlds had momentarily lifted to give me a glimpse of extraordinary powers beyond the visible, sensory realm.

Some days later, on an ordinary day full of blue sky and bright sunshine, I encountered a street vendor of crystals and stopped to admire his wares. There on his table was a green tourmaline, a replica in miniature of the crystal I had been given in the vision! Astounded, but by now accustomed to synchronous events, I purchased it and two other specimens. On my way home, I stopped at a supermarket for groceries and was lugging two full bags along my street when, I heard—as if someone had spoken at my shoulder—*"The Temple of the Horned Moon."*

I almost dropped my groceries. Stunned, I looked for the speaker, whom there was none. For a long moment I stood disoriented on the street, as if transported to another dimension, wondering what the words could mean. Finally, I continued on my way home—half a block later to be once again stopped in my tracks by the same voice saying,

"The last Scribe. You were the last Scribe of the Temple of the Horned Moon."

"What?" I said aloud, and the voice repeated itself.

I would like to report that the sky darkened, as with an eclipse, or some other dramatic moment, but absolutely nothing atmospheric changed. The sun continued to shine; the sky remained a clear and untroubled blue. Only I was out of sync. Stunned that in bright sunny daylight I was simultaneously inhabiting two different worlds, I stood stock-still, struggling to get a grip on myself.

As I walked the short distance to my apartment, without further incident, I searched my mind for the reference, "Temple of the Horned Moon," with no result. I had never heard of such a place. When I reached home I called a friend, who is expert in such matters, and asked him if such an appellation existed in antiquity. The answer was negative, but as I continued to puzzle over the incident, it occurred to me the two events were somehow connected and that my "accidentally" finding the green crystal was the link between them.

In time, I began to dwell on the theme of abandonment as a social and political, as well as personal, issue. This line of thought led me to Crete, c. 2500 B.C.E. I was perusing some visual research material in a book of reproductions of the art of Minoan Crete, when I was startled to see—by hands that drew and painted twenty-five hundred years ago—female and male figures matching the apparitions that had appeared in my bedroom!

So familiar did those slender, fine-boned people seem to me that I felt I had actually known them in real life. Next, I came across a drawing of the so-called "Horns of Consecration" from the Minoan site at Knossos on Crete. These great horns made of stone to resemble those on a bull, or the crescent Moon, had once adorned the temple there to the Great Goddess, c. 2500 B.C.E. With a "shock of recognition," I suddenly realized I had found the Temple of the Horned Moon. The sense of *déja vu*—of having been there before—heightened, and I "remembered" the room where Ariadne, the last High Priestess of the Great Mother Goddess had, before the coming of the patriarchal Greeks, performed her sacred rituals. I "saw" it in complete detail, including the serpent-entwined thronelike chair where she sat, *as* the Goddess. An awesome sense of power emanated from the precinct.

The question arose: was I being summoned to again serve this holy place? As with the function of symbols generally, the answer was not given directly nor immediately. It required a search—and the awareness that a message had been given and received. Interpretation of the signs of meaningfulness in one's life requires integrating them into the pattern of wholeness struggling to emerge. For a time, I sought a direct relationship—I had already been working for some time on Goddess material but the form it was to take remained elusive. It was only when the opportunity to write this book manifested that I understood I had mistakenly been looking for a relationship to a literal "temple," a concrete place that had once existed in antiquity. The realization dawned: my work now had to do with *The Temple Within*, the original title of this book.

Appendix
Astrological Services

Stargazer Productions offers a range of computerized astrological services via mail. These include a Simple Natal Chart, Personal Profiles (a detailed analysis of your chart), the Relationship Profile (a compatibility analysis between two people), A Child's Profile, and outerplanet transit lists with individual interpretations, as well as personal, non-computer astrological readings by telephone.

To receive a free discriptive brochure, please send a stamped, self-addressed envelope to the address below. Canadian and other non-U.S. correspondents can send $1.00 in lieu of SASE to:

Stargazer Productions
Rt. 7, Box 8180
Nacogdoches, TX 75961